Hayek: A Collaborative Biography

Archival Insights into the Evolution of Economics Series

This series provides a systematic archival examination of the process by which economics is constructed and disseminated. All the major schools of economics will be subject to critical scrutiny; a concluding volume will attempt to synthesise the insights into a unifying general theory of knowledge construction and influence.

Series Editor: Robert Leeson

Titles include:

Robert Leeson (*editor*)
THE KEYNESIAN TRADITION

Robert Leeson (*editor*)
THE ANTI-KEYNESIAN TRADITION

Robert Leeson (*editor*)
AMERICAN POWER AND POLICY

Roger Frantz and Robert Leeson (*editors*)
HAYEK AND BEHAVIORAL ECONOMICS

Robert Leeson (*editor*)
HAYEK: A COLLABORATIVE BIOGRAPHY PART 1

Forthcoming titles:

Robert Leeson (*editor*)
HAYEK: A COLLABORATIVE BIOGRAPHY PART 2

Robert Leeson (*editor*)
HAYEK AND THE AUSTRIAN SCHOOL

Archival Insights into the Evolution of Economics
Series Standing Order ISBN: 978-1-4039-9520-9 (Hardback)

You can receive future titles in this series as they are published by placing a standing order. Please contact your bookseller or, in case of difficulty, write to us at the address below with your name and address, the titles of the series and the ISBN quoted above.

Customer Service Department, Macmillan Distribution Ltd, Houndmills, Basingstoke, Hampshire RG21 6XS, England

Hayek: A Collaborative Biography

Part 1 Influences, from Mises to Bartley

Edited by

Robert Leeson
Visiting Professor of Economics, Stanford University

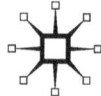
First published 2013 by
PALGRAVE MACMILLAN

Palgrave Macmillan in the UK is an imprint of Macmillan Publishers Limited, registered in England, company number 785998, of Houndmills, Basingstoke, Hampshire RG21 6XS.

Palgrave Macmillan in the US is a division of St Martin's Press LLC, 175 Fifth Avenue, New York, NY 10010.

Palgrave Macmillan is the global academic imprint of the above companies and has companies and representatives throughout the world.

Palgrave® and Macmillan® are registered trademarks in the United States, the United Kingdom, Europe and other countries

ISBN: 978–0–230–30112–2

This book is printed on paper suitable for recycling and made from fully managed and sustained forest sources. Logging, pulping and manufacturing processes are expected to conform to the environmental regulations of the country of origin.

A catalogue record for this book is available from the British Library.

A catalog record for this book is available from the Library of Congress.

Contents

List of Figures

Notes on Contributors

Samuel Bjork is a graduate student at Oxford University.

Rafe Champion is an independent scholar.

Selwyn Cornish is Adjunct Associate Professor of Economics, Australian National University and Official Historian of the Reserve Bank of Australia.

Steven Dimmick is an independent scholar and retired bank regulator.

Werner Erhard is the founder of Erhard Seminar Training.

Douglas French is Director of the Ludwig von Mises Institute.

Nils Goldschmidt is Professor of Social Policy, Department of Applied Social Sciences, Munich University of Applied Sciences and Affiliated Fellow at the Walter Eucken Institute, Freiburg.

Jan-Otmar Hesse is Professor of Economic History, Department of History, University of Bielefeld.

Stephen Kresge was the second General Editor of *The Collected Works of F.A. Hayek*.

David Laidler is Emeritus Professor of Economics, University of Western Ontario.

Melissa Lane is Professor of Politics, Princeton University and Director of the Program in Values and Public Life, University Center for Human Values, Princeton University.

Robert Leeson is Visiting Professor of Economics at Stanford University, Visiting Scholar at Hoover Institution and Adjunct Professor at the University of Notre Dame Australia.

Avner Offer is Chichele Professor Emeritus of Economic History, University of Oxford and Emeritus Fellow of All Souls College, Oxford University.

Gabriel Söderberg is a PhD candidate at Uppsala University.

Viktor J. Vanberg is Senior Research Associate, Walter Eucken Institut and Professor Emeritus of Economics, University of Freiburg.

1
Introduction

Robert Leeson

Austrians and World History

Friedrich August Hayek (8 May 1899–23 March 1992) was born towards the end of what came to be regarded as the pre-deluge (World War I) golden age, and died just after the end of the Cold War (World War III). Cold War victory was expected to lead to an era of triumphant democracy, *The End of History and the Last Man* (Fukuyama, 1992). Instead, capitalist democracies have faced intensified threats from theocratic-sponsored terrorism and plutocratic-sponsored financial crises.[1]

Had Hayek been largely an anonymous person, his interaction with the transformations of his era would still be worthy of social history attention: the increasing power of socialist and communist parties and the rise of the Welfare State; the final demise of the remnants of the *Ancien Régime* Empires (and the Habsburg Empire in particular); World War I and its repercussions; the inter-war dislocations that elevated a fellow Austrian into a Führer and the resulting reunification of Germans (*Anschluss*) and World War II; the Cold War; the libertarian revolt against collectivist trends; the deregulation movement and the decline of trade union power; the Thatcher–Reagan counter-revolutions; the collapse of Communism; and the rise of a new threat – revived fundamentalist religions. Hayek's life was shaped by nine of these ten forces: the average educated person reader has the 'knowledge' that he – more than any other individual – influenced five of them.

Yet little is currently known about the precise nature of his involvement in these forces. Hayek's public pronouncements – *The Road to Serfdom* (1944), for example – have been pored over by scholars and disciples; but so far there has been little or no attempt to *connect* Hayek's life to the sentiments he expressed. These chapters of collaborative

1

biography are the first systematic attempt to describe, interpret and integrate Hayek's life, beliefs and philosophy. They constitute an attempt to persuade scholars, disciples and other readers that there is something profoundly interesting and informative going on beneath the surface. No axe – ideological or otherwise – is being ground: the authors come from most parts of the appropriate spectrum. The merit of such a collaborative biographical approach is obvious: an expert perspective is brought to bear on each aspect of Hayek's life and work.[2]

The origins of the Austrian School of Economics can be traced back to Carl Menger's (1840–1921) 1871 *Principles of Economics* (*Grundsätze der Volkswirtschaftslehre*) *and* his 1883 *Investigations into the Method of the Social Sciences with Special Reference to Economics* (*Untersuchungen über die Methode der Socialwissenschaften und der politischen Ökonomie insbesondere*). The second book contained an attack on the inductive methods of the German Historical School; Gustav von Schmoller's (1838–1917) review of the book apparently used the derogatory label 'Austrian' to indicate an unfavourable contrast with the dynamism of Prussia.

The second generation Austrian School is associated with Friedrich von Wieser (1851–1926) and Eugen von Böhm-Bawerk (1851–1914) and the third generation with Hans Mayer (1879–1955), Ludwig von Mises (1881–1973) and Joseph Schumpeter (1883–1950). Hayek was the most famous member of the fourth generation, while Murray Rothbard (1926–1995) and others built an American-Austrian School to continue the Misean tradition. A fifth generation – split between Misesians and Hayekians – continues to prosper. Hayek was influenced by both traditions: Wieser and Mises were his most important early intellectual influences.

Hayek's published work has a life of its own; several additional layers of meaning and significance also need to be investigated. On the surface, there is the material contained in *The Collected Works of F. A. Hayek* (1988–) – a project initiated by Hayek's appointed biographer, William Warren Bartley III. A considerable amount of surface textual analysis has already been undertaken, mostly from somewhat predictable ideological positions. Below this surface, Hayek left a considerable number of recorded conversations, some of which have been 'doctored' and some of which remain in the private hands of a bogus 'doctored' disciple and look set to be destroyed on the implausible basis that Hayek intended them to be secret. In addition, Hayek left his archives for scholarly inspection at the Hoover Institution on War, Revolution and Peace.

Hayek's surface material influenced world history: these chapters will integrate that surface material with the insights provided by the underlying and parallel, archival reality.

Hayek (1994 [1972]: ix) concluded that he had lived 'an externally rather uneventful life'. At the time, Hayek was in the middle of the second of three major depressive episodes. Two years later he was awarded the Nobel Prize for Economic Sciences; in 1978 he reflected expansively on his life and influences in interviews (available on the UCLA oral history website). In the mid-1980s, Bartley recorded a large number of interviews, some of which have been reproduced in *Hayek on Hayek: An Autobiographical Dialogue* (1994). This introductory chapter will integrate these sources with an appropriate historical framework to illuminate Hayek's life and work.

Hayek explained that initially the term Austrian School meant 'marginal-utility analysis'.[3] The marginal revolution of the 1870s produced three overlapping traditions: Austrian (Menger), British (William Stanley Jevons, 1835–1882) and Swiss-French or Lausanne (Léon Walras, 1834–1910). All three traditions attempted to reconstruct classical economics by reaffirming social harmony as a framework within which to interpret and promote market exchange.

The relationship between government and the governed was transformed in the three centuries from John Locke's (1689) *Letter Concerning Toleration* to the fall of the Berlin Wall. A British king had been executed 40 years before Locke's *Letter*; the French Revolution began a wider assault on the *Ancien Régime* 100 years after the *Letter*. Almost simultaneously came the American colonists' 1776 Declaration of Independence, which Thomas Jefferson hoped would be 'the signal of arousing men to burst the chains under which monkish ignorance and superstition had persuaded them to bind themselves, and to assume the blessings and security of self-government'.

Adam Smith's *Inquiry into the Nature and Causes of the Wealth of Nations* (published four months before the Declaration) sought to provide a philosophy and a policy framework within which order could be maintained in an increasingly post-feudal social universe.

Classical economics was the product of the Enlightenment revolt against inter-State and intra-State conflict. Mercantilist (pre-Classical) State-based doctrine viewed international trade as a zero sum, conflict-ridden game; one of the unintended consequences of the religious wars of 1517–1648 was the emerging philosophy of tolerance. Classical economics emphasized harmony – both externally (trade as a positive sum game) and internally (self-interest was harnessed to produce social benefits when embedded in a competitive market environment).

The industrial revolution further undermined the *Ancien Régime*. Henry Sumner Maine's (1861) *Ancient Law: Its Connection with the Early History of Society and Its Relation to Modern Ideas* emphasized the associated transformation from status to contract. In the same year, an American dispute over labor contracts erupted into civil war.[4]

Two centuries after the 1648 Peace of Westphalia, *The Communist Manifesto* declared that

> a new spectre is haunting Europe – the spectre of Communism. All the Powers of old Europe have entered into a holy alliance to exorcise this spectre: Pope and Czar, Metternich and Guizot, French Radicals and German police-spies.

In *Capital: Critique of Political Economy*, Marx (1867) portrayed capitalism as a competitive effort to maximize the 'surplus-value' extracted from labour. Böhm-Bawerk's capital theory attempted to refute this analysis.

Marx expropriated the classical labour theory of value of Smith and David Ricardo as a theory of exploitation and thus a justification for revolution. The neoclassical revolution replaced the labor theory of value with the equilibrium intersection of privately optimal supply and demand curves. Thus marginal-utility analysis replaced class-based analysis: individual consumer choice became the basic unit of analysis. Trade allowed 'consumer surplus' and 'producer surplus' to be extracted from the anonymous market (surplus values that would otherwise be lost). Trade unions, tariffs, taxation and interferences with the price mechanism all produce 'deadweight losses' by reducing these surpluses.

Austrians saw marginalism 'as a deliverance from an ideological impasse' (Raico, 2012: 28). As deference to inherited status diminished, a new, more legitimate, king emerged: 'consumer sovereignty' (Hutt, 1990 [1936], Chapter 16). Simultaneously, producers earned zero economic profits in long-run competitive equilibrium.

The pre-1914 balance of power had been constructed by Otto von Bismarck, who dominated European affairs from the 1860s to his dismissal in 1890. Klemens von Metternich, Foreign Minister of the Holy Roman Empire and its successor state, the Habsburg Empire, dominated European diplomacy from the 1814 Congress of Vienna to his resignation in the wake of the liberal revolutions of 1848. Following Metternich's demise, Emperor Franz Joseph I (reigned 1848–1916) attempted to strengthen his multi-ethnic Empire through constitutional reform. Externally, Habsburg power was being eclipsed by the rise of Prussia; internally, there were German/non-German linguistic and cultural divisions (the German speakers pushed for a stronger central government; Czechs and Hungarians, however, wanted power to be dispersed).

According to Mises (2003: 2), from the middle of the 16th to the end of the 18th century, Austria was 'foreign to the intellectual effort of Europe'. The post-1848 reforms which initiated the beginnings of parliamentary government led 'in the realm of the spirit' to a 'flowering' which came 'suddenly after centuries of sterility and apathy'. Vienna became a centre for the interpretation of 'neurotic phenomena': Josef Breuer and Sigmund Freud developed psychoanalysis while Alfred Adler examined the inferiority complex.

The rise of the Austrian School was associated with this period of Habsburg decline. Defeat at the 1859 Battle of Solferino (the Second Italian War of Independence) had an additional significance: it was the last major battle in world history where all the armies were under the personal command of their monarchs (Franz Joseph I, Victor Emmanuel II and Napoleon III).

Prussian victories against Austria (1866) and France (1870) facilitated dominance over the German states and the emergence of the German Empire (1871) – the Second Reich. In 1867, Hungary gained some autonomy (*Ausgleich*) – a dual monarchy compromise that ended in independence in 1918. Simultaneously, Italian unification further diminished the size and strength of the Habsburg Empire. Metternich had declared that Italy was nothing more than 'a geographic expression'; by 1919, it became clear that Austria had never been a genuine nation: for over seven centuries its only unifying force had been loyalty to the Habsburgs. After 1974, such loyalty became a defining feature of many American-Austrians who lacked such a geographical connection – as Hayek later complained (see below).

In their *Manifesto*, Marx and Engels (1848: 22) declared that the Communist program could be summarized in 'a single expression: Abolition of private property'. In his Austrian Manifesto on *Liberalism*, Mises (1962 [1927]: 19) declared that

> the program of liberalism, therefore, if condensed into a single word, would have to read: *property*, that is, private ownership in the means of production. ... All the other demands of liberalism result from this fundamental demand [emphasis in original].

For Miseans, Marx and Engels were

> not altogether wrong when in the *Manifesto* they said, 'The history of all hitherto existing society is the history of class struggles'. But the conflict lies not among conflicting groups in the free market but rather between producers and those who seize their wealth, principally through statist predation (Gordon, 2012: xix).

This fits rather well with the Fox News distinction between 'makers' (the private sector) and 'takers' (governments and those who receive handouts).

For Miseans, Hayek was a 'taker'-tolerating renegade:

> once you have reached a certain level of wealth, I think it's in the common interest of all citizens to be assured that if their widows or their children by some circumstances become unable to support themselves, they would be assured of a certain very low minimum, which on current standards would be miserable but still would secure them against extreme deprivations... Most of the people I have in mind would really not be able to make much of an extra income. But if some widow who had to live on that small minimum income did take in some washing in her kitchen, I just would not notice it.[5]

In 'Liberty and its Antithesis', a review of Hayek's *Constitution of Liberty*, Mises (1961) criticized Hayek for believing that the

> Welfare State is under certain conditions compatible with liberty. In fact the Welfare State is merely a method for transforming the market economy step by step into socialism

– as had been demonstrated by Bismarck,

> the American New Deal and British Fabian Socialism... What separates the Communists from the advocates of the Welfare State is not the ultimate goal of their endeavours, but the method by means of which they want to attain a goal that is common to both of them.

The second generation British neoclassical School was dominated by Alfred Marshall (1842–1924) and his *Principles of Economics* (1890), which became the standard text for subsequent generations. The third generation was dominated by Arthur Cecil Pigou and John Maynard Keynes (1883–1946).

Pigou (1877–1959) succeeded Marshall as Professor of Political Economy at Cambridge at the age of 30. In his 1908 Inaugural Professorial Lecture, Pigou stated that he would be glad if a student would come to study economics as a result of having

> walked through the slums of London and is stirred to make some effort to help his fellow men…social enthusiasm, one might add, is the beginning of economic science (cited by Hutchison, 1953: 284, 416).

Forty-five years later, Pigou (1953: 65) reminded a Cambridge audience how Marshall kept a painting of a 'down and out' on his wall to guide him back to 'the right path' when beguiled by distracting but shallow academic controversies.

The British, or Cambridge School, tended to see a positive role for the State as a supplement to market forces. Pigou's (1912) monumentally titled *Wealth and Welfare* addressed

> the misery and squalor that surrounds us, the injurious luxury of some wealthy families, the terrible uncertainty overshadowing many families of the poor – these are evils too plain to be ignored.

Pigou used marginal analysis to provide remedies for market failure through taxes and subsidies. In *A Study in Public Finance*, Pigou (1928: 29) developed the concept of 'human capital'.

In Keynes' (1936) equally monumentally titled *General Theory of Employment, Interest and Money*, consumption and government spending were the vehicles by which unemployment could be minimized. If the externalities of the business cycle were caused by the animal spirits of investors, then government-based interference with the price mechanism (permanently low interest rates) could, he argued, be used as a remedy. The 'socialization of investment' might be permanently required.

Hayek found that his London School of Economics (LSE) colleagues, such as Lionel Robbins and Arnold Plant (1898–1978) displayed a 'certain critical attitude' towards Marshall because of the influence of Edwin Cannan (1861–1935), who had taught at the LSE since foundation (1895) and subsequently became Professor of Economics (1907–1926).[6] Cannan's focus was not on Marshallian price theory but on the Smithian search for the origins and causes of the wealth of nations (Howson, 2011: 81–82). According to Hayek, outside the LSE,

> Marshall established almost a monopoly ... England was dominated by Marshallian thinking. And this idea that if you knew Marshall there was nothing else worth reading was very widespread.[7]

Hayek believed that the Austrian and British Schools had previously been converging:

> So long as British economics at least aimed at being microeconomics (and that was true at that time), there was no such fundamental difference, though there must have been inherent in it a greater propensity to shift over to macroeconomics than there was in the Austrian tradition. I think historically it is true that most of the people in the Marshallian School readily switched over to macroeconomics, but the Austrians did not. It would be interesting, especially, to investigate the reasons why this happened. But my general feeling was that before Keynes helped macroeconomics to this complete temporary victory, the two traditions were closely approaching. Perhaps this was due to my making the acquaintance with English tradition very much in the form of Lionel Robbins's exposition, which was half-Austrian already. If I had moved not to the London School of Economics but to Cambridge, I might not have felt like this.[8]

According to Hayek, Mises was 'the real founder of the American School of Austrian economics' which was 'very largely a Mises School'. According to Hayek, this led to resentment:

> I am now being associated with Mises, but initially I think it meant the pupils whom Mises had taught in the United States. Some rather reluctantly now admit me as a second head, and I don't think people like [Murray] Rothbard or some of the immediate Mises pupils are really very happy that they are not – The rest are not orthodox Misesians but only take part of their views from Mises.

The Austrian School experienced a revival after Mises' death (10 October 1973): the 'first' Austrian Economics Conference met at Royalston College, Vermont, in June 1974, three months before the announcement of Hayek's Nobel Prize. Participants believed they were de-homogenizing neoclassical thought by separating out specifically Austrian contributions.

Hayek was scheduled to give the keynote address but declined to attend for a variety of reasons: chronic depression, general ill-health and the award of an honorary degree by the University of Salzburg. Conference participants sent Hayek a signed card with a letter that stated that his ideas would 'continue to inspire us in the future'.[9] The American-Austrian Nobel 'joy' was transmitted via the US telephone networks: 'From now on it will be more difficult to look upon libertarianism as an ideological oddity that surely must have died with Herbert Spencer' (Raico, 1975).[10] (The US Bell telephone system was already under anti-trust pressure from the Department of Justice. The deregulation movement, which gathered pace in the years after Hayek's Nobel Prize, culminated in the 1999 repeal of the 1933 Glass Steagal Act, which had separated investment from commercial banking.)

Hayek received an anonymous letter (23 July 1975) which quoted his opening remarks at the 'second' conference (June 1975): 'why economists with no geographical connection with Vienna should nevertheless choose to call themselves Austrian'. The letter explained that for conference participants

> spiritually and intellectually Vienna will always be our home: and we will always return to the charge against the forces of macro-darkness now threatening to overwhelm the world, carrying aloft the intellectual flag of Austria-Hungary...we still love you: and we feel that by continued association with us, we may yet show you the light and truth of anarcho-Hayekianism...And so, ladies and gentlemen, I give you two toasts to victory in the future, and to the best legacy of Vienna to the world, Professor Hayek. [emphases in original][11]

The following year, Hayek objected to Percy Greaves' (1973: xxiii, 284–285) *Understanding the Dollar Crisis* lectures. In a question-and-answer session Greaves was asked: 'Is the original explanation of the monetary theory of the trade cycle from Mises or from Hayek?' to which he replied, 'It is from Mises, and Mises alone...Hayek was Mises' assistant for many years in Austria'. Then Hayek went to the LSE where he published an English-language book

> on this monetary theory...So the first presentation of the Mises theory in English was by Hayek. Unfortunately the Hayek presentation had some errors in it. This was undoubtedly one reason why the theory has not been received as well as it deserves to be, or even as well as it has been received in German-speaking countries.

Mises (1973) wrote the Foreword and, according to Greaves (1973: xxiii), had 'kind words' for his lectures. Hayek (17 June 1976) objected both to the assertion that he was Mises' assistant and to the chronology and Misean origins of the Austrian business cycle theory. Greaves (5 July 1976) – George Wallace's successor as 1980 Presidential candidate for the American Party (formerly the American Independent Party) – was in no mood to retreat: he doubted that anyone had been misled. Moreover, Mises had approved the lectures. Greaves condescendingly stated that he was confused about which trade cycle theory Hayek now subscribed to.[12]

When asked about the Austrian School and 'libertarian ideology' Hayek (UCLA interviews) responded:

I would very definitely maintain that [Misean] methodological individualism does lead to political individualism. I don't think they would all admit it, but in the form in which I have now been led to put it – this idea of utilization of dispersed knowledge – I would maintain that our political conclusions follow very directly from the theoretical insights. But that's not generally admitted. I'm not speaking about the opponents, of course, but among those of the original group, I think it's even – Well, I think in the American-Austrian School, yes, it is now generally admitted. The young people would not call one an Austrian who is not both a methodological individualist and a political individualist. But that applies to the younger school and was not the tradition.[13]

In his Hillsdale College Ludwig von Mises Lecture on 'Coping with Ignorance', Hayek (1978) reflected that Wieser

unlike most of the other members of the Austrian School...had a good deal of sympathy with the mild Fabian socialism to which I inclined as a young man. He in fact prided himself that his theory of marginal utility had provided the basis of progressive taxation, which then seemed to me one of the ideals of social justice.

This was reinforced in his UCLA interviews: Wieser was a 'liberal' in the American sense:

slightly tainted with Fabian socialist sympathies. In fact, it was his great pride to have given the scientific foundation for progressive taxation ... Wieser and the whole tradition really believed in a measurable utility.

The American-Austrian School of Böhm-Bawerk 'and Mises even more' were 'liberals' in the European or 'classical liberal' sense.

Immediately after World War I, Hayek (1978) had 'looked in' at one of Mises' lectures 'and found that a man so conspicuously antipathetic to the kind of Fabian views which I then held was not the sort of person to whom I wanted to go'. Later, Mises provided 'continuous inspiration throughout a decade' – but Hayek believed that he had an advantage over Miseans:

> I have perhaps most profited from his teachings because I was not initially his student at the university, an innocent young man who took his word for gospel, but came to him as a trained economist, trained in a parallel branch of Austrian economics from which he gradually, but never completely won me over.

During World War II, *The Road to Serfdom* was designed as a parallel conversion process to persuade

> my English – what you would call liberals – Fabian colleagues that they were wrong. That the book caught on in America was a complete surprise to me; I never thought the Americans would be the least interested in that book.[14]

In summer 1924, on his return to Vienna after his first visit to America, Hayek was more fully introduced to the 'Menger/Böhm-Bawerk/Mises' classical liberal wing through the Mises seminar where

> the shade of Böhm-Bawerk was dominating; he was the common base upon which we talked and understood each other. But even in his work, his writings on marginal utility were perhaps more important than his work on interest. I think nearly everybody had some reservations on his interest theory, while everybody accepted his article on marginal utility as the standard exposition, really, of the marginal-utility theory.[15]

Hayek sought to distance Menger from the Menger/Böhm-Bawerk/Mises tradition: Menger was 'rather sceptical of the capital theory of Böhm-

Bawerk and his followers'.[16] Hayek represented the Menger/Wieser/Mayer tradition – to which Mises objected on a variety of counts, including perceived associations with Germany. According to Mises (2003: 13)

> British free trade philosophy triumphed in the nineteenth century in the countries of Western and Central Europe. It demolished the shaky ideology of the authoritarian welfare state (*landesfürstlicher Wohlfahrisstaat*) that had guided the policies of the German principalities in the eighteenth century. Even Prussia turned temporarily toward liberalism.

But after victory over Austria in 1866, the

> King's party – the Conservative Party of the Junkers, led by Bismarck – triumphed over the Prussian Progressive party that stood for parliamentary government, and likewise over the democratic groups of Southern Germany.

Mises (2003: 7, 13) described what he believed to be 'The German Rejection of Classical Economics'. There was 'no room left' in the Second Reich 'for the "alien" doctrines of Manchesterism and laissez faire'. In its place, Bismarck introduced a version of the German Historical School's

> *Sozialpolitik*, the system of interventionist measures such as labor legislation, social security, pro-union attitudes, progressive taxation, protective tariffs, cartels, and dumping.

The only disagreement in this 'state socialism' related to which group should

> operate the supreme planning board: the Junkers, the professors and the bureaucracy of Hohenzollern Prussia, or the officers of the Social-Democratic party and their affiliated labor unions.

Initially, the influence which led Hayek to study economics was 'Walter Rathenau's conception of a grand economy';[17] 'German *Sozialpolitik*, state socialism of the Rathenau type'.[18] Rathenau (1867–1922), a Jewish industrialist and Foreign Minister of Germany during the Weimar Republic (1919–1933), was assassinated on 24 June (which became a holiday of celebration during the Third Reich). During the war, Rathenau had been the

> raw materials dictator in Germany, and he wrote some very persua-
> sive books about the reconstruction after the war. And [those books]
> are, of course, socialist of a sort – central planning, at least, but not
> a proletarian socialism. They were very persuasive, indeed. And I
> found that really to understand this I had to study economics.[19]

One of Menger's students, Othmar Spann, introduced Hayek to Menger's (1871) *Principles of Economics*:

> That was the first book which gave me an idea of the possibility
> of theoretically approaching economic problems. That was probably
> the most important event.[20]

The book was influential for Hayek because of

> what it says on general sociology. This conception of the sponta-
> neous generation of institutions is worked out more beautifully there
> than in any other book I know.[21]

At a student in the immediate post-war years, Hayek initially found the University of Vienna to be

> dreadful ... There was nobody there. Wieser had left the university to
> become a minister in the last Austrian government; Böhm-Bawerk
> had died shortly before; [Eugen von] Philippovich, another great
> figure, had died shortly before; and when I arrived there was nobody
> but a socialist economic historian.[22]

Hayek (1994: 47) was referring to Karl Grünberg who later became the 'founder of the famous Marxist Freudian Frankfurt Institute of Social Research'.

All this changed when Wieser returned:

> he became my teacher. He was a most impressive teacher, a very distin-
> guished man whom I came to admire very much, I think it's the only
> instance where, as very young men do, I fell for a particular teacher.
> He was the great admired figure, sort of a grandfather figure of the
> two generations between us. He was a very kindly man who usually,

I would say, floated high above the students as a sort of God, but when he took an interest in a student, he became extremely helpful and kind. He took me into his family; I was asked to take meals with him and so on. So he was for a long time my ideal in the field, from whom I got my main general introduction to economics.[23]

As a lecturer, Wieser was

His Excellency, the ex-minister, nobody would dare to ask a question or interrupt. We were just sitting, 200 or 300 of us, at the foot of this elevated platform, where this very impressive figure, a very handsome man in his late sixties, with a beautiful beard, spoke these absolutely perfect orations.[24]

Hayek was also interested in psychology, but around 1918–1919

got definitely hooked by economics by becoming acquainted with a particular tradition through the textbook of Carl Menger, which was wholly satisfactory to me. I could step into an existing tradition, while my psychological ideas did not fit into any established tradition. It would not have given me an easy access to an academic career. So I became an economist, although the psychological ideas continued to occupy me.[25]

Hayek observed that in addition to two Austrian traditions there were two types of thinkers:

the one, whom I call the 'master' of his subject, who had complete command of all his subject areas, and who can give you a prompt answer about what is the answer of current theory to this-and-this problem ... Böhm-Bawerk was the master of his subject; Wieser was much more what one commonly would call an intuitive thinker. Then, later in life, I have known two types who are typical masters of the subject, and who, because they have the answer for everything ready, have not done as much original work as they would have been capable of. The one is Lionel Robbins; the other is Fritz Machlup. They both, to an extent, have command of the present state of economics which I could never claim to. But it's just because I don't remember what is the standard answer to a problem and have to think it out anew that occasionally I get an original idea.[26]

Hayek saw similarities between himself and Keynes, who

> was rather my type of mind, not the other. He certainly could not
> have been described as a master of his subject, as I described the other
> type. He was an intuitive thinker with a very wide knowledge in
> many fields, who had never felt that economics was weighty enough
> to – He just took it for granted that Marshall's textbook contained
> everything one needed to know about this subject. There was a
> certain arrogance of Cambridge economics about – They thought
> they were the centre of the world, and if you have learned Cambridge
> economics, you have nothing else worth learning.[27]

According to Hayek (1994: 81–88), Keynes knew little economics:

> I don't think he spent more than a year learning economics ... I liked
> Keynes and in many ways admired him, but do not think he was a
> good economist ... He knew his Marshall, but very little else. He had
> had to at one stage take an interest in Malthus, but I had to tell him
> about Henry Thornton.

Uneventful Austrian lives?

The label 'uneventful' does not adequately describe the lives of Hayek
and most of his fellow Austrians. Carl Menger began his career as a
journalist (1863) and apparently became a confidant of Count Richard
Belcredi, Minister of State and Prime Minister (1865); and in 1870
obtained a civil service appointment in the cabinet press department
(Mises, 2003: 2). In 1876, he became tutor to the 18-year-old Crown
Prince Archduke Rudolf von Habsburg, and travelled with him for two
years on a Grand Tour of Europe. On his return to Vienna, Rudolf's
father, the Emperor, appointed Menger to the Chair of Political Economy
in the Law Faculty at the University of Vienna.

Rudolf's lecture notes reveal that Menger was teaching material that
would assist Rudolf as Habsburg ruler: 'Heads of State must pay particular attention to ... ' Menger taught Smithian, pre-marginal economics:

> the notebooks of Crown Prince Rudolf are wholly imbued with the
> mid-nineteenth century's unlimited confidence in progress, espe-
> cially the economic progress of mankind (Streissler, 2000: 123).

Menger may have assisted Rudolf to write a pamphlet (published anony-
mously in 1878) which was critical of the Habsburg aristocracy (Schulak

and Unterkofler, 2011: 31). In 1889, the married 30-year-old Rudolf and his 17-year-old mistress died in an apparent suicide pact. Hayek (1994: 32) reported that this had adverse consequences for his grandfather Gustav von Hayek who hoped for 'higher prospects' after Rudolf had engaged him to organize an ornithological exhibition in 1881. The suicide had wider repercussions: Franz Joseph's brother, Archduke Karl Ludwig Joseph Maria (1833–1896) renounced his succession rights in favour of his son, Archduke Franz Ferdinand (1863–1914), whose assassination sparked World War I.[28] Hayek's (1915) diary contained an image of the martyred saint, Franz Ferdinand.[29]

Carl Menger dropped the inherited title of nobility in early adulthood; in 1900, he was appointed to the Austrian Imperial Herrenhaus (House of Lords). Shortly afterwards – in his early sixties – he fathered an illegitimate son, Karl Menger (1902–1985) with a journalist, Hermine Andermann (1869–1924), who was 29 years his junior (Schulak and Unterkofler 2011: 32).[30] According to Herbert Furth, Karl's mother was Menger's Jewish housekeeper. Menger got his son legitimized by imperial decree – but Karl never forgave his father for not marrying his mother.[31]

According to Schulak and Unterkofler (2011: 32), fathering an illegitimate child violated Viennese social conventions, and in 1903 Carl was forced into early retirement and withdrawal from public life. Members of the Austrian School maintained the *esprit de corps* posture that he had taken voluntary retirement for the sake of further studies: a '"true Viennese secret" – which everyone in Vienna knew but did not talk about in public'. The animosity between Austrians and the German Historical School was no secret: in 1910, Menger requested that every economist in the world should send him a photograph of themselves as a 70th birthday present, which, apparently, only Gustav Schmoller and Lujo Brentano refused to provide (Kauder, 1965: 236).

Wieser and Böhm-Bawerk were brothers-in-law;[32] Hayek became 'very friendly' with Wieser who 'asked me many times to his house. How far that was because he was a contemporary and friend of my grandfather's, I don't know'.[33] Böhm-Bawerk had been his grandfather's mountaineering companion,[34] and a 'close friend' of his parents. Hayek (1994: 48) 'used to meet his widow, a maternal friend of my mother; my mother called his widow "aunt," because of the years they were together in Salzburg'.

Hayek recalled that Wieser and Böhm-Bawerk had been

personally very close friends, although Wieser always refused to discuss economics. In fact, I am told he began to avoid Böhm-Bawerk because Böhm-Bawerk insisted on talking economics all the time. Of course, there's a famous episode which is rather similar: before the war, immediately before, Marshall used to go to the Austrian Dolomites for his summer holiday, and for a time Wieser went to the next village. They knew of each other but made no attempt to make contact. Then Böhm-Bawerk came on a visit and insisted on visiting them both, bringing them together to talk economics, with the result that neither Wieser nor Marshall returned.[35]

Böhm-Bawerk (1895, 1897–1898, 1900–1904), Wieser (1917) and Schumpeter (1919) all served as Finance Ministers. Böhm-Bawerk (1899) and Wieser (1917) were elevated to the Herrenhaus; Böhm-Bawerk had represented the government in the lower house on taxation questions from 1889.

According to Mises (2003: 17) although the 'greatness' of Menger, Wieser and Böhm-Bawerk 'cannot be overrated' they did not embrace optimism:

History shows that again and again periods of marvelous mental accomplishments were followed by periods of decay and retrogression. We do not know whether the next generation will beget people who are able to continue along the lines of the geniuses who made the last centuries so glorious.

Wieser retired in the year that Hayek finished his first degree and was succeeded by

Mayer, his favorite disciple. An extremely thoughtful man, but a bad neurotic...a man who could never do anything on time, who was always late for any appointment, for every lecture, who never completed things he was working on, and in a way a tragic figure, a man who had been very promising.[36]

Mayer was also a

difficult person to get on with, and Mises was, contrary to his reputation, an extremely tolerant person. He would have anyone in his seminar who was intellectually interested. Mayer would insist that you swore by the master, and anybody who disagreed was unwelcome.[37]

Hayek (1978) 'expected much' of the Wieser tradition, but Mayer had 'constant quarrels with Othmar Spann', who was

> semicrazy and changed violently from different political persua-sions – from socialism to extreme nationalism to Catholicism, always a step ahead of current fashions. By the time the Nazis came into power, he was suspect as a Catholic, although five years before he was a leading extreme nationalist.[38]

Spann always had

> rather fantastic philosophical ideas. He soon ceased to be interested in technical economics and was developing what he called a univer-salist social philosophy. But he, being a young and enthusiastic man, for a very short time had a constant influence on all these young people. Well, he was resorting to taking us to a midsummer cele-bration up in the woods, where we jumped over fires and – It's so funny.[39]

The dynamics of influence

Hayek (1994: 64) hurried to finish his degree because he

> had hoped before taking a job to spend an additional year at a German university. Max Weber had taught in Vienna the year I was fighting in Italy, and when I returned the following year, the univer-sity was full of talk about that great man. I in fact got a half-promise from my father that after getting my degree at Vienna I might go for a year to Munich.

Weber (1864–14 June 1920), the author of *The Protestant Ethic and the Spirit of Capitalism*, associate of the youngest German Historical School and promoter of methodological individualism, died before Hayek could visit. In addition, post-war Austrian inflation prohibited Hayek's father from funding the trip.

The 1919 Treaty of Saint-Germain-en-Laye confirmed the dissolution of the Habsburg Empire; *Anschluss* was prohibited without the agree-ment of the council of the League of Nations. Mises was a Director of the Office of Accounts (*Abrechnungsamt*) which had been established to carry out the financial clauses of the Peace Treaty. After December 1920,

Mises apparently became an 'unofficial spokesman for Austrian business and banking' in the reparations negotiations, through which he met Theodore Gregory, Professor of Economics at the LSE (Hülsmann, 2007: 480).

1921 became a pivotal moment in Austrian School history. According to Mises (2003: 19) 'About the time of Menger's demise (1921), one no longer distinguished between an Austrian School and other economics'. (Referring to his own *Theory of Money and Credit* (1912), Mises added: 'There was, of course, one exception'.) In 1922 Mises (1922: 25) published *Socialism*, which – citing Sidney Webb, the founder of the LSE – began with the assertion that 'the word Capitalism expresses for our age, the sum of all evils'. In November 1922, Mises 'talked to an English professor' – probably Gregory – about an English translation of *Socialism*; in November 1924 he travelled to London to discuss a translation with Robbins (Hülsmann, 2007: 480). Robbins later used his influence to create an Austrian outpost at LSE (Howson, 2011: 2).

In consequence of hyperinflation and Weber's death, in 1921 'after a long summer vacation', Hayek began looking for a job. In October 1921, having passed his examinations, but prior to graduation, Hayek (1994: 64) was recruited by Mises to work at the Office of Accounts. From the 1880s, the term 'Austrian School of Economics' was for its German Historical School critics a term of derision symbolizing the decline of the House of Habsburgs relative to the Prussia House of Hohenzollern. The Office of Accounts symbolized the consequences of the joint defeat of the Habsburgs and Hohenzollerns.

Moreover, two strands of the Austrian School met in that October 1921 job interview: Wieser recommended Hayek to Mises. The Austrian–LSE connection and Mises' influence on Hayek were, in a sense, part of the economic consequences of the peace.

The 1921 job interview was the beginning of Hayek's exposure to Mises. Hayek acknowledged his debt to both Menger's *Principles of Economics* and Mises's *On Socialism:*

> Menger I at once absorbed; Mises's was a book with which I struggled for years and years, because I came to the conclusion that his conclusions were almost invariably right, but I wasn't always satisfied by his arguments. But he had probably as great an influence on me as any person I know. On political ideas, I think the same is true of the two men I mentioned before in another connection: [Alexis de] Tocqueville and Lord [John] Acton.[40]

Hayek attempted to heal or at least moderate the breach between the two strands of Austrian thought by resurrecting the Austrian Economic Association (*National Okonomische Gesellschaft*):

> I rather regretted the division which had arisen between the Mises and the Mayer circle. There was no forum in which they met at all, and by restarting this no longer existing society there was at least one occasion where they would sit at the same table and discuss. [41]

Hayek's intention was to bring Mayer's seminar and 'Mises's admirers' together

> because they were not on very good relations, really. That had created some difficulty for us younger people – we had to be on good terms with Mayer in order to have any prospects at the university. We were more attracted by Mises... [42]

Mayer's seminar was almost completely

> confined to marginal-utility analysis... Mayer was a coffeehouse man, mainly. If there was any place he was to be found, it was at the coffeehouse at Kunstlercafe, opposite the university; and I did sit there with him and a group of his students many times in quite informal talk, which I'm afraid was much more university scandal than anything serious.

But

> Mayer – and also [Paul] Rosenstein[-Rodan], perhaps – kept away from the Mises circle for political reasons. There were no very good Mayer pupils. [43]

Mises (2003) believed that he, not Hayek, had revived the *Gesellschaft*:

> Immediately after the war I sought to revive the group. In order to avoid coming into conflict with the authorities, however, we had to establish a formal association, which we called the *Nationalökonomische Gesellschaft*. A short while later we began having difficulties yet again and it became clear that cooperation with Spann was not possible. In time we succeeded in excluding Spann, and the society was able to resume its activities.

Mises (2003: 78) reported that

> Spann and Mayer were jealous of my success, and tried to alienate my students from me...Spann was barely acquainted with modern economics; he did not teach economics. Instead he preached universalism, that is, National Socialism.

Mayer's awareness of his own

> sterility and lack of creativity depressed him gravely and caused him to be unstable and malicious. He occupied his time with an open war against Spann and with spiteful intrigues directed against me.

Nevertheless, Mises was conciliatory or at least diplomatic towards the Wieser strand:

> As the *Gesellschaft* did not want to be an affront to university professors, it felt it necessary to make Hans Mayer its president. I, myself, was vice president. When I left for Geneva in 1934, after which I only returned to Vienna for short visits, the *Gesellschaft* slowly began to fade away.

In 1931 Spann adopted the derogatory label 'neoliberal' to assault the Austrian School and engaged in anti-Semitic diatribes about marginal utility (Schulak and Unterkofler, 2011: 106, 112). Mises (2003: 78) recalled that

> On March 19, 1938, Hans Mayer wrote to all members issuing notice that all non-Aryan members were to take leave of the *Nationalökonomische Gesellschaft*, 'in consideration of the changed circumstances in German Austria, and in view of the respective laws now also applicable to this state'. This was the last that was heard of the society.

Anschluss united Austria and Germany – but ended Robbins' (1971: 91) 15-year 'love affair with Vienna, its setting and its culture'.

Hayek initially disliked Mises:

> At first we all felt he was frightfully exaggerating and even offensive in tone. You see, he hurt all our deepest feelings, but gradually he won us around, although for a long time I had to – I just learned he

was usually right in his conclusions, but I was not completely satisfied with his argument. That, I think, followed me right through my life. I was always influenced by Mises's answers, but not fully satisfied by his arguments. It became very largely an attempt to improve the argument, which I realized led to correct conclusions. But the question of why it hadn't persuaded most other people became important to me; so I became anxious to put it in a more effective form.[44]

Mises had a 'great influence' on Hayek

but I always differed, first not consciously and now quite consciously. Mises was a rationalist utilitarian, and I am not. He trusted the intelligent insight of people pursuing their known goals, rather disregarding the traditional element, the element of surrounding rules. He wouldn't accept legal positivism completely, but he was much nearer it than I would be. He would believe that the legal system – No, he wouldn't believe that it was invented; he was too much a pupil of Menger for that. But he still was inclined to see [the legal system] as a sort of rational construction. I don't think the evolutionary aspect, which is very strongly in Menger, was preserved in the later members of the Austrian School. I must say till I came, really, in between there was very little of it.[45]

In the year of Mises' death, Bartley (1973) published a biography of Hayek's cousin, Ludwig Wittgenstein (1889–1951). Bartley (1934–1990) was regarded by Popper (1902–1994), his PhD supervisor, as the best young philosopher he had met. Hayek had been aware of Bartley since the early 1960s; in the last nine years of his life Bartley became a major influence on Hayek's life. He stressed the 'evolutionary aspect' of Hayek's methodology. These chapters will explore these various influences on Hayek.

Hayek's influence: phase one

Hayek and his work became influential in four phases. During Hayek's time (1931–1950), the LSE became the epicentre of Austrian economics. Like Pigou, Robbins (1898–1984) and Hayek became full professors when barely out of their twenties. Robbins' (1932) *Essay on the Nature and Significance of Economic Science* emphasized the Austrian *a priori* perspective. The Benthamite goal of 'maximizing the greatest good of the greatest number' as measured by the number of 'utils' was part of the classical tradition; the ordinalist revolution associated with Robbins (1932; 1938), and John Hicks and R. G. D. Allen (1934) removed the cardinal notion of the measurability of utility and thus the foundation of interpersonal comparisons of utility (the basis of redistributive taxation).

Hayek recalled that he had

> spent all my early years on utility analysis...I was very attracted, in a way, by the indifference-curve analysis. I thought it was really the most satisfactory form, particularly when it became clear that it unified the theory of production and the theory of utility with a similar apparatus.

Hayek reflected:

> I don't know whether I ought to mention it – I doubt whether John Hicks remembers it – but it's almost a joke of history that I had to draw Hicks's attention, who came from Marshall, to indifference curves. ... the blackboard was used much by people like Hicks and Allen.[46]

Hicks had been

> a complete Marshallian when he came, and it was really in discussion – I probably had more theoretical discussions with John Hicks in the early years of the thirties than with any of the other people.[47]

Hayek recalled a conversation after a seminar when Hicks 'had been talking in Marshallian terms, when I drew his attention to Pareto'.[48] Hicks and Kenneth Arrow won the Nobel Prize in 1972; when Armen Alchian asked, 'Perhaps it might have been more appropriate for the Nobel Prize to have gone to you and Hicks together, and Arrow and [Gunnar] Myrdal together', Hayek replied, 'Oh, surely'.[49]

Jack High quoted Hicks to Hayek:

> When the definitive history of economic analysis during the 1930s comes to be written, a leading character in the drama – it was quite a drama – will be Professor Hayek.

Hicks was not just referring to the ordinalist revolution but also to the Keynesian revolution.[50]

Hayek (1931) and Robbins (1934) became major opponents of Keynes. Hayek stated that for about 'twenty years' he and Keynes jointly dominated economics until Keynes was elevated to sainthood:

I bitterly regretted having once mentioned to my [first] wife after Keynes's death, that now Keynes was dead I was probably the best-known economist living. But ten days later it was probably no longer true. At that very moment Keynes became the great figure, and I was gradually forgotten as an economist.

Indeed, Hayek (1979) believed that he 'became a Satan'.

Yet Hayek's influence continued. After winning the Nobel Prize, Hayek campaigned for Ronald Coase (1910–) to be likewise elevated. The last Prize to be awarded before Hayek's death went to Coase for two essays. First, 'The Nature of the Firm' (1937) which according to the Nobel press release became the basis for rapidly expanding research on principal-agent relations. It has also influenced vital aspects of financial economics, such as the lively research devoted to explaining the pattern of financial intermediaries; and, second, 'The Problem of Social Cost' (1960) in which 'frictionless markets' could eliminate the need for government intervention to correct for market failure.

In the *Journal of Law and Economics* symposium on 'The Fire of Truth', Ben Klein (1983: 202) noted that Coase's 1937 'Nature of the Firm' article 'seems to have been widely cited', and although it was reprinted in the American Economic Association (AEA) volume readings 'it didn't seem to influence anybody – everybody sort of nodded'. George Stigler (1983: 202) added: 'Not even Ronald...I chose the article' to be reprinted in the AEA volume on *Readings in Price Theory* (Stigler and Boulding, 1952).

In his Nobel Lecture, Coase (1991) referred to

the infamous Coase Theorem, named and formulated by Stigler, although it is based on work of mine. Stigler argues that the Coase Theorem follows from the standard assumptions of economic theory. Its logic cannot be questioned, only its domain. I do not disagree with Stigler. However, I tend to regard the Coase Theorem as a stepping stone on the way to an analysis of an economy with positive transaction costs. The significance to me of the Coase Theorem is that it undermines the Pigovian system. Since standard economic theory assumes transaction costs to be zero, the Coase Theorem demonstrates that the Pigovian solutions are unnecessary in these circumstances.

The famous 1960 'Coase versus Pigou' evening at Aaron Director's house in Chicago was 'the most exciting intellectual event' of Stigler's life. Coase attempted to persuade 20 Chicago economists (including Stigler, Director, Milton Friedman, Arnold Harberger, Gregg Lewis, Lloyd Mints, Reuben Kessel, Martin Bailey, and John McGee) that Pigouvian externalities need not restrain markets in the absence of transaction costs. According to Stigler, (1988: 75) during the course of the evening the vote changed from 20 for Pigou to 21 for Coase. This effectively partitioned economics into two epochs: After Coase (A.C.) and Before Coase (B.C.).

Coase (1983: 192) recalled, 'When I came to the University of Chicago (1964) I regarded my role as that of Saint Paul to Aaron Director's Christ. He got the doctrine going, and what I had to do was bring it to the gentiles'.

According to Stigler (1988: 75) 'Before Coase' economists accepted the 'gospel' of a disharmony between private and social interests in the same way they accepted supply and demand as the forces determining prices 'instinctively and without misgivings'. Denying externalities was 'heresy' – but this heresy became the foundation of renewed faith in market success. This was the only 'Eureka' moment of Stigler's life.

Stigler developed a theory of – and strategy for – knowledge construction and destruction (Leeson, 2000a). Stigler implied that Coase's insights revealed a redundancy in the second generation British School of Economics. Presumably referring to Marshall's (1890) *Principles of Economics*, Stigler stated that the 'Before Coase' epoch had confused 'all economists...from at least 1890 until 1961' (Stigler, 1983: 221; 1988: 148–169; 1992: 456).[51]

Coase (1983: 217, 211–213) was an important link between Hayek, the LSE and the creation of the Chicago School: 'Hayek was terribly important at the LSE in ways that perhaps people wouldn't realize. He helped to make our theory more precise'. In 1928, Coase attended an LSE lecture at which Allyn Young (1876–1929) 'spoke about the Austrians and the importance of their work...he was introducing von Mises who then gave a lecture'. Referring to *The Ethics of Competition* (1935), a volume of Frank Knight's collected essays (selected and edited by Friedman, Homer Jones, Stigler and Allen Wallis), Coase explained:

You might have thought that I got my views from Marshall and Pigou but that wasn't true, I got it both from studying particularly the Ethics of Competition [Knight] and actually having heard Knight in 1932 at Chicago.

The title of Coase's paper on 'The Problem of Social Cost' came from Knight's (1924) 'Fallacies in the Interpretation of Social Costs'.

With respect to Cambridge, Coase (1983: 218) stated: 'Marshall had wanted to encourage the study of law. When Pigou took over that seems to have disappeared ... It's obvious to anybody who knows Pigou that he isn't interested in this subject'.

Hayek's influence: phase two

The second phase of Hayek's influence relates to both a wide and an elite audience. The wider constituency was reached via *The Road to Serfdom* (1944). In 1947, Hayek also created the libertarian Mont Pelerin Society (MPS): fellow Europeans plus some hand-picked Americans, some of whom, like Friedman and Stigler, were undertaking their first overseas trip (Friedman and Friedman, 1996: 159). They were parochial in another sense: Friedman (2 January 1947) informed Hayek that several of the European names on his proposed list of attendees were 'unfamiliar to us' (the 'us' apparently included Director and Knight).[52] According to Stigler (1988: 148), 'There was no Chicago School of Economics' before the foundation of the MPS.

Hayek believed that the popular *The Road to Serfdom* component of this second phase simultaneously reduced his influence amongst mainstream economists: 'For the following thirty years, it was only Keynes who counted, and I was gradually almost forgotten ... I was known to a few specialists but not by the public at large'.[53]

This neglect ended with the 1974 Nobel Prize awarded jointly with the left-wing Myrdal (1898–1987).

Chapters 2–4 describe two of these four phases. Melissa Lane (Chapter 2) outlines the genesis of *The Road to Serfdom*, emphasizing that one aspect of Hayek's advocacy – his attack on political nationalism – has tended to be ignored by his conservative supporters. The book's influence in American derived from a cartoon (by *Look* magazine, distributed by General Motors) plus Max Eastman's condensed version (*Reader's Digest*, subsequently distributed by the Book of the Month Club).[54]

Hayek's influence: phase three

Since 1968, expectations and outcomes associated with the award of the Nobel Prize in Economic Sciences have contributed to the transformation of social science and public policy. Some aspirants began to see themselves as 'prize fighters' confronting competitors; some ideologically-driven economists have also aggressively promoted fellow-travellers. Prize aspirations may have driven Don Patinkin and Harry Johnson to make accusations about Friedman's honesty with respect to monetarism and the Chicago 'oral tradition'. In the frenzy of accusations, no-one – not even Friedman – thought that the relevant evidence should be examined: Friedman's 1932–1933 University of Chicago lecture notes (Leeson, 2003a, b).

The origins of Hayek's third phase of influence are controversial and difficult to document. In the late 1960s, he descended into a lengthy depression which lasted into 1974. According to the Nobel Press statement (9 October 1974) Hayek and Myrdal had 'always' been on the list of proposed winners. Hayek's merits were delineated under the title 'The Functional Efficiency of Economic Systems': Hayek's profundity allowed him to give a 'warning of the possibility of a major economic crisis before the great crash came in the autumn of 1929'. With respect to 'the problems of centralized planning' Hayek

> gave a profound historical exposé of the history of doctrines and opinions in this field. He presented new ideas with regard to basic difficulties in 'socialistic calculating', and investigated the possibilities of achieving effective results by decentralized 'market socialism' in various forms. His guiding principle when comparing various systems is to study how efficiently all the knowledge and all the information dispersed among individuals and enterprises is utilized. His conclusion is that only by far-reaching decentralization in a market system with competition and free price-fixing is it possible to make full use of knowledge and information ... For him it is not a matter of a simple defence of a liberal system of society as may sometimes appear from the popularized versions of his thinking.

The original Nobel Prize Selection Committee – Bertil Ohlin (chairman), Erik Lundberg, Assar Lindbeck, Ingvar Svennilson, Herman Wold and Sune Carson – no doubt thought carefully about how to maximize the prestige of their judgments. The Prize altered incentives for both economists and members of the Committee. Their deliberations are supposed to be kept secret until the archives are opened: yet Lindbeck apparently revealed that Roy Harrod would have been awarded the Prize had he lived long enough (Eltis, 1987: 596).

At least four Selection Committee members were associated with Hayek: Carson (who attended Mises' seminar in the 1920s), Ohlin,[55] Lundberg and Lindbeck. Hayek invited Ohlin – the leader of the right-of-centre Liberal People's Party (1944–1967) – to become a foundation MPS member;[56] at the first meeting Stigler also proposed that Ohlin be elected.[57] It appears, however, that Ohlin was participating in a rival organization: Eli Heckscher (30 December 1946) informed Hayek that an 'international Liberal Association' had been proposed and that 'The only one among us that seemed willing to take a personal part in their undertaking was Ohlin'.[58] Hayek declined an invitation to join the Executive of 'Liberal International' – possibly because of that organisation's attachment to the ideals of William Beveridge. But attempts were apparently made to coordinate MPS and 'Liberal International' meetings.[59]

Lundberg of 'Skandinaviska Banken, Stockholm' was elected to MPS membership in 1958.[60] 'Erik Lundberg and/or Bertil Ohlin' were listed as part of the fourteen 'Possible Advisors' to the 1963 Principles of Freedom Project.[61] Lindbeck (2006: 13), in *An Essay on Economic Reforms and Social Change in China*, stated that

> markets are the only realistic method for coordinating decentralized decision-making and hence exploit decentralized and fragmented knowledge in society (a point emphasized, in particular, by Hayek, 1945).

The 1970s were a poor decade for macroeconomic outcomes; indeed, the discrediting of Keynesian macroeconomics tended to elevate both anti-Keynesian macroeconomics and pre-Keynesian marketeconomics (which Hayek represented). Arthur Burns, a second-year MPS member, ran an inflationary monetary policy during his Chairmanship of the Federal Reserve System (1970–1978) whilst also promoting price and wage controls (Leeson, 2003c). Most neoclassical economists objected to such interferences with the price mechanism.

Keynes (1919: 235–236) typified the objection to inflation:

> Lenin is said to have declared that the best way to destroy the capitalist system was to debauch the currency... Lenin was certainly right. There is no subtler, no surer means of overturning the existing basis of society than to debauch the currency. The process engages all the hidden forces of economic law on the side of destruction, and does it in a manner which not one man in a million is able to diagnose.

The emergence of the Cold War (1947–1948) and then the fear of Richard Nixon being elected President of the USA in 1960 may have weakened this opposition to inflation (Leeson, 1997a, b). On 15 August 1971, President Nixon introduced price and wage controls: the New Economic Policy – a name derived from Lenin.

In 1971, the Nobel Selection Committee invited Machlup – Hayek's close friend, fellow Austrian School economist and founding MPS member – to write an 'appraisal' of Hayek's worthiness for a Nobel Prize – which he completed in September 1971.[62] Between 5 and 9 September 1971, Machlup and Hayek and other MPS Board members met to plan the 25th MPS anniversary meeting, to be held in 1972.[63]

Initially the MPS was an elite group of intellectuals and their donors. Friedman (2 January 1947) informed Hayek that

> Our faith requires that we be skeptical of the efficacy, at least in the short run, of organized efforts to promulgate it. But it also requires a belief in the long-run efficiency of the kind of discussion this conference is intended to promote.[64]

By 'faith', Friedman may have been referring to neoclassical production theory: in the short run, their labours were being added to the fixed factor of an intellectual climate which would become a variable factor in the long run. The initial 38 MPS members combined human capital (academics), access to financial capital (donors and think tankers: F. A. Harper, Albert Hunold, Leonard Read and Orval Watts) plus access to public opinion (journalists: John Davenport, Trygve Hoff, Herbert Tingsten and Cicely Wedgwood).

According to Friedman and Hayek, in its third decade the MPS long run arrived. In 1977 Hayek (1992) proclaimed that 'its main purpose has been wholly achieved'. Prior to 1957, Friedman attended only one MPS meeting – the first (Friedman and Friedman, 1996: 33). As MPS President, Friedman (October 1970) proposed that a special board of directors meeting consider holding a 'grand 25th anniversary meeting' in 1972 'and then disbanding... in a blaze of glory... Organizations have a tendency to persist after they have outlived their function. Unlike old soldiers, they generally do not even fade away'.[65]

By 1974, Hayek had largely faded from professional significance. Gabriel Söderberg, Avner Offer, and Samuel Bjork (Chapter 3) reveal that Hayek's citation pattern was quite different from the average Nobel Prize winner. In eighteen years, seven early MPS members joined the Nobel elite: Hayek (1974), Friedman (1976), Stigler (1982), James Buchanan (1986), Maurice Allais (1988), Coase (1991) and Gary Becker (1992). In a sense, they were the beneficiaries of the long run. In the two decades after Becker, only one MPS member has been similarly acknowledged: Vernon Smith (2002).

Tensions between Hayek and Myrdal apparently stretched back to the 1930s. In 1933, Hayek – apparently reluctantly – published an essay by Myrdal which was critical of Hayek's (and Keynes') work on monetary economics (Barber, 2008: 25). The *New York Times* reported that both Hayek and Myrdal 'are said to have been annoyed by the [1974 Nobel] pairing'.[66] With the possible exception of John Nash in 1994, no other Economics Prize has generated as much speculation: was Myrdal the balance to Hayek, vice versa, or neither? In her biography of her mother, Alva Myrdal, Sissela Bok (1991: 305) speculated that her father's Prize was a 'condescending joke on the part of the members of the Swedish economics establishment'. Certainly, it appears that there were personal, as well as ideological and methodological tensions between the two. If the intention was to aggravate Myrdal, it succeeded: he later regretted accepting the Prize (Barber, 2008: 164–5).

The editor of this volume participated in a 1995 conversation with several distinguished social scientists at which it was asserted that a foundation member of the Selection Committee had stated that there had been pressure for an early award to the Swedish Myrdal. But Myrdal had been co-chair of the International Commission of Inquiry into US War Crimes in Indochina (Barber, 2008: 160); he was also allegedly personally (and politically) disliked by members of the Committee. A compromise was apparently reached: he was given the Prize jointly with the right-wing Hayek, someone he despised.[67]

David Laidler (Chapter 4) recounts a similar conversation in autumn 1973 between himself, Lundberg and Herbert Giersch, a foundation member of the German Council of Economic Experts (1964–1970). Giersch overlapped with Hayek at the LSE (1948–1950, as a British Council Fellow) and was one of his friends and intellectual colleagues. Giersch (1985) was also an MPS Director and later President (1986–1988) and one of fourteen participants at the 1985 Liberty Fund conference on 'The Mont Pelerin Society and the Revival of Liberalism' at which he presented a paper which documented how Hayek, indirectly, and Walter Eucken and Erhard, directly, rescued the economy and thus the society of post-war Germany.[68]

The London *Times* and the *Daily Telegraph* promoted Hayek throughout the third phase of his influence. In 1978 Hayek stated:

You see, I'm very interested in politics; in fact, in a way I take part. I now am very much engaged in strengthening Mrs. [Margaret]

Thatcher's back in her fight against the unions. But I would refuse to take any sort of political position or political responsibility. I write articles; I've even achieved recently the dignity of an article on the lead page of the London *Times* on that particular subject. I'm represented in England as the inspirer of Mrs. Thatcher, whom I've only met twice in my life on social occasions.[69]

The editors of the *Times* during this period were William Rees-Mogg (1967–1981), Harold Evans (1981–1982), Charles Douglas-Home (1982–1985) and Charles Wilson (1985–1990); Peter Jay was the *Times* Economics Editor (1967–1977). This process culminated in a *Times* profile by Mises' daughter-in-law, Gitta Sereny (1985), on 'The Sage of the Free Thinking World'. During this period, the power of both the Soviet Union and British unions declined (the latter associated with the defeat of the National Union of Mineworkers, 1984–1985, and the Fleet Street production workers, 1986–1987).

In 1978 Hayek had

just published an article in the London *Times* on the effect of trade unions generally. It contains a short paragraph just pointing out that one of the effects of high wages leading to unemployment is that it forces capitalists to use their capital in a form where they will employ little labour. I now see from the reaction that it's still a completely new argument to most of the people.[70]

In response to Leo Rosten's statement that 'Unions are part of the establishment in the United States', Hayek replied. 'Well, so they are in England – much more so'.[71] *The Times* had long been considered the voice of the British establishment; in 1981 it was acquired by Murdoch's News International in controversial circumstances. In 1986 Murdoch sacked 6000 Fleet Street production employees and relocated his four main titles, *The Times*, *The Sunday Times*, *The Sun* and the *News of the World*, to a new plant in Wapping. Murdoch's defeat of the Fleet Street unions transformed industrial relations in Britain.

Two years later, in the Manhattan Institute's third annual Walter B. Wriston Lecture in Public Policy, Murdoch (1990) described 'The War on Technology' in Hayekian terms:

We were encouraged by Mrs. Thatcher's victory in the miners' strike and by signs that authorities were prepared to protect private property from the actions of massed pickets...The war between new technology and outmoded social institutions continues. At stake is the very idea of human progress ... The great truth, which being an immigrant perhaps I can see more clearly than the average citizen, is this: Modernization is Americanization. It is the American way of organizing society that is prevailing in the world ... The decision to rely on market forces is the essence of modernization. Yet technological change often provokes atavistic, authoritarian responses. The real danger of the present technological revolution is that we may be panicked by future shock into regressive schemes of regulation ... The immediate result of our victory was greater freedom and flexibility, and higher profits, for News Corp. But the Battle of Wapping also ushered in a silver age of British newspaper journalism.[72]

From the Suez debacle (1956) to the onset of the Global Financial Crisis (2007), Great Britain was obliged to address the lost status associated with the demise of Empire, non-white immigration from the former colonies plus intensified industrial disputation. Attempts were made to find a post-imperial role. For example, Harold Macmillan (Prime Minister, 1956–1963) embraced the decolonizing 'wind of change', and under Edward Heath (1970–1974) the country joined the European Economic Community. But Heath's free market rhetoric collapsed into price and wage controls, and his government was unable to overcome the industrial power of the National Union of Mineworkers. Under Harold Wilson's Labour Governments (1964–1970 and 1974–1976) attempts to reduce trade union power were abandoned.

At the intersection of ideas and politics, British decline was addressed by Anthony Fisher's Institute of Economic Affairs (1955–) plus two Conservative Party groups: the free market Selsdon Group (1973–) and the anti-decolonization and immigration-restricting Monday Club (1961–). Hayek was an inspiration for – and an associate of – all three.

As noted above, the term 'Austrian School of Economics' was for its German Historical School critics derisory – a reflection of Habsburg decline relative to Prussia. Hayek and Otto von Habsburg (1976) saw similarities with British decline. Mrs. Thatcher and *The Times* derived inspiration from these sources. Peter Jay regarded the era of the 'two Harolds', Macmillan and Wilson (1956–1976), as a period of 'shame ... of short-termism, of political manipulation, of cynicism'.[73] In 1978, *The Times* juxtaposed this era with the 'age of Hayek' plus a photograph captioned 'F. A. Hayek, the greatest economic philosopher of the age'.[74]

A few weeks before the announcement of his Nobel Prize, Hayek stated in an interview:

> It may be said that effective and rational economic policies can be implemented only by a superior leader of the philosopher-statesman type under powerful autocracy. And I do not mean a communist-dictatorship but rather a powerful regime following democratic principles.

The interviewer, Seigen Tanaka (1974), reported, 'Saying this, Prof. Hayek shifted his eyes to the snow capped mountains at a distance'.[75]

In the 1978 UCLA interviews with Leo Rosten, Hayek reflected about the insights of one of his Austrian predecessors:

> You see, I believe Schumpeter is right in the sense that while socialism can never satisfy what people expect, our present political structure inevitably drives us into socialism, even if people do not want it in the majority. That can only be prevented by altering the structure of our so-called democratic system. But that's necessarily a very slow process, and I don't think that an effort toward reform will come in time. So I rather fear that we shall have a return to some sort of dictatorial democracy, I would say, where democracy merely serves to authorize the actions of a dictator. And if the system is going to break down, it will be a very long period before real democracy can reemerge. My present aim is really to prevent the recognition of this turning into a complete disgust with democracy in any form, which is a great danger, in my opinion. I want to make clear to the people that it's what I call unlimited democracy which is the danger, where coercion is not limited to the application of uniform rules, but you can take any specific coercive measure if it seems to serve a good purpose. And anything or anybody which will help the politician be elected is by definition a good purpose. I think people can be made to recognize this and to restore general limitations on the governmental powers; but that will be a very slow process, and I rather fear that before we can achieve something like this, we will get something like what [J. L.] Talmon has called 'totalitarian democracy' – an elective dictatorship with practically unlimited powers. Then it will depend, from country to country, whether they are lucky or unlucky in the kind of person who gets in power. After all, there have been good dictators in the past; it's very unlikely that it will ever arise. But there may be one or two experiments where a dictator restores freedom, individual freedom.

Americans typically embrace Benjamin Franklin in this context: 'those who give up a little liberty to gain a little security, deserve neither'. Rosten exclaimed: 'I can hardly think of a program that will be harder to sell to the American people. I'm using "sell" in the sense of persuade. How can a dictatorship be good?' To which Hayek replied: 'Oh, it will never be called a dictatorship; it may be a one-party system'.

Hayek had little hope for America:

> But if I may say so – I hope you are not offended – I don't believe the ultimate decision is with America. You are too unstable in your opinion, and if opinion has been turning in the right direction the last few years, it may be turning in the wrong direction again in the next few years. While it's sometimes a great advantage to be able to change opinion very rapidly, it also creates a certain amount of instability. I think it must become a much more general movement, and for that reason, I am rather more hopeful about what is happening among the young people in Europe nowadays than what's happening here, perhaps also because in Europe the intellectual tendencies are more likely to capture public opinion lastingly.

Hayek concluded that

> Socialism has never been an affair of the proletarians. It has always been the affair of the intellectuals, who have provided the workers' parties with the philosophy.

Hayek's strategy for revolution involved marginalizing the 'fathers' of other neoclassical schools:

> I believe there is a chance of making the intellectuals proud of seeing through the delusions of the past. That is my present ambition, you know. It's largely concerned with socialism, but of course socialism and unlimited democracy come very much to the same thing. And I believe – at least I have the illusion – that you can put things in a way in which the intellectuals will be ashamed to believe in what their fathers believed... what I always come back to is that the whole thing turns on the activities of those intellectuals whom I call the 'secondhand dealers in opinion', who determine what people think in the long run. If you can persuade them, you ultimately reach the masses of the people.[76]

Hayek told Robert Bork that 'this is my present attempt to make the intellectuals feel intellectually superior if they see through socialism'.[77]
Hayek concluded that:

> The net effect of John Stuart Mill on economics has been devastating, and [W. Stanley] Jevons knew this. Jevons regarded Mill as a thoroughly pernicious influence ... In assessing the difference between the Austrians and the Cambridge School, it was Marshall, with his harking back to Mill and his famous two blades of a sisal [scissors?] – it's not demand only, it's not supply only, it's a sisal [*sic*] that determines values – that preserved this tradition. And it's out of this tradition that the whole of English socialism has sprung.[78]

Rosten (18 February 1979) informed Hayek that President 'Carter is a disaster – but who will follow him? The world map is godawful these days'.[79] But within two years of the UCLA interviews, the 'two Jameses', Callaghan and Carter, were defeated by Mrs. Thatcher (May 1979) and Ronald Reagan (November 1980) respectively. While convalescing from the 1984 Irish Republican Army bombing of the Conservative Party conference, Norman Tebbitt, Thatcher's Secretary of State for Trade and Industry, read up on two of his favourite characters: the 'two Freds' – Hayek and Truman (the cricketer). These chapters will explore the roles that Hayek played in these policy revolutions.

Hayek's influence: phase four

The fourth phase of influence – the 21st-century promotion of Hayek by Murdoch's Fox News – created a bull market. Selwyn Cornish (Chapter 5), the Official Historian of the Reserve Bank of Australia, critically examines part of this Hayek-promotion wave: Nicholas Wapshott's (2001) *Keynes Hayek: The Clash That Defined Modern Economics*. Later chapters in this series of collaborative biographical chapters will systematically examine other contributions to the Hayek literature.

Austrians and the social market economy

Chapters 6, 7 and 8 examine the divisions and dynamics within the Austrian and libertarian tradition. Douglas French (Chapter 6), the Director of the Ludwig von Mises Institute, describes the relationship between Hayek and Mises and the two Austrian School traditions.

Viktor Vanberg (Chapter 7) elaborates on some of the conflicts within the classical liberal tradition. In 1962, Hayek moved to Freiburg where he remained (with an interlude at Salzburg, 1970–1977) until his death. Hayek (1994: 118) was intellectually and personally close to Walter Eucken – who he regarded as having challenged Mises' claim 'to represent the only authoritative liberalism'. Eucken was an 'ordo-liberal', and some of his colleagues, such as Alexander Rüstow, believed both Mises and Hayek to be 'Palaeoliberals'. Hayek's connections to Eucken and the ordo-liberals was, for some, further evidence of Hayek's deviation from the Misean or neoliberal tradition.

Nils Goldschmidt and Jan-Otmar Hesse (Chapter 8) examine aspects of the Hayek–Eucken relationship via a 1946 letter. Three conclusions emerge: First, Eucken perceived that societal order must prevail over individual freedom; second, Eucken argued that the state must intervene to prevent the cartelization of industry while Hayek tended to reject such intervention and later publicly opposed a ban on cartels; and third, Eucken assigned to the state the role of organizing competition, while Hayek saw competition as a natural state requiring a substantial *absence* of state intervention.

Bartley

Chapters 9–12 explore Bartley and his interactions with Hayek. No philosopher could be persuaded to provide a biographical account of Bartley: the present author, an economist, was therefore obliged to write Chapter 9.

Rafe Champion (Chapter 10), an authority on Bartley's philosophy, outlines the salient aspects of that philosophical tradition. After Bartley's premature death, his partner, Stephen Kresge, took over the *Collected Works of F.A. Hayek* project: Chapter 11 provides an illuminating interview with Kresge.

In addition to his biography of Wittgenstein, Bartley (1978) wrote *Werner Erhard the Transformation of a Man: The Founding of est* (Erhard Seminars Training). Jack Rosenberg renamed himself after Werner Heisenberg, the physicist and author of the uncertainty principle, and Ludwig Erhard, the author of the post-war German economic 'miracle'. Ludwig Erhard (20 June 1948) introduced a currency reform and abolished the price-fixing and production controls initiated by the occupying military forces; shortly afterwards he became an MPS member (1950). Like Hayek, he was associated with Eucken, the Freiburg School and the social market economy of ordo-liberalism.

Werner Erhard developed the personal development 'est Training' (1971–1983) and 'The Forum' (1984–1991) which became the 'Landmark Forum' (1991–). In Chapter 12, he reflects on his interactions with Bartley and two MPS foundation members (Friedman and Popper), plus Michael Jensen, the founder (1973) and editor of the *Journal of Financial Economics* and the co-author of two seminal, Coase-inspired, essays on stock options as incentive-compatible executive compensation tools (Jensen and Meckling, 1976; Jensen and Murphy, 1990).

This series has its origins in a Reserve Bank of Australia analysis of policy outcomes and knowledge dynamics in the economics profession (Leeson, 2000b). The first three volumes in this series examined *The Keynesian Tradition* (volume 1), *The Anti-Keynesian Tradition* (volume 2) and *American Power and Policy* (volume 3). Implausible neoclassical assumptions of rationality have stimulated behavioural economics – an area in which Hayek was a pioneer (volume 4, *Hayek and Behavioural Economics*). If the current era of endemic financial crises accelerates this reconstruction of economics, Hayek's life and influence may continue to shed light on the market for knowledge.

Notes

1. Sometimes referred to as the Taliban and the Talibank.
2. Previous biographies have not directly attempted to undertake this task.
3. 1978 UCLA interview with Axel Leijonhufvud.
4. The dispute over labor contracts was simultaneously a dispute about the rights of the States relative to the power of the Federal government.
5. 1978 UCLA interview with Leo Rosten.
6. 1978 UCLA interview with Armen Alchian.
7. 1978 UCLA interview with Leo Rosten.
8. 1978 UCLA interview with Jack High.
9. Hayek Papers Box 27.1.
10. Hayek Papers Box 165.
11. Hayek Papers Box 26.28.
12. Hayek Papers Box 22.18.
13. 1978 UCLA interview with Axel Leijonhufvud.
14. 1978 UCLA interview with Armen Alchian.
15. 1978 UCLA interview with Armen Alchian.
16. Hayek (10 June 1981) to Frank Tipler. Hayek Papers Box 53.9.
17. 1978 UCLA interview with Leo Rosten.
18. 1978 UCLA interview with Earlene Craver.
19. 1978 UCLA interview with Leo Rosten.
20. 1978 UCLA interview with Axel Leijonhufvud.
21. 1978 UCLA interview with James Buchanan.
22. 1978 UCLA interview with Earlene Craver.
23. 1978 UCLA interview with Earlene Craver.

24. 1978 UCLA interview with Armen Alchian.
25. 1978 UCLA interview with Robert Chitester.
26. 1978 UCLA interview with James Buchanan.
27. 1978 UCLA interview with Leo Rosten.
28. Mises offered a different perspective: http://mises.org/daily/3512
29. Hayek Papers Box 121.2.
30. Hayek (2 February 1984) to William Johnson, Hayek Papers Box 29.38.
31. Seminar notes (16 February 1993). Furth Papers, Hoover Institution, Box 12.
32. As, coincidently, were influential members of the Chicago School (Friedman and Director) and the Keynesian Neoclassical Synthesis (Paul Samuelson and Kenneth Arrow).
33. 1978 UCLA interview with Armen Alchian.
34. 1978 UCLA interview with James Buchanan.
35. 1978 UCLA interview with Axel Leijonhufvud.
36. 1978 UCLA interview with Earlene Craver.
37. 1978 UCLA interview with Jack High.
38. 1978 UCLA interview with Armen Alchian.
39. 1978 UCLA interview with Earlene Craver.
40. 1978 UCLA interview with Leo Rosten.
41. 1978 UCLA interview with Axel Leijonhufvud.
42. 1978 UCLA interview with Armen Alchian.
43. 1978 UCLA interview with Axel Leijonhufvud.
44. 1978 UCLA interview with Earlene Craver.
45. 1978 UCLA interview with James Buchanan.
46. 1978 UCLA interview with Armen Alchian.
47. 1978 UCLA interview with Armen Alchian.
48. 1978 UCLA interview with James Buchanan.
49. 1978 UCLA interview with Armen Alchian.
50. 1978 UCLA interview with Jack High.
51. 1890 was also the year of the Sherman Anti-trust Act.
52. Hayek Papers Box 73.40.
53. 1978 UCLA interview with Robert Chitester.
54. The founders, editors and publishers of *Reader's Digest*, De Witt and Lila Bell Wallace, left part of their wealth to the Hoover Institution. Eastman became an MPS member in 1948. Hayek Papers Boxes 73.20.
55. Like many others, Ohlin visited the LSE during Hayek's time (Robbins, 1971: 132).
56. Hayek Papers Boxes 46.25 and 80.33.
57. Hayek Papers Box 80.34.
58. Hayek Papers Box 75.1.
59. Hayek (30 May 1949) to Dr Salvadore de Madariaga. Hayek Papers Box 36.22.
60. Hayek Papers Boxes 83.6 and 71.3.
61. Hayek Papers Box 67.23.
62. Machlup (19 November 1974) to Hayek. Hayek Papers Box 36.18.
63. Hayek Papers Box 74.30.
64. Hayek Papers Box 73.40.
65. Hayek Papers Box 73.40.
66. http://www.nytimes.com/1987/05/18/obituaries/gunnar-myrdal-analyst-of-race-crisis-dies.

67. Gustav Lennart Jörberg (1927–1997), an associate member (1993) of the Nobel Selection Committee, reportedly asserted during a seminar at Lund University that it had been decided that Myrdal's discomfort would be maximized by his pairing with Hayek because Hayek had 'paired' with Myrdal's wife, Alva, in an extra-marital affair. It is *possible* that someone initially had reliable knowledge about this – but the chain (from the inter-war period?) to Jörberg may have had many steps and so is flimsy at best. However, the gossip is indicative of the unusual nature of the 1974 award.
68. Hayek Papers Box 21.31.
69. 1978 UCLA interview with Robert Chitester.
70. 1978 UCLA interview with Robert Chitester.
71. 1978 UCLA interview with Leo Rosten.
72. http://www.city-journal.org/article01.php?aid=1631
73. http://www.meg.qmul.ac.uk/Transcripts/IMF/index.html
74. 1978 UCLA interview with Thomas Hazlett.
75. Hayek Papers Box 52.28.
76. 1978 UCLA interview with James Buchanan.
77. 1978 UCLA interview with Robert Bork.
78. 1978 UCLA interview with Jack High.
79. Hayek Papers Box 46.46.

Bibliography

Archival insights into the evolution of economics

Leeson, R. (ed.) 2008. *Vol. 1: The Keynesian Tradition* (New York: Palgrave Macmillan).
Leeson, R. (ed.) 2009a. *Vol. 2: The Anti-Keynesian Tradition* (New York: Palgrave Macmillan).
Leeson, R. (ed.) 2009b. *Vol. 3: American Power and Policy* (New York: Palgrave Macmillan).
Franz, R. and Leeson, R. (eds) 2012. *Vol. 4: Hayek and Behavioural Economics*. (New York: Palgrave Macmillan).

Other works cited

Barber, William J. 2008. *Gunnar Myrdal: An Intellectual Biography* (New York: Palgrave Macmillan).
Bartley, W.W. 1973. *Wittgenstein* (New York: Lippincott Co.).
Bartley, W.W. 1978. *Werner Erhard The Transformation of a Man: The Founding of est* (New York: Clarkson N. Porter).
Bok, S. 1991. *Alva Myrdal: A Daughter's Memoir* (Boston: Addison Wesley).
Caldwell, B. 2000. (ed.) Carl Menger and his Legacy in Economics. *History of Political Economy* (Annual Supplement).
Coase, R. 1937. The Nature of the Firm. *Economica*, 4 (16): 386–405.
Coase, R. 1960. The Problem of Social Cost. *Journal of Law and Economics*, 3 (1): 1–44.
Coase, R. 1983. The Fire of Truth: A Remembrance of Law and Economics at Chicago, 1932–1970. *Journal of Economics and Law* (April), XXVI: 163–234.
Coase, R. 1991. Nobel Lecture.

Eatwell, J., M. Milgate and P. Newman. (eds) 1987. *The New Palgrave Dictionary of Economics* (London: Macmillan).

Eltis, W. 1987. Roy Forbes Harrod. In Eatwell J. Milgate M. and Newman P. (eds) *The New Palgrave Dictionary of Economics* (London: Macmillan).

Friedman, M., H. Jones, G. Stigler and W. A. Wallis. (eds) 1935. *The Ethics of Competition and Other Essays* (London: George Allen & Unwin).

Friedman, M. and R. D. Friedman. 1996. *Two Lucky People* (Chicago: University of Chicago Press).

Fukuyama, F. 1992. *The End of History and the Last Man* (Free Press: New York).

Giersch, H. 1985. Liberal reform in Europe with Special Reference to Germany (Mimeo), Hayek Papers Box 21.31.

Gordon, D. A. 2012. Preface. In Raico, *Classical Liberalism and the Austrian School* (Auburn, Alabama: Ludwig von Mises Institute).

Greaves, P. 1973. *Understanding the Dollar Crisis* (Western Islands: Belmont, Mass).

Habsburg, O. 1976. Our Finest Hour. *Daily Telegraph*

Hayek, F. A. 1931. *Prices and Production* (London: Routledge).

Hayek, F. A. 1944. *The Road to Serfdom* (London: Routledge).

Hayek, F. A. 1945. The Use of Knowledge in Society. *American Economic Review*, 35 (4): 519–530.

Hayek, F. A. 1978. Coping with Ignorance. *Imprimus*, 7 (7) (July, 1–6).

Hayek, F. A. 1979. A Period of Muddle Heads. Interview. *Newsweek,* (5 November), Hayek Papers Box 109.33.

Hayek, F. A. 1992. The Road from Serfdom: Forseeing the fall. *Reason* (July), http://reason.com/issues/july-1992.

Hayek, F. A. 1994. *Hayek on Hayek: an Autobiographical Dialogue* (Chicago: University of Chicago Press). Edited by Stephen Kresge and Leif Wenar.

Hicks, J. R. and R. Allen 1934. A Reconsideration of the Theory of Value. *Economica*, 1 (1): 52–76

Howson, S. 2011. *Lionel Robbins* (Cambridge: Cambridge University Press).

Hülsmann, J. G. 2007. *Mises: The Last Knight of Liberalism* (Auburn, Alabama: Ludwig von Mises Institute).

Hutchison, T. 1953. *A Review of Economic Doctrines, 1870–1929* (Oxford: Oxford University Press).

Hutt, W. 1990. *Economics and the Public: A Study of Competition and Opinion* (New Jersey: Transaction).

Jensen, M. and W. Meckling. 1976. Theory of the Firm: Managerial Behaviour, Agency Costs and Ownership Structure. *Journal of Financial Economics* (October), 3 (4): 305–360.

Jensen, M. and K. Murphy. 1990. CEO Incentives – It's Not How Much you Pay, But How. *Harvard Business Review ,* 3 (May June), 138–149.

Kauder, E. 1964. *A History of Marginal Utility Theory* (Princeton: Princeton University Press).

Keynes, J. M. 1919. *The Economic Consequences of the Peace* (London: Macmillan).

Keynes, J. M. 1936. *General Theory of Employment, Interest and Money* (New York and London: Harcourt, Brace).

Klein, B. 1983. The Fire of Truth: A Remembrance of Law and Economics at Chicago, 1932–1970. *Journal of Economics and Law* (April), XXVI: 163–234.

Knight, F. 1924. Fallacies in the Interpretation of Social Costs. *Quarterly Journal of Economics* (May), 38: 582–606.

Leeson, R. 1997a. The Political Economy of the Inflation Unemployment Trade-Off. *History of Political Economy* (Spring), 29 (1): 117–156.

Leeson, R. 1997b. The Eclipse of the Goal of Zero Inflation. *History of Political Economy* (Fall), 29 (3): 445–496.

Leeson, R. 2000a. *The Eclipse of Keynesianism: The Political Economy of the Chicago Counter-Revolution* (New York: Palgrave Macmillan).

Leeson, R. 2000b. Inflation, Disinflation and the Natural Rate of Unemployment: A Dynamic Framework for Policy Analysis. In *The Australian Economy in the 1990s* edited by David Gruen (Reserve Bank of Australia: Sydney), pp. 124–175.

Leeson, R. (ed.) 2003a. *Keynes, Chicago and Friedman*, Vol. 1 (London: Pickering and Chatto).

Leeson, R. (ed.) 2003b. *Keynes, Chicago and Friedman*, Vol. 2 (London: Pickering and Chatto).

Leeson, R. 2003c. *Ideology and the International Economy: The Decline and Fall of Bretton Woods* (New York: Palgrave-Macmillan).

Lindbeck, A. 1971. *The Political Economy of the New Left: An Outsider's View*, First edition (New York: Harper and Row).

Lindbeck, A. 1977. *The Political Economy of the New Left: An Outsider's View*, Second edition (New York: Harper and Row).

Lindbeck, A. 2006. *An Essay on Economic Reforms and Social Change in China* (World Bank Working Policy Research, Working Paper 4057).

Locke, J. 1689. *Letter Concerning Toleration.* (London: Awnfham Churchill).

Maine, H. 1861. *Ancient Law: Its Connection with the Early History of Society, and Its Relation to Modern Ideas* (London: John Murray).

Marx, K. 1915 [1867]. *Capital: Critique of Political Economy* (Chicago: Charles Kerr).

Marx, K. and F. Engels. 2011 [1848]. *Communist Manifesto* (England: Penguin).

Menger, C. 1881 [1871]. *Principles of Economics* (New York: L. Schneider).

Menger, C. 1985 [1883]. *Investigations into the Method of the Social Sciences with Special Reference to Economics* (New York: L. Schneider).

Mises, L. 1951. *On Socialism* (New Haven: Yale University Press).

Mises, L. 1953 [1912]. *Theory of Money and Credit* (New Haven: Yale University Press).

Mises, L. 1961. Liberty and its Antithesis: A review of Hayek's Constitution of Liberty. *Christian Economics*, 1 (August), 3.

Mises, L. 1962 [1927]. *Liberalism* (New York: Foundation for Economic Education).

Mises, L. 1973. Foreword. In Greaves, P., *Understanding the Dollar Crisis* (Western Islands: Belmont, Mass).

Mises, L. 2003. *The Historical Setting of the Austrian School of Economics* (Auburn, Alabama: Ludwig von Mises Institute).

Pigou, A. C. 1912. *Wealth and Welfare* (London: Macmillan).

Pigou, A. C. 1953. *Alfred Marshall and Current Economic Thought* (London: Macmillan).

Raico, R. 1975. A Libertarian Maestro. *The Alternative American Spectator*, 8, 8 (May), 21–23.

Raico, R. 2012. *Classical Liberalism and the Austrian School* (Auburn, Alabama: Ludwig von Mises Institute).

Robbins, L. 1932. *Essay on the Nature and Significance of Economic Science* (London: Macmillan).

Robbins, L. 1934. *The Great Depression* (London: Macmillan).

Robbins, L. 1938. Interpersonal Comparisons of Utility: A Comment. *Economic Journal*, 43 (4): 635–641.

Robbins, L. 1971. *Autobiography of an Economist* (London: Macmillan).

Samuelson, P. A. 1971. Foreword. In Lindbeck, *The Political Economy of the New Left: An Outsider's View*, First edition (New York: Harper and Row).

Schulak, E.-M. and H. Unterköfler. 2011. *The Viennese School of Economics* (Auburn, Alabama: Ludwig von Mises Institute).

Sereny, G. 1985. The Sage of the Free Thinking World. *Times* (9 May).

Smith, A. 1776. *Inquiry into the Nature and Causes of the Wealth of Nations* (W. Strahan and T. Cadell: London).

Steissler, E. 2000. Carl Menger on Economic Policy the Lectures to Crown Prince Rudolf. In Caldwell ed. *Carl Menger and his Legacy in Economics. History of Political Economy* (Annual Supplement).

Stigler, G. 1983. The Fire of Truth: A Remembrance of Law and Economics at Chicago, 1932–1970. *Journal of Economics and Law* (April), XXVI: 163–234.

Stigler, G. 1988. *Memoirs of an Unregulated Economist* (New York: Basic Books).

Stigler, G. 1992. Law or Economics? *Journal of Law and Economics* (October), XXXV: 455–468.

Stigler, G. and K. Boulding. (eds) 1952. *Readings in Price Theory* (American Economic Association New York: R.D. Irwin).

Tanaka, S. 1974. What Will Happen to the World as Keynesian Economic Theories are Disproved? Views of Professor Hayek, a World-Famous Authority on Inflation Sought. *Shuukan Post* (17 May).

Wapshott, N. 2001. *Keynes Hayek: The Clash That Defined Modern Economics* (New York: W.W. Norton).

Weber, M. 2002 [1905]. *The Protestant Ethic and the Spirit of Capitalism* (England: Penguin).

2
The Genesis and Reception of *The Road to Serfdom*

Melissa Lane

In 1963, Friedrich Hayek looked back on his life as an economist in London in the 1930s:[1]

> I found myself differing very strongly from the view then gener-
> ally current in England and particularly held by the majority of my
> socialistically inclined colleagues in the other departments of the LSE
> [London School of Economics and Political Science, where Hayek had
> taught]. They all tended to interpret the National Socialist regime of
> Hitler as a sort of capitalist reaction to the socialist tendencies of the
> immediate post-war period, while I saw it rather as the victory of a
> sort of lower-middle-class socialism, certainly thoroughly anti-capi-
> talistic and anti-liberal but taking over all the methods of socialism.
> It was in the end one of the memoranda which we occasionally did
> to prevent Sir William Beveridge from committing himself publicly
> to a thesis which we thought wrong that I first sketched the thesis. It
> caused so much surprise and disbelief... (Hayek, [1963] 1995, 62–63)

...that he decided to publish it as an article: 'Freedom and the Economic System' in the *Contemporary Review* of April 1938.[2]

This is the backstory of *The Road to Serfdom* (RtS),[3] which is an expanded version of a previously expanded version of 'Freedom and the Economic System' (FES) itself – and indeed the memorandum which Hayek mentions as lying at the bottom of the chain seems to have been identified as a Spring 1933 memo titled 'Nazi'-Socialism (Caldwell, 2007a: 5–6); Hayek, [1933] 2007). As Bruce Caldwell has demonstrated in his *Collected Works* edition of RtS in which the 1933 memo is reprinted, the backstory is striking in at least two respects.

The first is that the backstory reveals the British, rather than Austrian or German, context in which the ideas at the heart of RtS were conceived – or rather, the British context in which the Austrian and German experiences were being rethought by Hayek in the formation of those ideas. As he would write in the introduction to RtS in December 1943, having been evacuated with the rest of the LSE to safety in Peterhouse, Cambridge, he had twice watched a 'very similar evolution of ideas' (RtS: 57), that is, in Austria and Germany, and now in England, for 'it is Germany whose fate we are in some danger of repeating'. (RtS: 58)

The second is that the backstory shows that RtS is in its essence a *pre-war* book (pre-World War II, that is). For all that it has been received as part of a formulation of a pan-collectivist conception of totalitarianism – tarring British and American wartime ally Stalin with the same socialist label as Hitler – there is actually almost nothing in the book that is specific to the wartime experience of planning in Britain or America. That is because the ideas at the heart of RtS grew not out of the experience of wartime planning – as casual readers might have assumed – but rather out of the economic theory and practice debates of the peacetime 1920s and 1930s. No doubt, part of the prompt for the book were the debates about extending wartime planning into peacetime (Caldwell, 2007a: 8–9). But the attack on planning itself had already been formulated in its essentials by Hayek by the end of the 1930s.

To the now recognized origins of RtS in FES and even in the 1933 memo, the present chapter adds an exploration of a key set of texts which Hayek wrote between 1933, when he penned 'Nazi'-Socialism as the very earliest gestation of RtS, and December 1943, when he completed the book's final element, its preface, in Cambridge. These are the three English-language contributions to the 'Socialist Calculation Debate', as Hayek brought the original Austrian debates to the attention of an English-speaking public (two of them in the collection he edited on *Collectivist Economic Planning*, the third published in *Economica* in 1940), and 'Economics and Knowledge', which he delivered as the presidential address to the London Economic Club in November 1936 and published in *Economica* in 1937. The latter, which was stimulated by reflection on socialist calculation again a decade or so after the original debates, was considered by Hayek perhaps his most important intellectual insight. And it was made just two years before the first FES article was written. Thus, even though Hayek did not direct the reader interested in RtS to 'Economics and Knowledge' when publishing a collection including the latter in 1948 (see preface to *Individualism and Economic Order*), the conjunction of its insight into the division of knowledge, with the consideration of both the logical and the practical possibilities of socialism in the revived 'socialist calculation' debate, may shed light on the fused analysis and passion which became RtS.[4]

Gathering all these texts together, what emerges as most distinctive of Hayek's thought is that he does not simply argue that socialism is either relatively inefficient (compared to the market), or absolutely inefficient (such that it would be impossible to realize). Both of these would be claims on which the general equilibrium approach could potentially agree: socialist calculation represented an effort to make planning achieve the equilibrium which idealized markets had been mathematically proven capable of attaining. For Hayek, schooled in the Austrian approach to economics, the proofs of what idealized markets could do had to be juxtaposed to the temporal dynamics which real markets experienced. So the assumptions behind the idealization had to be scrutinized. And in scrutinizing them, Hayek developed three related points which became the backbone of RtS. First, the idealization assuming perfect universal knowledge assumes away the heart of the economic situation: the essentially distributed nature of knowledge. Second, knowledge is of one's ends and not only of available means: each individual knows what they value and how much they value it, so that their own personal planning can be rational and can achieve (changing) states of equilibrium, whereas society neither knows nor has a rational basis to reconcile the diverse valuations of its members. Therefore, conjoining the two points, the free interaction on the basis of such knowledge will be disrupted and destroyed by attempts to plan coercively, which can neither aggregate knowledge accurately nor choose fairly among the different values of the individuals who possess the knowledge. This conclusion is succinctly stated in Hayek's much later work, *Law, Legislation, and Liberty* (volume II):

it is thus due to the freedom of choosing the ends of one's activities that the utilization of the knowledge dispersed through society is achieved (Hayek, 1976: 9).

The first of these points is developed in 'Economics and Knowledge', yet it was already anticipated by Hayek's interventions in the socialist calculation debates. In the 1936 lecture, Hayek insists that the central problem of economics –

how the spontaneous interaction of a number of people, each possessing only bits of knowledge, brings about a state of affairs in which prices correspond to costs, etc.

– has been assumed away by surreptitious fiat in which

> instead of showing what bits of information the different persons must possess in order to bring about results, we fall back in effect on the assumption that everybody knows everything and so evade any real solution of the problem. (Hayek, [1936] 1948: 50–51)

The real 'marvel' (a word he uses elsewhere) is not the idealized plan, but rather that

> the spontaneous action of individuals will, under conditions which we can define, bring about a distribution of resources which can be understood as if it were made according to a single plan, although nobody has planned it (Hayek, [1936] 1948: 54).

The zeal for planning had assumed that it could eliminate waste and secure a rational use of resources, but it had ignored the remarkable mechanism which could succeed in doing so (albeit that this was a dynamic process, in which any one state of equilibrium could not last).

The second point is made clearly in Hayek's Anglophone contributions to the revived socialist calculation debate. Already in the 1935 *Collectivist Economic Planning* volume, in his introductory essay on 'The Nature and History of the Problem', he identifies the fundamental economic problem as arising 'as soon as different purposes compete for the available resources' (Hayek, [1935] 1997: 56). Yet as he tartly remarks

> the fact that in the present [capitalist] order of things such economic problems are not solved by the conscious decision of anybody has the effect that most people are not conscious that such problems exist. (Hayek, [1935] 1997: 56)

In the case of socialism, by contrast

> one central authority has to solve the economic problem of distributing a limited amount of resources between a practically infinite number of competing purposes (Hayek, [1935] 1997: 62)

and the question is whether and how any such authority can make such a determination of values, given that there

> are no scientific criteria which would enable us to compare or assess the relative importance of needs of different persons. (Hayek, [1935] 1997: 68)

Here, the focus is on the problem of comparing values and valued needs; in the concluding essay in the same volume ('The State of the Debate'), Hayek stresses the sheer problem of aggregating all the detailed knowledge relative to such a comparison. Later, in his 1940 consideration ('The Competitive "Solution"') of the more recent proposals by Lange and Taylor, and by Dickinson, both of which tried to incorporate consumer prices into a socialist economy, he combines both points. These hopeful socialist economists must still assume that the planning board 'will possess at least as much knowledge as the individual entrepreneurs' (Hayek, [1940] 1997: 134) – the point which 'Economics and Knowledge' had undermined. And despite their concern with individual freedom, their plans cannot do without

> a much more extensive agreement among the members of the society about the relative importance of the various needs is required than will normally exist

– and therefore

> this agreement will have to be brought about and a common scale of values will have to be imposed by force and propaganda. (Hayek, [1940] 1997: 138)

In support of this point, Hayek cites his 1939 FES pamphlet (the 1948 *Individualism and the Economic Order* reprint also cites RtS) – and so we have come to the point where the critique of socialist calculation and the backstory of RtS converge into one. Indeed, the 1939 FES pamphlet had put the point more succinctly: planning presupposes

> a complete moral code in which the relative values of all human ends, the relative importance of all the needs of all the different people, are assigned a definite place and a definite quantitative significance. (FES, 1939: 201)

At the heart of both FES and RtS are the claims that planning the full economy will inevitably mean supplanting the price system (despite the brave attempts by Oskar Lange and Frederick M. Taylor, and by Henry Douglas Dickinson, to prevent this), and that planning therefore substitutes individual determination and market pursuit of ultimate ends with a collective decision that will have to be made arbitrarily. Planning threatens not only liberty, but also democracy, since democratic parliaments will be incapable of reaching the decisive yet inevitably arbitrary determination of value required, and freedom of discussion will have to be curtailed if it is not to undermine that determination. Already in the 1939 version of FES, Hayek saw democratic governments as straining to cope with the planning tasks that had already been assigned to them. And he already foresaw (though of course with the experience of the First World War behind him) that war would be one of the few situations in which such widespread planning could be popular and accepted, insofar as it rested on a genuine if temporary singleness of purpose. Wrote Hayek:

> 'Rational' action is only possible in the service of a given system of ends, and if society as a whole is to act rationally it must be given such a common scale of values. The dictator will find at a very early stage that if he wants to carry out the will of the people he will have to tell them what to want. (FES, 1939: 206)

As a peacetime warning, this was powerful; in wartime, when RtS appeared in 1944, it was ironically less applicable, since precisely a common scale of values – winning the war – had been effectively agreed upon. As we will see, however, with the end of the war to which people were already looking in 1944, and in the British general election of 1945, this point would be seized upon.

There are two further arguments added about planning, one already in FES, the other in RtS, which had not been present in the socialist calculation debate essays or in 'Economics and Knowledge'. The first is the attack on the idea of desert in FES, which would become both a major theme of RtS, constituting the whole of Chapter VIII, and also a continuing leitmotif in Hayek's later work, particularly volume II of *Law, Legislation, and Liberty* ('The Mirage of Social Justice'), which attacks social justice on the basis that in the economic game, 'only the conduct of the players but not the result can be just', precisely because the *'values which their services will have to their fellows will often have no relations to their individual merits or needs'* (Hayek, 1976: 72, emphasis original). He had already brought out the political implications of this point in FES. For if government starts planning as a substitute for the price mechanism, it will have to make judgments about precisely all these services and their values. And every interest group will feel itself maligned and misunderstood by such a ranking. Thus the state

> will not be able to refuse protection against the consequences of any change which are regarded as undeserved. (FES, 1939: 200)

The second is a point on which RtS is the first text to focus, in Chapter 6: that planning requires discretion to deal with individual cases, so it is in principle hostile to the rule of law. This will again remain a major theme in Hayek's later work. *The Constitution of Liberty* is devoted to the study of the rule of law and to elaborating the distinction between what in 'The Nature and History of the Problem' was admitted to be 'the product of rational planning' but limited only to 'the permanent frame-work of institutions', versus a system of central direction. (Hayek, [1935] 1997: 66) (Compare FES, 1939: 194–196, which lauds the 'application of reason to social problems' (194) in the general, 'good' kind of planning – this is a point on which the late Hayek of *The Fatal Conceit* would break with his earlier self.)[5] In effect, Hayek here extends his diagnosis of the liberty threatened by planning, from the liberty of choosing one's own economic activity and goals to the liberty from subjection to the exercise of arbitrary power. Deprivation of the former, in line with his earlier argument, requires deprivation of the latter as well, since economic activity cannot be planned without the plan being imposed.

The critique of planning, then, whether employed by socialists or by fascists or by well-meaning leftish 'fellow travellers', is at the heart of FES and so of RtS. But this critique is embedded in a more general political analysis, and it is this perhaps which lifted RtS out of the narrow frame-work of economic debates into appearing to have much broader relevance. There are two elements to this political analysis. The most important, dating back to FES and indeed to the 1933 memorandum, is that of the kinship in intellectual and organizational approach between fascism and communism. Hayek made this point both logically and also, perhaps more persuasively, empirically, adducing cases of socialists who had crossed over to the fascist side and of ex-fascists who were now diagnosing their previous beliefs; socialist youth group features which the fascists had adopted; and the like. One summary of these claims was offered at the outset of FES:

> The similarity of many of the most characteristic features of the 'fascist' and 'communist' regimes is becoming steadily more obvious... The intellectual past of the authoritarian leaders as well as the fact that in the fascist states a socialist is often regarded as a potential recruit, while a liberal of the old school is recognized as the arch-enemy, point to a filiation of ideas which is very different from that commonly assumed (FES, 1939: 190).

This was hardly an unprecedented analysis. Hitler had after all called his movement 'National *Socialism*', and Hayek's strategy on this point in RtS is to adduce witnesses, such as the erstwhile Bolshevik sympathizers Max Eastman and William Henry Chamberlin, who had made exactly this kind of point.[6] Nevertheless, even before the intellectual dislocations caused by the Nazi–Soviet pact and then its rupture, left-wing economists and political thinkers had tended to reject the idea that fascism was a variant of socialism. Influential left-wing diagnoses of fascism treated it rather as the inevitable degenerate form, or perhaps the bastard child, of capitalism. So it was already antithetical to *bien-pensant* Anglo-American opinion in 1938 and 1939 to identify fascism as a form of socialism. But to insist on that identification in the midst of the wartime alliance – with implications for the socialist future to which many people in Western Europe were aspiring after the war, and for the New Deal present in American politics – was intellectually incendiary.

If this was incendiary to the left, RtS would also develop a political strand of argument which was incendiary to the right: an attack on political nationalism. Indeed, this was so contrary to most conservative world views that it has often been ignored in readings and remembrances of the volume. Yet it was central to Hayek's own world view. He averred that 'most "planners" are militant nationalists' (RtS: 163), while rejecting nationalism as a relevant principle in economic affairs:

> It is neither necessary nor desirable that national boundaries should mark sharp differences in standards of living, that membership of a national group should entitle to a share in a cake altogether different from that in which members of other groups share.

Otherwise

> we might indeed find that we have defeated National Socialism merely to create a world of many national socialisms ... (RtS: 224)

Indeed, he went so far as to reject the national monopoly on coining money as a dangerous and unjustified arrogation of monopoly power by the state.

This attack on nationalism relates to a broader point which connects FES to RtS: his distinction between political and economic power. We have already seen that Hayek did not idealize the market as frictionless. No more did he idealize it as a space of equality and freedom from domination. Inequality meant that the formal freedom of contract accorded to all would be experienced very differently by the rich and the

poor, by the capitalist and the worker. Hayek's defence of market capitalism was not that there was no domination or power in the market.
He acknowledged the power of big firms and rich individuals. But he
argued that the domination of the state, were it to control economic
life and supplant market competition instead, would be far worse. As he
wrote in RtS, the 'substitution of political for economic power' means
necessarily the substitution of power from which there is no escape for a
power which is always limited. What is called economic power, while it
can be an instrument of coercion, is in the hands of private individuals
never exclusive or complete power, never power over the whole life of a
person. But centralized as an instrument of political power it creates a
degree of dependence scarcely distinguishable from slavery (RtS: 166).

Hayek would make the same point against Beveridge himself, in a
review of his book on *Full Employment in a Free Society* which was a sort
of sequel to the 'Beveridge Report' of 1942. He contended that Beveridge
advocated subjecting

> all private investment to the direction of a National Investment
> Board [...] Sir William endeavours to show that, despite all the
> controls he wishes to impose, 'essential liberties' will be preserved.
> But private ownership of the means of production is, in his opinion,
> 'not an essential liberty in Britain, because it is not and never has
> been enjoyed by more than a very small proportion of the British
> people'.

His judgment of this claim is damning:

> It is surprising that he should not yet have learned that private
> ownership of the means of production is important to most people
> not because they hope to own such property, but because only such
> private ownership gives them the choice of competing employers
> and protects them from being at the mercy of the most complete
> monopolist ever conceived. (Hayek, [1945] 1995: 235)

Note the similar tenor of a remark by Keynes, on this point Hayekian
avant la lettre, in the final chapter of his *General Theory*:

> It is better that a man should tyrannise over his bank balance than
> over his fellow citizens and whilst the former is sometimes denounced
> as being but a means to the latter, sometimes at least it is an alterna-
> tive. (Keynes, [1935] 1936: 374)

Despite the fact that the core contentions of RtS had been fully anticipated in FES five and even (in the original article) six years earlier, the
book made a huge impact upon publication in the United Kingdom, the
United States, and also in occupied Germany. It was published in London
in March 1944, and went through six print runs in sixteen months
despite the wartime paper shortage – and even then it was difficult for
eager readers to obtain. In the United States, three publishers rejected
it before the University of Chicago Press accepted it in December 1943,
without particular hopes for high volume sales. The book appeared
on 18 September 1944 in a print run of 2000; a week later the press
printed 5000 more. Reader's Digest published a condensed version in
April 1945; the book was chosen for distribution by book of the Month
Club; and *Look* magazine published a cartoon version in 1945 (Caldwell,
2007a: 1). Meanwhile in 1945 the occupying powers banned its publication in occupied Germany, declaring officially that it might impair
good relations with the USSR – but excerpts circulated in typewritten
copies (Hayek, 1994: 21). I will consider the British and American recep-
tions further in turn.

Perhaps most famous in the RtS reception is Winston Churchill's
conservative party election broadcast of 4 June 1945 predicting that
election of a socialist government in Britian would lead to a Gestapo:

> No Socialist Government conducting the entire life and industry of
> the country could afford to allow free, sharp, or violently-worded
> expressions of public discontent. They would have to fall back on
> some form of Gestapo, no doubt very humanely directed in the first
> instance. And this would nip opinion in the bud; it would stop crit-
> icism as it reared its head, and it would gather all the power to the
> supreme party and the party leaders, rising like stately pinnacles
> above their vast bureaucracies of Civil Servants, no longer servants
> and no longer civil. And where would the ordinary simple folk –
> the common people, as they like to call them in America – where
> would they be, once this mighty organism had got them in its grip?
> (Churchill, [1945] 1974: 7172)

As Alan Ebenstein's biography of Hayek reports, Attlee accused Churchill
in reply (5 June) of retailing 'the second-hand version of the academic
views of an Austrian professor, Friedrich August von Hayek' (the full
German-sounding names doubtless deliberately spelled out); Hayek
retorted in the *Evening News* the next day that he was not interested
in party politics and that Attlee had misunderstood his book.[7] (He

was not at the time publicly associated with the conservative party, having been a member of the Liberal Party-focused Reform Club; his public association with the Conservatives came only in the Margaret Thatcher era.)[8] Churchill's tactic may have backfired. Public opinion was outraged by his seeming smear against colleagues with whom he had shared wartime responsibilities in the unity government (Gamble, 1996: 77). To accuse the mild-mannered Attlee of Gestapo tendencies seemed absurd (though that was exactly Hayek's point).

A more nuanced response was offered by Hayek's erstwhile duelling partner on the economic slump, more recently his personal host in arranging rooms in King's College, Cambridge, during the LSE's official sojourn in Peterhouse, and his companion in wartime fire patrols on the roof of King's College Chapel,[9] speaking of English literature – John Maynard Keynes. Keynes wrote to Hayek on 28 June 1944 about the publication of RtS, which he read on board ship to the Bretton Woods conference:

> morally and philosophically I find myself deeply in agreement with virtually the whole of it; and not only in agreement, but in deeply moved agreement.

But

> dangerous acts can be done safely in a country which thinks rightly, which could be the way to hell if they were executed by those who feel wrongly. (Gamble, 1996: 77)

The British reception was dominated primarily by the core themes that had already been advanced in FES: in particular, planning and its relationship to liberty. In America, it was the political twist emphasized by RtS – the lineage connecting socialism to fascism – which was rejected by many. For example, in the second of two reviews of the book published in the *American Economic Review* in March 1945, the distinguished public servant and historian of economic thought, Eric Roll, concludes:

> Perhaps the most vulnerable aspect of the book is the frequent identification...of all forms of collectivism and socialism with nazism. A few years ago this was a common tactic in popular journalism and in political speeches, but one would have expected something more searching in a book of this kind. Hayek might have stopped to reflect upon the very different development during the last few

pre-war years in Germany and in the Soviet Union, and he might have had the grace, at the least, to acknowledge the very different manner in which the war itself has been conducted by the enemy and by our ally: we have yet to be shown that Maidanek is an inevitable corollary of a collective economy. The truth is that Hayek's strong political prejudices show through the veneer of reasonableness coupled with high-mindedness with which he tries to impress the reader. (Roll, 1945: 180)[10]

This kind of left-wing criticism of the book has not worn well. Rather more penetrating was the observation that Hayek's appropriation by the libertarian and capitalist right in American debates had made him 'a pawn in a political game in a fashion which is hardly to his liking', being used as a 'made to order hand grenade for conservatives to hurl at planners – i.e., New Dealers, followers of Henry Wallace, the Communists and so on' (Grattan, 1945: 48–49). This was remarked by C. Hartley Grattan in a review of RtS in *Harper's Magazine* in July 1945. The 'basic weakness' of the book, he opined, is that Hayek

> comes down hard on what he believes to be abuses of governmental power and defines the abuses chiefly in extreme forms, without making equally clear his opposition to the abuses of power on the part of private business. (Grattan, 1945: 48)

(As noted above, however, Hayek's opposition to such abuses of private economic power had always to be seen in the context of his insistence that abuses of public economic power would be worse.)

Grattan remarked on Hayek's embarrassment at the popular reception of the book in America as an oversimplification, in which the book was welcomed as a weapon against Roosevelt and the New Deal as a form of planning akin (on its arguments) to nazism and socialism. But what was the reason for the embarrassment? Consider an interview given by Hayek to the Chicago *Sun* Book Week:

> For an author who never intended to write a popular book a reception like that accorded to *The Road to Serfdom* is a pleasant surprise but also something of an embarrassment. The problems to which the book addresses itself are inevitably difficult, and if I had been asked to write about them for a large public, I should almost certainly have refused ... the chief purpose in writing it was to persuade a few leaders in the current movement of opinion that they were on an extremely

dangerous path.... [I might add,] since I am frequently misunderstood on this point, that my contentions are mainly based not on historical parallels but on a theoretical argument which tends to show why, in the circumstances, the development which took place was inevitable. I must confess... that I was at first a little puzzled and even alarmed when I found that a book written in no party spirit and not meant to support any popular philosophy should have been so exclusively welcomed by one party and so thoroughly excoriated by the other. (Grattan, 1945: 49–50)

The same appropriation by the Conservative party, and excoriation (based on its use as a Tory weapon) by the Labour party, had taken place in Britain. But was Hayek's embarrassment disingenuous?

It is true, and important, that his theory of political change rested in this period on the role of opinion formers, and of ideas, rather than on the role of mass opinion. In the introduction to RtS he had written that

If in the long run we are the makers of our own fate, in the short run we are the captives of the ideas we have created. Only if we recognize the danger in time can we hope to avert it. (RtS: 58)

He would later advise Anthony Fisher that reaching the opinion formers with ideas was the crucial means of bringing about political change:

Society's course will be changed only by a change in ideas. First you must reach the intellectuals, the teachers and writers, with reasoned argument. It will be their influence on society which will prevail, and the politicians will follow.[11]

Elsewhere he would refer to these as the 'second-hand dealers in ideas' (Hayek, [1949] 1997: 222; cf. Mueller, 2011: 152). On this point, as on many broader liberal values (despite the misconception of them as philosophical enemies), Hayek and Keynes broadly agreed. Compare the famous statement by Keynes on the influence of ideas:

The ideas of economists and political philosophers, both when they are right and when they are wrong, are more powerful than is commonly understood. Indeed the world is ruled by little else. Practical men, who believe themselves to be quite exempt from any intellectual influence, are usually the slaves of some defunct economist. (Keynes, [1935] 1936: 383)

In a similar vein, acknowledging Hayek's liberalism, Joseph Schumpeter would dismiss Hayek's politics as that of a 'Gladstonian liberal' and his political sociology as that of John Stuart Mill (Schumpeter, 1946: 269–270; cf. Gamble, 1996: 82). For Schumpeter, both of these liberal pedigrees made Hayek blind to Marx's insights about group interests and the power of the proletariat created by capitalism itself. For his part, Hayek later acknowledged the similarity of his concern in RtS that liberal society might undermine itself politically, to Schumpeter's prediction of the inherent political instability of capitalism. But he remarked that Schumpeter's determinism was exactly the opposite of his own belief that people might come to think differently, to hold better or worse ideas, which intimated at least some modest power of reason (though in late writings such as *The Fatal Conceit* Hayek would claim to abjure any belief in reason). Hayek's diagnosis of Schumpeter's enjoyment of deterministic paradoxes is fascinating from this standpoint:

> Although he [Schumpeter] claimed the opposite, he had, in the last resort, really no belief in the power of argument. He took it for granted that the state of affairs *forces* people to think in a particular manner. This is fundamentally false. There is no simple understanding of what makes it necessary for people under certain conditions to believe certain things. The evolution of ideas has its own laws and depends very largely on developments which we cannot predict. I mean, I'm trying to move opinion in a certain direction, but I wouldn't dare to predict what direction it will really move. I'm hoping that I can just divert it moderately. But Schumpeter's attitude was one of complete despair and disillusionment over the power of reason. (Hayek, 1994: 155)[12]

In *Law, Legislation, and Liberty*, volume I, Hayek would remark that RtS had been misunderstood. It had not sought to assert an automatic or ineluctable link between planning and totalitarian deprivation of liberty. It was rather a warning: 'If you do not mend your principles, you will go to the devil' (Hayek, 1973: 58).[13]

Thus liberty rather than efficiency becomes the leitmotif of Hayek's defense of capitalism: spelled out as the liberty to think differently, so to act differently; liberty to choose and pursue one's values and goals; and also liberty from the arbitrary interference of a dominating state – but not the new socialist concocted ideas of freedom from necessity or freedom from economic care, both of which could only be purchased with the sacrifice of the other, older forms of liberty (RtS: 77). So too had liberty been central for the economic and political thought of his hero John Stuart Mill. But in the intervening period, the focus on mathematical models of efficiency had obscured the basic value of liberty relevant to the heart of economics as of politics. An economist as different from Hayek as Amartya Sen would later herald Hayek for his insistence on the importance of freedom as a human value. As RtS Chapter 6 makes clear, the real enemy of freedom is not inefficiency, but despotism. In his consistent commitment to the value of freedom and his identification of its home in the choices and the values of each individual, Hayek set a standard for even those interventions and political systems of which he would not himself approve.

Notes

1. This chapter was informed by the experience of lecturing and supervising students on Hayek in the Faculty of History at the University of Cambridge for more than a decade, and by the discussion at a 2004 meeting on the 60th anniversary of *The Road to Serfdom*, which I had the privilege of co-convening with Sylvia Nasar at the Centre for History and Economics, King's College, Cambridge, under the directorship of Emma Rothschild and Gareth Stedman Jones. I learned a great deal from all participants, and thank the Centre and its administrators for their support. I am also grateful to Robert Leeson for editorial advice and Julie Rose for research assistance supported by Princeton University.
2. The chapter was subsequently enlarged into a pamphlet of same title, University of Chicago Press 1939, Public Policy Pamphlet no.29 in a series edited by Harry D. Gideonse. The quotations here are from the original pamphlet, reprinted in the *Collected Works*, and it is to this that I refer as FES. I refer to the subsequent expanded pamphlet as FES 1939.
3. Hayek dedicated the work 'to the socialists of all parties' – presumably implying that the book was an offering to help them realize the error of their ways.
4. Strangely, while Caldwell is assiduous in sketching the British political backstory and the textual history of what became RtS, he remarks on Hayek's 'later and much fuller development' of knowledge in the marketplace in the context of Hayek's 1940 review of Lange et. al. ('Socialist Calculation: The Competitive "Solution,"' discussed in Caldwell, 2007a: 25). But 'Economics and Knowledge,' which was the breakthrough on this point, preceded the review of Lange by a good four years.
5. See also the acknowledgement in RtS Chapter 3 of the legitimacy of forms of social insurance, collective protection against externalities, and other forms of state regulation of the market.
6. In fact, the identification of 'totalitarianism' as a label uniting Hitler and Stalin was already advanced by Harry D. Gideonse's editorial introduction to the 1939 pamphlet version of FES: 'Could anything be more futile than the denunciation of dictators and the simultaneous support of the very policies

that have made dictatorship inevitable elsewhere? Is it mere accident that social-democratic Germany and Austria as well as communist Russia – which up to very recently were held up to us as examples of social advancement – have been the first to submit to totalitarian tyranny?' (Gideonse, 1939: iii). And consider the remark by Hayek's mentor, Ludwig von Mises, in a text published in 1940 and repeated in another in 1947, calling Nazism 'socialism with the outward appearance of capitalism' (Mises, [1940] 1998: 6; Mises, [1947] 1951: 529); it should be noted however that in 1927, Mises had suggested that Fascism had 'saved European civilization' (Mises, [1927] 2005: 51).

7. The accounts of both Attlee's speech and Hayek's response are in Ebenstein (2001: 138).
8. Shearmur (2006: 310), a reference I owe to Robert Leeson, argues that Hayek did have some 'very specific, if not publicly acknowledged contacts with the British Conservatives in the 1940s.'
9. The fire patrols with Keynes were mentioned by Laurence Hayek, F.A. Hayek's son, at a meeting in 2004 (see the first endnote for details); they are also mentioned in Ebenstein (2001: 106). Caldwell, who was also present at the 2004 meeting, nevertheless offers grounds for believing them to have been conducted with John Clapham rather than Keynes: see Caldwell (2007b: 268).
10. The other review was by Aaron Director, who had prompted the University of Chicago Press to consider publishing RtS (Caldwell, 2007a: 16).
11. Quoted in Blundell (2007: 41); I owe my awareness of this quotation to Angus Ritchie.
12. Schumpeter's actual review of RtS was more nuanced on this point, arguing that a genuinely conservative thinker should present a 'standpoint' from which 'a politically effective program *could* be presented' so must explain how existing social tendencies constrain and enable political action – not deal with ideas 'as if they floated in the air'. While Schumpeter remarked in a Marxist vein that the 'fundamental lines' of social development were 'probably ineluctable,' he (like Marx and Engels, in fact) still saw room for an individual and group conscious contribution to social change: 'much in the way in which the ever-present change comes about depends on individuals and groups, abilities and volitions'. So, he proposed, it is worth thinking about how to make 'transitions with a minimum loss of social values' (Schumpeter, 1946: 269–270).
13. On the question of 'inevitability' in RtS, see Caldwell (2007a: 28), and Hayek's (1976) preface to RtS (Hayek, [1976] 2007).

Bibliography

Blundell, John. 2007. *Waging the War of Ideas*, 3rd edn. London: Institute of Economic Affairs.

Caldwell, Bruce. 2007a. Introduction to *The Road to Serfdom: Text and Documents* by F. A. Hayek, edited by Bruce Caldwell. Chicago: The University of Chicago Press, pp. 1–33.

Caldwell, Bruce. 2007b. Acknowledgments in *The Road to Serfdom: Text and Documents* by F. A. Hayek, edited by Bruce Caldwell. Chicago: The University of Chicago Press, pp. 267–268.

Churchill, Winston S. (1945) 1974. 'Party Politics Again'. In 1943–1949, Vol. VII of *Winston S. Churchill: His Complete Speeches 1897–1963*, edited by Robert Rhodes James. New York: Chelsea House, pp. 7169–7174.

Ebenstein, Alan. 2001. *Friedrich Hayek: A Biography.* New York: Palgrave.

Gamble, Andrew. 1996. *Hayek: The Iron Cage of Liberty.* Oxford: Polity.

Gideonse, Harry D. 1939. Introduction to *Freedom and the Economic System* by F. A. Hayek. No. 29 in *Public Policy Pamphlets*, edited by Harry D. Gideonse. Chicago: The University of Chicago Press.

Grattan, C. Hartley. 1945. 'Hayek's Hayride: or, have you read a good book lately?' *Harper's Magazine*, 191 (1142): 45–50.

Hayek, F. A. (1933) 2007. 'Nazi-Socialism'. In *The Road to Serfdom: Text and Documents* (RtS) edited by Bruce Caldwell. Vol. II of *The Collected Works of F.A. Hayek* edited by Bruce Caldwell. Chicago: The University of Chicago Press, pp. 245–248.

Hayek, F. A. (1935) 1997. 'The Nature and History of the Problem'. In *Socialism and War: Essays, Documents, Reviews* edited by Bruce Caldwell. Vol. X of *The Collected Works of F.A. Hayek* edited by Stephen Kresge. Chicago: The University of Chicago Press, pp. 181–188. Originally published in 1935 as the introduction to *Collectivist Economic Planning: Critical Studies on the Possibilities of Socialism* edited by F. A. Hayek. London: George Routledge and Son, pp. 1–20.

Hayek, F. A. (1936) 1948. 'Economics and Knowledge'. In *Individualism and Economic Order,* Chicago: The University of Chicago Press, pp. 33–56. Originally presented at the London Economic Club, November 1936 and originally published in *Economica*, 1937: 33–54.

Hayek, F. A. (1938) 1997. 'Freedom and the Economic System (FES)'. In *Socialism and War: Essays, Documents, Reviews* edited by Bruce Caldwell. Vol. X of *The Collected Works of F.A. Hayek* edited by Stephen Kresge. Chicago: The University of Chicago Press, pp. 181–188. Originally published in *Contemporary Review*, April 1938: 434–442.

Hayek, F. A. (1939) 1997. 'Freedom and the Economic System [1939]'. (FES 1939) In *Socialism and War: Essays, Documents, Reviews* edited by Bruce Caldwell. Vol. X of *The Collected Works of F. A. Hayek* edited by Stephen Kresge. Chicago: The University of Chicago Press, pp. 189–211. Originally published in 1939 in a series edited by Harry D. Gideonse as Public Policy Pamphlet No. 29, Chicago: The University of Chicago Press.

Hayek, F. A. (1940) 1997. 'Socialist Calculation: The Competitive "Solution"'. In *Socialism and War: Essays, Documents, Reviews* edited by Bruce Caldwell. Vol. X of *The Collected Works of F. A. Hayek* edited by Stephen Kresge. Chicago: The University of Chicago Press, pp. 117–140. Originally published in *Economica*, 1940: 125–149 and reprinted in *Individualism and Economic Order*: 181–208.

Hayek, F. A. (1944) 2007. *The Road to Serfdom: Text and Documents* (RtS) edited by Bruce Caldwell. Vol. II of *The Collected Works of F. A. Hayek* edited by Bruce Caldwell. Chicago: The University of Chicago Press. Originally published in March 1944, London: George Routledge and Son.

Hayek, F. A. (1945) 1995. Review of Sir William Beveridge, *Full Employment in a Free Society.* In *Contra Keynes and Cambridge: Essays, Correspondence* edited by Bruce Caldwell. Vol. IX of *The Collected Works of F. A. Hayek* edited by Stephen Kresge. London: Routledge, pp. 233–236. Originally published in *Fortune*, March 1945: 204–206.

Hayek, F. A. (1949) 1997. 'The Intellectuals and Socialism'. In *Socialism and War: Essays, Documents, Reviews* edited by Bruce Caldwell. Vol. X of *The Collected Works of F. A. Hayek* edited by Stephen Kresge. Chicago: The University of Chicago Press, pp. 221–237. Originally published in *University of Chicago Law Review*, 16: 417–433.

Hayek, F. A. (1963) 1995. 'The Economics of the 1930s as Seen from London'. In *Contra Keynes and Cambridge: Essays, Correspondence* edited by Bruce Caldwell. Vol. IX of *The Collected Works of F. A. Hayek* edited by Stephen Kresge. London: Routledge, pp. 49–63. Originally presented as a Charles O. Walgreen Foundation lecture at the University of Chicago, October 1963.

Hayek, F. A. 1973. *Rules and Order.* Volume I of *Law, Legislation and Liberty.*Chicago: The University of Chicago Press.

Hayek, F. A. 1976. *The Mirage of Social Justice.* Volume II of *Law, Legislation and Liberty.*Chicago: The University of Chicago Press.

Hayek, F. A. [1976] 2007. Preface to the 1976 edition of *The Road to Serfdom: Text and Documents* (RtS) edited by Bruce Caldwell. Vol. II of *The Collected Works of F. A. Hayek* edited by Bruce Caldwell. Chicago: The University of Chicago Press.

Hayek, F. A. 1994. *Hayek on Hayek: An Autobiographical Dialogue.* Edited by Stephen Kresge and Leif Wenar. London: Routledge.

Keynes, John Maynard. (1935) 1936. *The General Theory of Employment, Interest, and Money.* New York: Harcourt, Brace & World.

Mises, Ludwig von. (1927) 2005. *Liberalism: The Classical Tradition*, edited by Bettina Bien Greaves. Translated by R. Raico. Indianapolis: Liberty Fund. Originally published as *Liberalismus* (Jena: Fischer).

Mises, Ludwig von (1940) 1998. *Interventionism: An Economic Analysis*, edited by Bettina Bien Greaves. Translated by T. F. McManus and H. Bund. Irvington-on-Hudson, NY: Foundation for Economic Education.

Mises, Ludwig von (1947) 1951. *Epilogue in Socialism: An Economic and Sociological Analysis [Die Gemeinwirtschaft: UntersuchungenUber den Sozialismus].* Translated by J. Kahane. 2nd ed. New Haven: Yale University Press, pp. 525–592. Originally published in 1947 as *Planned Chaos.* Irvington-on-Hudson, NY: Foundation for Economic Education.

Mueller, Jan-Werner. 2011. *Contesting Democracy: Political Ideas in Twentieth-Century Europe.* New Haven: Yale University Press.

Roll, Eric. 1945. 'Review of *The Road to Serfdom* by F. A. Hayek'. *American Economic Review,* 35: 176–180.

Schumpeter, Joseph A. 1946. 'Review of *The Road to Serfdom* by F. A. Hayek'. *Journal of Political Economy,* 54: 269–270.

Shearmur, Jeremy. 2006. 'Hayek, *The Road to Serfdom*, and the British Conservatives'. *Journal of the History of Economic Thought,* 28: 309–314.

3
Hayek in Citations and the Nobel Memorial Prize

Gabriel Söderberg, Avner Offer and Samuel Bjork

Citations

Citations are a currency of academic standing. Among scholars, priority of discovery is acknowledged in footnotes and references, and the number of citations is a measure of the impact of conceptual innovations. Citation counts were first assembled in the 1920s. The Science Citation index was launched in 1960, and a companion Social Science Citation index was added in 1975.[1] Both are now part of the Thomson-Reuters ISI database, which is the most prominent citation database in use today. All citation counts have biases.[2] ISI is proprietary and is not easy to work with; its coverage dwindles the further back you go, it has a restricted range of journals, only counts first authors, and only takes account of books if they appear in journal citations. Elsevier's more recent Scopus database covers many more journals, but has a poor coverage of the distant past. An online source of citations, Google Scholar, is easy to use, and it counts books as well as publications in languages other than English. That is not a decisive argument against it, since most important journals are available online, but the findings are weighted towards the present and the scores are always in flux. It is also difficult to extract citation on a yearly basis.

The data we use come from a different source, the JSTOR project to digitize scholarly journals, which has not been used for this purpose before. This database was started in 1995 with a core of the most important USA academic journals in most academic fields, and has since expanded to include the main English-language journals, and increasingly the peripheries of scholarship.[3] For each journal, JSTOR typically goes back to the origin, and stops a few years before the present. The journals can be taken to comprise the most highly regarded scholarship of every period in the English language since the late nineteenth century. The most important finding in citation studies is that the bulk of cited articles are published by a minority of authors in a minority of journals.[4] On that basis, JSTOR, as a collection of the most important journals, is a good sample to be using. It does not encompass everything, but is unlikely to misrepresent scholarly trends. The total number of journals in JSTOR in January 2012 was 1984, with 409 of them in economics, business and finance.[5] Current total citations in Google Scholar are substantially higher, in some cases by an order of magnitude, so JSTOR (like Thomson-ISI and Scopus) should be considered as a selective and high-quality sample.

Citations are derived from JSTOR articles, by year of publication, and provide a continuous record over time. JSTOR does not include books directly, but like ISI it does count them in journal citations, so books are amply represented. Citations are only taken from the reference and footnotes sections, and not from the body of the text. One feature of the database is that a name is only counted once, regardless of the number of times it is cited in an article (that is also the case with ISI). The main disadvantage of JSTOR is the virtual exclusion of publications that are not in English. In consequence, a few reputations appear abruptly, after a previous history of publication in a different language. JSTOR makes it possible to begin the count from a scholar's first publication in English. We begin our counts in 1930 and for most purposes stop in the year 2005; at the time of writing, JSTOR totals drop steeply after that year.

The number of journals and their size have grown over this period, so it would be misleading to report raw citation figures. A low citation count in 1970 might be a greater achievement in relative terms than a high one in 2000. To control for the changing size of the literature, citations are reported as an index number. Several economists have also had an impact beyond economics, and a few of the Nobel Prize winners in economics (henceforth NPW) were not even economists. Consequently, the index is calculated as the ratio of a person's JSTOR citations in all disciplines to the total of all JSTOR articles (the total number of citations is not available, and the number of articles is a suitable deflator). Kenneth Arrow, one of the very top economists, had the highest individual NPW annual score up to the year 2000, and this provides an intuitive benchmark for comparison with the others. This index number is expressed as a percentage of his highest single year citation ratio (in 1976), which is given the score of 100. These percentages are termed 'Arrows'. In that year, Arrow was cited in 0.335 per cent of all JSTOR articles. His absolute number of citations that year was 289.

An 'Arrow' was therefore worth 2.89 JSTOR citations in 1976. This value changed from one year to another, depending on the number of JSTOR articles and the number of NPW citations. 100 Arrows equals 0.335 per cent of JSTOR articles in any year. In 2000, for example, an Arrow was worth 3.54 citations.

A similar method is used for specific publications. Here the benchmark used is Hayek's own *The Road to Serfdom*. Its best year was 1945, when it was cited 13 times in JSTOR, which was 0.0401 per cent of all JSTOR articles. This constant is used to construct a 'Road to Serfdom Index' that is similar to the Arrow Index.

The Bass model of the diffusion of innovations

The citation trajectory can be understood as the diffusion of an innovation. In marketing research, the Bass model is widely used to investigate the diffusion of new products, and can also be applied to intellectual innovation. Diffusion follows a rising trend, which can be modelled as a logistic growth curve. In such models, the probability and timing of new adoptions (in our case, of new citations) is determined by the quantity and pace of previous ones. The cumulative diffusion curve, which describes the pace of diffusion and its upper limit, has a sigmoid (s-shaped) shape, with an inflection point halfway up the curve vertically. A derivative curve, which represents the number of citations in each unit of time, is approximately bell-shaped, peaking at the point of inflection of the cumulative curve (Figure 3.1). Adoption is a learning (or 'contagion') process. At the start, a few acolytes embrace the innovation. Information and emulation spread the word, and take-up

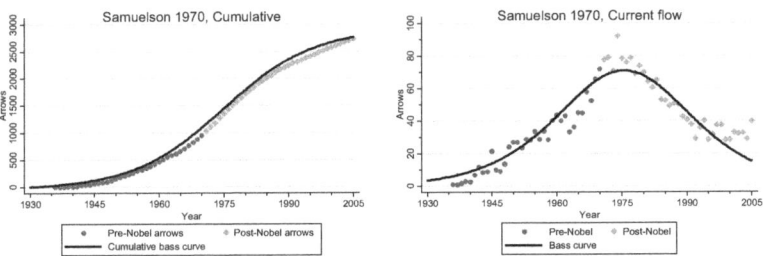

Figure 3.1 Bass innovation diffusion curves of citations: the example of Paul Samuelson

Note: 1970 is the year of the Nobel award.

accelerates. Diffusion then slows down as the innovation approaches its maximum appeal. The flow of citations takes a typical bell shape, rising towards a maximum at the inflection point as diffusion accelerates, and declining when most new adoptions have taken place.

The model has three unknown variables that describe the pace of adoption and its maximum. For prediction, three initial values need for be guessed at, the computation will then converge iteratively on a stable value. Advocates of the model claim some explanatory meaning for these variables. We think this can be ignored: the Bass model is essentially a mathematical curve-fitting procedure. To achieve good prediction requires that data should be available at least up to the inflection point. We have data for the whole curve, and are interested in description rather than prediction. Nothing needs to be guessed, except for the initial seeding values. The Bass model provides a remarkably useful tool for characterizing NPW citation trajectories, and a suitable benchmark to analyze the effect of the Prize on Hayek's academic reputation.[6]

Figure 3.2 shows an average of the Nobel Prize citation trajectories, with all 57 Nobel Memorial Prize winners 1969–2005 normalized to centre on their prize year. The average citation trajectory fits well with

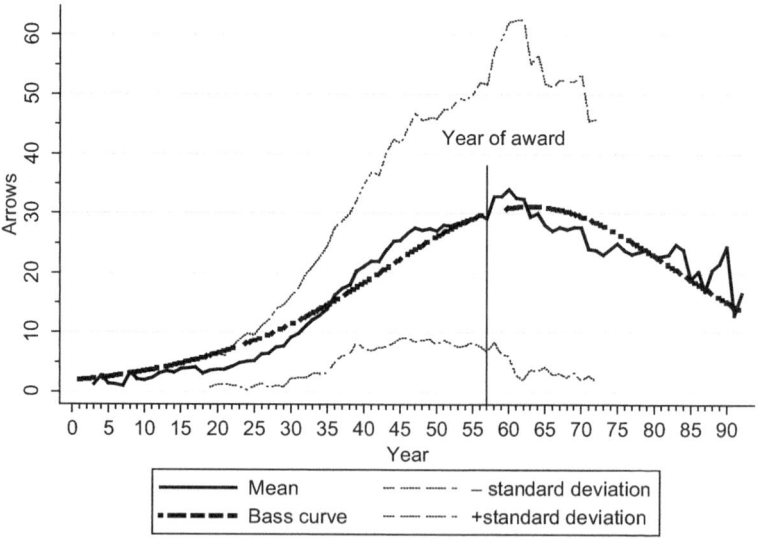

Figure 3.2 Average citation trajectory of 57 Nobel Prize winners, centred on their prize year

Note: One standard deviation, where number is 30 or more.

an almost symmetrical Bass curve (the skew is largely imparted by the later winners, who have fewer years after the prize). There is a small and brief 'prize citation premium', and reputational decline then sets in a few years after the award. At its most basic, the good fit indicates that old novelties are displaced by new ones over time in the discourse of the discipline, and that what goes up eventually comes down, at least as far as direct citation is concerned.

Hayek's Nobel Prize

On average, the Nobel Prize Committee tended to award the prize near the winners' citation peaks, that is, close to the height of a winner's reputation. This is also confirmed by our analysis of all individual winners, which is to be published elsewhere. The committee tended to play it safe, and awarded prizes to those already endorsed by the profession as being currently productive; this had the effect of enhancing the credibility of the prize. But their discretionary power could be used to diverge from the prudent course, and to make a few choices that were more controversial. Hayek's prize (joint with Myrdal) in 1974 may well be the most significant Nobel Prize in economics ever. Hayek's claim to the Prize was not obvious. His work in the Austrian tradition on monetary and price theory and business cycles, from the 1920s and early 1930s, while quoted as the nominal reason for the Prize, had been overshadowed by the Depression and by Keynes' *General Theory*. *The Road to Serfdom* (1944) positioned Hayek to lead the ideological resistance to the welfare state, and earned Hayek 'his fifteen minutes of fame' (see Figure 3.3 for the book's citation record).[7] Its popular success also served to alienate Hayek from academic economists. He searched for credibility in other fields. In an interview much later he stated:

> After *The Road to Serfdom*, I felt that I had so discredited myself professionally ... I wanted to be accepted in the scholarly community. To do something purely scientific and independent of my economic view.[8]

In the mid-1950s Hayek shifted his focus to expounding on classical liberal political philosophy, most notably in *The Constitution of Liberty* (1960).

Hayek's other notable contribution to economics was to argue the importance of markets as a means for discovering and transmitting price information. This originated as a contribution to the 'socialist planning' controversy, was acutely written but was not entirely original, and followed prior work by Ludwig von Mises (who had also inspired his work on capital theory).[9] Economic agents were circumscribed in their knowledge by their circumstances and individual capacities. But the personal economic decisions of millions of uncoordinated individuals added up to the price signals that allowed a market economy to function efficiently. This richness of information could not be matched by the efforts of the socialist central planner.

This view was not consistent with the premises of the dominant neoclassical economics, which assumed that rational agents operated with complete knowledge of prices. It was also inconsistent with the Walrasian approach to general equilibrium. A perfectly informed central planner would be little different from a Walrasian auctioneer. The Two Theorems of Welfare Economics, proven in the 1950s by Arrow and Debreu (both of them NPWs), which dominated high theory in the 1960s and 1970s, also assumed that agents had complete information. From the 1950s onwards Hayek no longer published any economics, but engaged in elaborating a classical liberal political philosophy. In the 1960s, his reputation had fallen well below his previous and subsequent peaks (Figure 3.3). The only publication that was fitfully alive was his 1945 article, 'The Use of Knowledge in Society'.

Hayek shared the 1974 Prize with the Social Democrat economist, politician and development scholar Gunnar Myrdal. As a social-democratic non-mathematical economist, and a Swedish native son to boot, Myrdal's award offset the recognition of such a right-wing figure. At the time, his reputation was as high as Hayek's was low. Myrdal had a much stronger citation record, and was only overtaken by Hayek in the 1980s (Figure 3.4). Like Hayek, Myrdal had made interesting and even important contributions to macroeconomic theory in the 1920s and 1930s, which were cited by the committee; but he had moved away from theory and had acquired a much larger reputation as the author of two great studies in social development, *An American Dilemma* (about blacks in America) and *Asian Drama* (on South Asian development), in addition to periods in ministerial office and international agencies.

The choice of Hayek may be linked to the role he had played in Swedish policy debates. *The Road to Serfdom* was immediately translated into Swedish in 1944, and served as a focal point for resistance to the welfare state.[10] Several leading Swedish economists were influenced by Hayek's writings. Assar Lindbeck, Nobel Prize Committee chairman between 1980 and 1994, and member since 1969, states in an interview

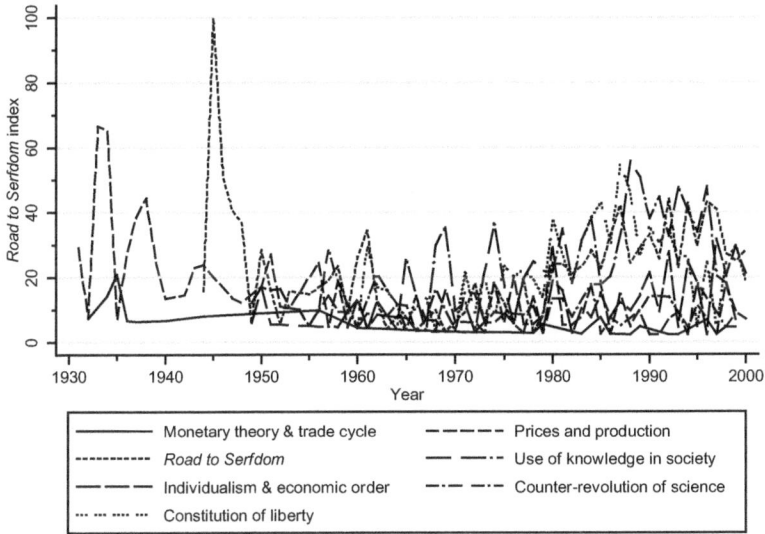

Figure 3.3 Average JSTOR Citation Scores Indices for Hayek's major works, 1969–1973

Note: *Road to Serfdom* in 1945 = 100.

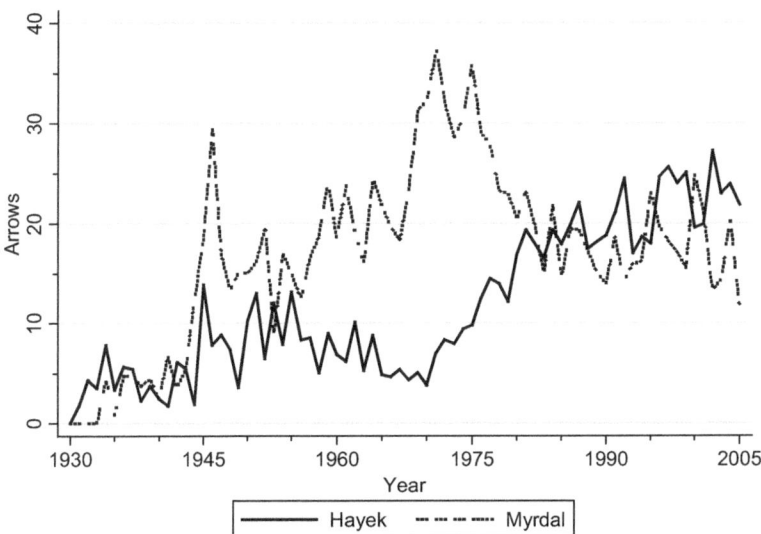

Figure 3.4 Hayek and Myrdal Arrow citations scores, 1930–2005

that Hayek's 'The Use of Knowledge in Society' was the most important text for him in clarifying the rationale for markets, and that the
same article was highly appreciated by another Committee member
at the time of Hayek's Prize, Erik Lundberg.[11] Lindbeck described an
essay of his of 1977 as having a Hayekian flavour.[12] He had spent the
previous year at the Hoover Institution, a bastion of American academic
conservatism.

Despite their almost polar differences, the 1974 winners had one
thing in common. Among all recipients of the Prize, these two were its
only public critics. In his acceptance speech, Hayek criticized the scien-
tistic pretensions of the Nobel Prize, in accordance with his view that
economic agents (and economists as well) had only imperfect information and understanding.[13] Two years later, Myrdal criticized what
he saw as the politicization of the prize, when it was given to Milton
Friedman.[14]

Hayek's biographers acknowledge that his reputation had reached a
low ebb in the early 1970s. He was depressed and financially insecure.
Assar Lindbeck later stated in an interview that the decision to give
the Prize to Hayek was an important personal gesture for him: 'He'd
been in a very deep depression he told me. It was terribly satisfying to
indicate his greatness'.[15] One of his biographers wrote 'If Hayek had not
received the Nobel Prize in Economic Science; it is an open question
what his reputation would be now'.[16] This is confirmed in a Bass model
of Hayek's citations.

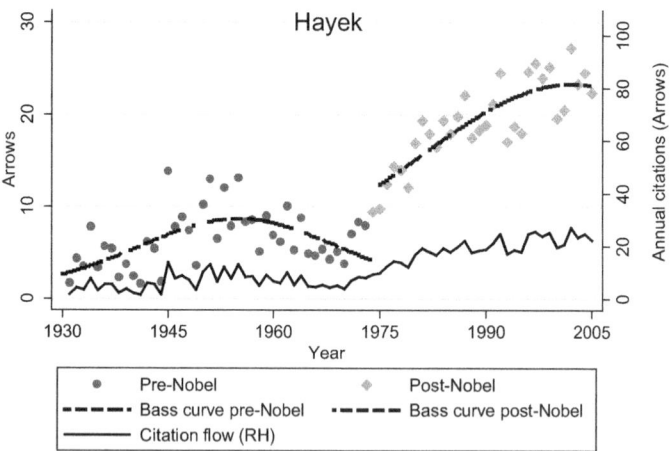

Figure 3.5   Arrow citation scores and Bass diffusion curves for Hayek, before and
after the Nobel Prize

Figure 3.5 shows Hayek's citation record over time (solid line, right-hand scale), and fits two Bass flow trajectories, the first up to the Prize in 1974, and second beginning in 1975. The first trajectory shows Hayek as having exhausted his potential as an innovator by 1974. Receiving the Prize shifted him onto a much higher trajectory (although he had reached the second inflection point by 2005). Of the 57 Nobel Prize winners up to 2005, only two others experienced such a dual-peak pattern: Stone (1982) and Vickrey (1996).

The Prize also raised the prestige of the Mont Pelerin Society, which Hayek had founded in 1947. Several members received the Prize in the years to come: Friedman in 1976, Stigler in 1982, Buchanan in 1986, Allais in 1988, Coase in 1991, and Gary Becker in 1992. The official historian of the Mont Pelerin Society wrote in 1995:

> A main reason for the heightened profile of the Society was the awarding of the Nobel Prize in economics to seven of its members ... There is no doubt that the Nobel prizes, with their world-wide recognition, strengthened the intellectual status of the Society and thus, in the world at large, its influence in the formation of a more liberal conception of society and its workings.[17]

Conclusion

Hayek had only limited salience in academic economics in the years immediately prior to receiving his Nobel Prize. His citations pattern is quite different from the average NPW, in that his award arrived at the tail end of a Bass trajectory, and not (like most others) close to his citation peak. The prize came early enough in the rise of neo-liberalism to reinforce his authority with a citation boost. His late career might have been different had he not received it.

Notes

1. De Bellis, *Bibliometrics*, chapter 2.
2. Harzing, *The Publish or Perish Book*, pp. 4–6.
3. Schonfeld, *JSTOR: A History*.
4. De Bellis, *Bibliometrics*, chapter 4.
5. See dfr.jstor.org.
6. A succinct account in Lilien and Rangaswamy, *Marketing Engineering*, 195–203.
7. Caldwell, *Hayek's Challenge*, 258.
8. Hayek in a 1994 interview, quoted in ibid., 257.

9. Mises, 'Economic Calculation in the Socialist Commonwealth'.
10. Lewin, *Planhushållningsdebatten*, 267–273.
11. Gylfason, 'Interview with Assar Lindbeck', 108.
12. Lindbeck, 'Introduction', *Selected Essays*, Vol. 2, xiii.
13. Hayek, 'The Pretence of Knowledge'.
14. Myrdal, 'The Nobel Prize in Economic Sciences', 50.
15. Assar Lindbeck in a 1997 interview, quoted in Nasar, *A Beautiful Mind*, 367.
16. Ebenstein, *Friedrich Hayek*, 261.
17. Hartwell, *History of the Mont Pelérin* Society, 160.

References

Bruce Caldwell, *Hayek's Challenge: An Intellectual Biography of F. A. Hayek* (Chicago, London: University of Chicago Press, 2004).
Nicola De Bellis, *Bibliometrics and Citation Analysis: From the Science Citation Index to Cybermetrics* (Lanham, Md., Plymouth: Scarecrow Press, 2009).
Alan O. Ebenstein, *Friedrich Hayek: A Biography* (New York: Palgrave for St Martin's Press, 2001).
T. Gylfason, 'An Interview with Assar Lindbeck', *Macroeconomic Dynamics*, 10 (2006): 101–130.
R. M. Hartwell, *A History of the Mont Pelerin Society* (Indianapolis: Liberty Fund, 1995).
Anne-Wil Harzing, *The Publish or Perish Book: Your Guide to Effective and Responsible Citation Analysis*, 1st edn. (Melbourne: Tarma Software Research Pty Ltd, 2011).
F. A.Hayek, 'The Pretence of Knowledge', in Assar Lindbeck (ed.) *Nobel Lectures: Economic Sciences 1969–1980*, vol. 1 (Singapore: World Scientific, 1974), pp. 179–188.
JSTOR, *Data for Research* (2012), in http://dfr.jstor.org/.
Leif Lewin, *Planhushållningsdebatten*. 2nd edn. (Stockholm: Almqvist & Wiksell, 1967).
Gary L. Lilien, and ArvindRangaswamy, *Marketing Engineering: Computer-Assisted Marketing Analysis and Planning* (Reading, Mass., Harlow: Addison-Wesley, 1997).
Assar Lindbeck, *Economic Sciences, 1969–1980: The Sveriges Riksbank (Bank of Sweden) Prize in Economic Sciences in Memory of Alfred Nobel* (Singapore; London: World Scientific, 1992).
Assar Lindbeck, 'Introduction', in *The Selected Essays of Assar Lindbeck. Vol. 2, The Welfare State* (Aldershot , 1993).
Ludwig vonMises, 'Economic Calculation in the Socialist Commonwealth', in F. A. Hayek (ed.) *Collectivist Economic Planning* (London: George Routledge & Sons, 1935), pp. 87–130.
Gunnar Myrdal, 'The Nobel Prize in Economic Science', *Challenge* (March–April, 1977), pp. 50–52.
Sylvia Nasar, *A Beautiful Mind* (London: Faber and Faber, 1998).
Roger C. Schonfeld, *JSTOR: A History* (Princeton, NJ.; Oxford: Princeton University Press, 2003).

4
The 1974 Hayek–Myrdal Nobel Prize

David Laidler

I was aware of Friedrich Hayek even when an undergraduate, and as a rather muddled left-winger (recently radicalized by Suez) I 'knew' he was on the 'other side', one of those responsible for the prolongation of the Great Depression and the author of a book called *The Road to Serfdom* (1944) which was a right-wing attack on the welfare state. However, I actually read almost nothing by him, nor was I ever asked to – his Introduction to *Paper Credit* was the only exception here, in my third undergraduate year at the LSE, probably at Lionel Robbins' suggestion. I don't recall being troubled in the least by the evident contrast between the even-tempered scholarship of the latter work and the allegedly repellent nature of Hayek's work in general.

At the University of Chicago, I knew Hayek was there but never saw him. Rumour had it that he was uninterested in the economics department because of its quantitative empirical orientation, but that again was at second hand.

Back in the UK, and particular in the years after I had migrated to Manchester, he re-appeared on the horizon, largely, I think, under the auspices of the Institute of Economic Affairs. I recall him being hailed as someone who had anticipated Friedman (1968) during the 1930s, and apparently being willing to accept this interpretation of his work.

I now know that the famous passage in *Prices and Production* (1931) upon which this claim was based referred to the dangers of inflation of the *money supply,* not the *price level,* and that his views on the monetary policy problems of the early 1930s were therefore diametrically opposed to Friedman's and had nothing to do with the natural rate hypothesis – but I didn't know that then. I also recall his advocacy some time in the early 1970s of a 'cold-turkey' approach to inflation control. I seem to remember that Robbins once did me the honour of comparing my gradualist proposals to Hayek's and coming down on my side, but I don't remember when or where that was – maybe in one of his Lords speeches on inflation?

Now to the Nobel Prize: in the autumn of 1973 I was invited by Herbert Giersch to give a lecture in the Kieler Vortrage series. My topic was 'Information, Money and the Macroeconomics of Inflation' (Chapter 1 of my *1975 Essays on Money and Inflation*).[1] The timing of my lecture immediately preceded a forecasting conference that Giersch's institute was hosting (which I also sat in on). It was a pretty high-level affair, with directors of various European institutes in attendance. The Swedish representative was Erik Lundberg, who arrived early and came to my lecture. He was very enthusiastic about my presentation, which did my ego no end of good, and at dinner afterwards (I think) began to discuss the relationship between what I was talking about and Swedish work in the 1930s, about which, at that time, I knew nothing – though I had already written a piece on Wicksell, of course. This was the context of the exchange between Lundberg and Giersch that I think I recall.

Roughly speaking, Lundberg argued that Gunnar Myrdal's work had been enormously important, and noted that there was local pressure on the Nobel Prize Committee to recognize him, but wondered how it would be received abroad if this was done. (Remember that the Prize was then rather new, and Lundberg had to be careful about its reputation.) Giersch's reply was that the quality of the work surely merited the award, but maybe the politics of it would be easier if there was a joint recipient who was neither Swedish nor shared Myrdal's views – what about Hayek? That's it – is this where Hayek's prize came from, or was he already high on the list, or what? I haven't the faintest idea.

As to 'me and Hayek' in the following years, Lundberg's comments on my lecture were surely one source of my subsequent interest in post-Wicksell macro, though it took a few years for this to go anywhere. I did, and still do, think that New Classical Economics has quite a bit in common with the Austrians (so did Robert Lucas, and I am surprised to find that I did not refer to this in the early 1980s, so I was either careless or did not know about it until a bit later).

But it was a great mistake to trot out this view in 1982 in my *Monetarist Perspectives* without explaining or defending my reasons. It annoyed a lot of people and, more important, it distracted their attention from the substance of my book's analysis and helped it to sink with very few ripples – my fault entirely, and a salutary lesson.

Even so, Axel Leijonhufvud's (1991) later comment – on my paper 'The Austrians and the Stockholm School – two failures in the History of Macroeconomics?' 'that while the Austrians and the New Classicals may both be ideological non-interventionists, the difference between the two belief systems is that in the Austrian one things can very easily go wrong' and that when it came to classifying ideas this all-important difference completely outweighed all the similarities, long ago persuaded me to take great care with this line of argument, and not to push it too far. As my subsequent work shows, I've come to appreciate the Austrians more as time has passed, and particularly those aspects of it that explain how things can go wrong.

Note

1. As an aside, this turned out to be an awkward choice. No-one at Kiel had bothered to tell me that they planned to publish the lecture and expected exclusive rights to do so, and it was already committed to a Lund conference proceedings edition of the *Scandinavian Journal*. The issue was eventually resolved by having the thing translated into German – by Klaus Hennings – for publication by Kiel, but they were miffed, nonetheless.

Bibliography

Friedman, M. 1968. The role of monetary policy. *American Economic Review*, 58 (March): 1–18.

Hayek, F. A. 1931. *Prices and Production* (London: Routledge).

Hayek, F. A. 1939. Introduction to Henry Thornton. *An Enquiry into the Nature and Effects of the Paper Credit of Great Britain* 1802, as reprinted and edited F. A. Hayek (London, Allen and Unwin).

Hayek, F. A. 1944. *The Road to Serfdom* (London: Routledge and Kegan Paul).

Laidler, D. 1975. *Essays on Money and Inflation* (Manchester: University of Manchester Press, Chicago: University of Chicago Press).

Laidler, D. 1982. *Monetarist Perspectives* (Deddington, Philip Allan, Cambridge MA: Harvard University Press)

Leijonhufvud, A. 1991. Comment (on D. Laidler 'The Austrians and the Stockholm School – two failures in the History of Macroeconomics?') in Lars Jonung (ed.) *The Stockholm School of Economics Revisited* (Cambridge: Cambridge University Press).

5
The Hayek Literature: Nicholas Wapshott, *Keynes Hayek: The Clash That Defined Modern Economics*

Selwyn Cornish

Opinion about the role government should play in the macroeconomy tends to conform to a rhythm, an ebb and flow, determined by circumstances and influenced by ideas. This book examines the ideas of John Maynard Keynes and Friedrich Hayek from the 1920s to the present, and concludes that interest in their theories and policy proposals waxed and waned according to changes in economic conditions. It is at once a study of the development of modern macroeconomic theory and policy, and a review of competing political philosophies. The author is a Reuters contributing columnist and former senior editor at *The Times* of London. He writes with an engaging style and adopts a light touch, calculated no doubt to attract a wide audience. The book, to be sure, is a good read. But historians of economic thought – and economists in general – will be disappointed perhaps with the superficial nature of much of the argument. Yet the book may assist the general reader to understand the evolution of economic ideas, as long as it is recognized that substantial liberties have been taken to simplify the argument.

The author's intention may have been to write a book about Keynes. But there are now so many books about him, and about his economics, that it is difficult to conjure up new ways of presenting his ideas. Following the method adopted by the Greek essayist Plutarch, who wrote about parallel lives, Wapshott has come up with the idea of discussing the progression of Keynes' ideas by comparing them with those of one of his chief rivals, Friedrich Hayek. The discussion focuses in particular on the high point of their rivalry in the early 1930s. First, Keynes' major works in economics are discussed, and Wapshott then contrasts Keynes' conclusions with Hayek's ideas on monetary economics and capital theory. While Keynes' call for government expenditure on public works to alleviate unemployment began as early as 1924, it originally lacked an analytical foundation. As unemployment in Britain grew, Keynes spent the next ten years trying to develop a theory to justify government expenditure on public works. On the other hand, Hayek's economics was influenced by the work of his Austrian forebears and by the hyper-inflation in Austria and adjoining countries in the early 1920s. This led him to conclude that government intervention in the economy led inevitably to distortions in the underlying economic structure and to inflation.

In this battle of ideas and policies, Wapshott directs particular attention to the marked divisions in the 1930s between the economists in Cambridge led by Keynes and his associates, including Richard Kahn, Piero Sraffa and Joan Robinson, and Hayek's supporters at the London School of Economics, where his great champion was Professor Lionel Robbins. In fact, Wapshott asserts that Robbins brought Hayek to London from Vienna for the express purpose of halting the spread of Keynes' influence on contemporary economic thought and policy.

The highlight of the book for many readers will be those sections that cover the exchanges between the rival parties in the early 1930s. They pulled no punches when criticizing the economics of the other side. But notwithstanding the ferocious attacks on each other's work, Keynes and Hayek were able to maintain a high personal regard for each other. Keynes, for example, went out of his way to take care of Hayek and his family when they were forced to vacate London during the war and move to Cambridge. Hayek, for his part, had no hesitation in adjudging that Keynes was 'the one really great man I ever knew'. This ability to retain a high personal regard for each other while conducting a heated public debate against each other's ideas and proposals says a great deal about the two men; it recalls the earlier debate between two great rivals, namely David Ricardo and Thomas Robert Malthus.

While discussion of their ideas and the intellectual and personal exchanges between Keynes and Hayek and their associates absorb a significant portion of the book, the central theme is the fluctuating fortunes of their ideas and related policy positions. Thus Keynes seemed initially to win the battle, dominating economic thought and policy from the 1930s to the early 1970s. In defeat, Hayek moved from economics to political philosophy, beginning with *The Road to Serfdom* and continuing with *The Constitution of Liberty*. These publications slowly created a new interest in Hayek, which accelerated with the stagflation of the 1970s and early 1980s. Now Hayek's early writing in economics won new adherents, and in 1974 he was the joint winner, with Gunnar Myrdal, of the Nobel Memorial Prize in Economic Science. The eclipse of Keynes and the resurgence of Hayek lasted until the Global Financial Crisis in 2008. In later chapters, Wapshott records the swing back to Keynes, and then gives brief attention to the subsequent questioning of the validity of Keynesian policies as sovereign debt crises materialized and excessive monetary easing rekindled fears about the recurrence of inflation.

As an organizing conception, the differences between Keynes and Hayek might seem to be a promising device to capture the general reader's attention. The problem is that such a framework leaves open the possibility of oversimplification. An example is the stress that is placed on the idea that Keynes' economics failed when stagflation arrived in the early 1970s, since it was thought incapable of handling the coexistence of inflation and unemployment. But one only has to read Chapter 21 of the *General Theory of Employment, Interest and Money* to know that Keynes well understood the possibility of inflation occurring when the economy operated at less than full employment, which for him meant an unemployment rate of 4–5 per cent. The idea that inflation and unemployment were necessarily incompatible was taken from the so-called Phillips Curve. The apparent trade-off between unemployment and inflation, however, has nothing to do with Keynes' economics, but was rather a concoction formulated by Samuelson and Solow decades after the publication of the *General Theory*. As to policy, there was nothing Keynesian about the desire of American administrations in the second half of the 1960s and early 1970s to boost government expenditure and allow budget deficits to accelerate at a time of full employment and rapid inflation. Nor was there anything Keynesian about the decisions of Australian governments in the early and mid 1970s permitting the continuation of a grossly overvalued exchange rate and massive increases in government expenditure when the foreign reserves quadrupled within the space of two years and unemployment was at near record lows and inflation at peacetime highs. Here are to be found the origins of the stagflation in the 1970s, rather than the work of Keynes. Further, there is nothing Keynesian about the excessive stimulus measures in 2008 and 2009 when the Australian economy was scarcely touched by the GFC, or about the continuation of these measures into 2010 and the perpetuation of budget deficits in 2011 and 2012. Rather than being inspired by Keynes, all these developments were the result of political expediency and should be seen in that light.

What, then, was the essence of 'the clash' between Keynes and Hayek that 'defined modern economics'? Whereas Hayek believed that attempts to subvert the market mechanism, though they might be undertaken with the best of intentions, would lead inevitably to inefficiency, unemployed resources and ultimately to the loss of freedom. Keynes believed that the market system had a tendency to operate at below capacity, and required fiscal and monetary measures to boost aggregate demand.

Keynes had two major problems with Hayek, one to do with the latter's economics, the other with his political philosophy. As with members of the 'classical school', Hayek's economics was based on the implicit assumption of full employment. Perhaps the most important point that Keynes made in the *General Theory* was that when the economy operated at less than full employment – and for him, this was the general case – there were spare resources that could be drawn upon by public authorities without having to divert resources from existing employment. In this sense, the structural distortions between capital goods and consumer goods industries that Hayek argued would occur when governments spent on public works, or when the monetary authorities allowed excessive monetary easing, would not occur. At full employment, Keynes conceded that the classical analysis was valid; in those circumstances, market forces should be allowed to do their job, governments should scale back their expenditures, and central banks should tighten monetary policy. While Arthur Pigou, for example, had been signing the same letters to newspapers as Keynes, calling as they did for increased government expenditure to stimulate activity, Keynes criticized Pigou's continued adherence to the economics of the classical school because it presupposed that there could not be any unemployment. As Keynes (1936) wrote in the Preface to the *General Theory*:

> if orthodox economics is at fault, the error is to be found not in the super-structure, which has been erected with great care for logical consistency, but in a lack of clearness and of generality in the premises.

He had made the same point in 1931 when criticizing Hayek, saying that his analysis

> is an extraordinary example of how, starting with a mistake, a remorseless logician can end up in Bedlam. (Moggridge, 1973)

The other issue that troubled Keynes – and many others, including Frank Knight and Jacob Viner – was an inconsistency that lay at the heart of *The Road to Serfdom*. Keynes saw great merit in the book's attack on excessive government intervention. Writing to Hayek in June 1944, he considered *The Road to Serfdom* to be a grand book. We have the greatest reason to be grateful to you for saying so well what needs to be said... morally and philosophically I find myself in agreement with virtually the whole of it; and not only in agreement with it, but in a deeply moved agreement. (Moggridge, 1980)

For many, however, this praise by Keynes for Hayek's most popular work has often been difficult to square with their differences on matters of economic theory and policy. But that was not the point, for when it came to politics it is often forgotten that Keynes and Hayek had much in common: both were liberals, and both saw a limited role for government in economic and social affairs. Unlike Marx, for example, the objective of both Keynes and Hayek was to preserve capitalism; that aim, according to Keynes, required the government to stabilize the economy, while Hayek supported government intervention in various areas of social policy (as did Adam Smith). Of *The Road to Serfdom*, Keynes told Hayek that his 'only serious criticism of the book' was

the question of knowing where to draw the line [on government intervention]... You agree that the line has to be drawn somewhere, and that the logical extreme is not possible. But you give us no guidance whatever as to where to draw it. In a sense, this is shirking the practical issue. It is true that you and I would probably draw it in different places... But as soon as you admit that the extreme is not possible, and that a line has to be drawn, you are, on your own argument, done for, since you are trying to persuade us that so soon as one moves an inch in the planned direction you are necessarily launched on the slippery path which will lead you in due course over the precipice. (Moggridge, 1980)

In 1971, after reviewing the debates of the 1930s, which to some degree he had initiated, Lionel Robbins (1971) – now Lord Robbins – wrote that the

historian of the future, if he wishes to treat of the relations between London and Cambridge during this period, should be warned that any generalizations that he may wish to make must fit facts of considerable complexity if they are not seriously to misrepresent the situation.

Regrettably, Wapshott failed to heed this advice, since he has over-generalized and ignored the complexities involved. As to his part in the debates of the 1930s, Robbins later confessed that he

> was certainly an anti-expansionist where public expenditure was concerned, at a time when, as I now think, I should have been on the other side.

The problem was that the prevailing 'theory was inadequate to the facts'; he was prepared to admit 'my dispute with Keynes as the greatest mistake of my professional career'. Like Hayek, Robbins agreed that he 'would certainly regard Maynard Keynes as the most remarkable man I have ever met'.

One final point: there are an inordinate number of factual and biblio-graphical mistakes in this book. In the early 1980s the distinguished English novelist Graham Greene wrote a letter to *The Times* in which he took Wapshott to task for manifold errors in an article Wapshott had written for the paper; Greene suggested that Wapshott should be described as 'Mr Badshott'. (Hawtree, 1989). It is a pity that Wapshott did not learn from his encounter with Greene.

Bibliography

Hawtree, C. 1989. *Graham Greene. Yours etc. Letters to the Press 1945–1989.* Reinhardt Press .

Keynes, J. M. 1936. *The General Theory of Employment, Interest and Money.* London: Macmillan.

Moggridge, D. 1973. *The Collected Writings of John Maynard Keynes: XIII, The General Theory and After, Part 1, Preparation.* London: Macmillan.

Moggridge, D. 1980. *The Collected Writings of John Maynard Keynes: XXVII, Activities 1940–1946, Shaping the Post-War World, Employment and Commodities.* London: Macmillan.

Robbins, L. 1971. *Autobiography of an Economist.* London: Macmillan.

Wapshott, N. 2011. *Keynes Hayek: The Clash That Defined Modern Economics.* Scribe Publications.

6
Hayek and Mises

Douglas French

There are no two Austrian economists linked as closely as Friedrich A. von Hayek and Ludwig von Mises. If an educated man on the street knows the name of an Austrian economist at all it is however, likely to be that of Hayek. This recognition is all the more likely since the Global Financial Crisis of 2008, as shorthand for the debate as to how to fix the economy has become 'Keynes vs. Hayek'.

Mises is mentioned in the same breath, for it was Mises's Austrian Business Cycle Theory that Hayek refined, earning him a share of the 1974 Nobel Prize a year after Mises passed away. It was as a result of their work in this area that Mises and his protégé Hayek 'were among the very few economists in the world to predict the 1929 depression' (Rothbard, 1974: 18).

The two men met in October of 1921 when the 22-year-old Hayek (1994: 64, 67), possessing a freshly minted law degree, came to the office known as *Abrechnungsamt* [Office of Accounts] in Vienna to apply for a job. This office was created 'to carry out certain provisions of the peace treaty of 1918 – the settlement of pre-war private debts between nations'.

Hayek hadn't wanted to go to work so soon after getting his first degree. He had hoped to study in Munich under Max Weber. However, Weber died and the Austrian inflation made it impossibly expensive for Hayek's father to pay for another year of study in Germany.

Mises, working for the chamber of commerce, was a director at the office. Applicants with a law degree and speaking two languages not only had a better chance of being hired, but were qualified for higher paid positions. Hayek had both, as well as a letter from his teacher Friedrich von Wieser, who recommended Hayek for the job.

Mises read Wieser's recommendation, looked at Hayek and smiled, but was sceptical, commenting, 'Wieser says you're a promising young economist. I've never seen you at my lectures' (Hayek, 1994: 67–68). However, Mises hired the young Hayek on the spot, believing it would be rude to reject him given Wieser's recommendation (Hülsmann, 2007: 453).

Mises put Hayek to work researching money and banking, and Hayek was quickly useful to his boss, 'alerting Mises to the case for free banking' (Hülsmann, 2007: 453). This was an important topic as the inflation was so bad that Hayek's initial salary of 5,000 kronen a month was bumped to 15,000 kronen on his second month on the job, and by the next July 'it reached one million a month' (Hayek, 1994: 70).

At the same time Hayek began work on a doctorate in economics. In the summer of 1922 he began work on a thesis on the theory of imputation of value, and completed his second degree in early 1923.

Hayek became convinced that an economist must become familiar with the United States and after completing his second degree and saving enough money for a one-way ticket, Mises's protégé sailed for New York with his boss's blessing, arriving with less than US$20 to his name.

Professor Jeremiah W. Jenks had committed to employing Hayek as a research assistant. But when Hayek arrived, he was told that Professor Jenks had left for vacation and was not to be disturbed.

It didn't take long for the young Austrian to run through his limited funds, and jobs were scarce for someone with limited English skills. Although he had letters of recommendation from the likes of Joseph Schumpeter, Hayek was forced to look for unscholarly work: 'I was finally accepted as a dishwasher in a Sixth Avenue restaurant – but I never actually started on it', writes Hayek (1994: 65), 'since an hour before I was to report to work a telephone call came through saying that Professor Jenks had returned and was prepared to employ me'.

Hayek made $100 a month working for Jenks, and managed to spend only $60 of it for living expenses, staying at a YMCA. The rest he saved for his return trip. During his 14 months in New York, Hayek was enrolled at New York University, but he gate-crashed a number of lectures at Columbia, especially those of Wesley C. Mitchell, who Hayek did side work for. 'At present I am at the National Bureau for Economic Research collecting material for Professor Mitchell's study of the Business Cycle'. Hayek wrote in a letter to Mises (Hülsmann, 2007: 454f).

Mitchell was a great admirer of Professor Wieser, and Hayek also talked to him about his boss back in Vienna.

To Mitchell's mild astonishment, Hayek put Mises in the same class as Voltaire, Montesquieu, Tocqueville, and John Stuart Mill (Hülsmann, 2007: 454).

In his spare time, Hayek turned his imputation thesis into an article and began gathering material for a book on the Federal Reserve. He had hoped to continue his stay in New York with funds from a Rockefeller fellowship. Professor Wieser was the main contact for the fellowship, and he made sure his old student was granted the first one (Hülsmann, 2007: 455). However, the fellowship notification passed Hayek's (1994: 67) ship in the night, while he was returning to Vienna. When the notification caught up to him, he 'was then unwilling and unable, in view of my job, to take it up at once, hoping to go instead a few years later'.

Once Hayek turned down the Rockefeller fellowship, Mises attempted to hire Hayek for the Kammer library, a position Mises had corresponded with Hayek about while Hayek was in New York. But the young Austrian didn't obtain that position either, and his friend Gottfried von Haberler eventually filled the post: 'These early problems foreshadowed Hayek's lifetime lack of talent as a careerist' (Hülsmann, 2007: 455).

However, Hayek had a friend in Mises, having worked in the *Abrechnungsamt* office under him (Haberler, 2000). Mises created a suitable position for Hayek by forming the Österreichisches Institut für Konjunkturforschung (Austrian Institute for Business Cycle Research), one of the first business cycle institutes in central Europe (Hülsmann, 2007: 455; Schulak and Unterköfler, 2010: 117). According to Mises' secretary, Mrs. Wof-Thieberger, Mises created the Institute 'because he had to help Hayek find the right start in life' (Margit Mises, 1976: 48).

Hayek (1994: 68–69) writes that his relationship with Mises was

the personal contact from which I profited most, not only by way of intellectual stimulation but also for his direct assistance with my career.

Hayek credits Mises with creating the Austrian Institute for Business Cycle Research, believing it was conceived

largely for the purpose of providing scope for me after he had failed to get me as a sort of scientific assistant into the chamber of commerce where he held his main job (for the purpose of building up there under his direction an economic research division).

Mises did the necessary lobbying of government agencies and trade organizations to provide funding for the institute and to put Hayek in charge.

For the four years between 1927 and 1931 Hayek organized the Institute from the ground up, with just him and his secretary. Later Oscar Morgenstern was added as a collaborator. Morgenstern would take over when Hayek left for London. The Institute job came just in time for Hayek, as he had recently married and the pay and prospects of the temporary civil servant post were not good.

Hayek describes the relationship with his mentor as 'curious' in the sense that although Mises was never Hayek's teacher in the conventional sense, Hayek wrote that he learned more from Mises than from any other man. As a regular student he attended only one Mises lecture, 'but rather disliked him'. Along with working with Mises during the day, Hayek (1994: 69) joined Mises's *Privateseminar* held twice a month on Friday evenings at Mises' office. Hayek describes these meetings as 'the most important centre of economic discussion at Vienna'.

Monetary theory was the focus of the seminar in the winter semester of 1921–1922, a semester that included not only Hayek, but Haberler, Fritz Machlup, and Alfred Schütz. But over time the seminar developed an interdisciplinary spirit. Although no degree credit was being received for attending the seminar, the debates were gruelling (Hayek, 1994: 71). Hayek was happy for a reprieve when he spent a year in New York (Hülsmann, 2007: 461–462).

When Hayek returned, only a third of the twenty-odd participants were economists, so the discussions turned much more philosophical. The seminars started at 7:00 p.m. with one member giving a short talk. This was followed by discussions until 10:30 pm, the official end of the meeting. At that point the discussion moved to a restaurant – typically an Italian eatery known as Ancora Verde – where the discussion continued:

> The most ardent debaters, Mises usually among them, finally went on to the Café Künstler and stayed until 2 or 3 a.m.

Mises would typically leave at 1:00 am, with Fritz Machlup and philosopher Alfred Schütz staying till 3:00 a.m. (Hülsmann, 2007: 461–462).

Members of the seminar even sang songs written by philosopher and member Felix Kaufman about the seminar. The 28 songs were based upon Austrian folk melodies and songs popular at the time. Even in his late 80s, Gottfried von Haberler remembered the words to many of the songs.

Haberler said in a 1990 interview:

> In the first place, they [the songs] dealt with interesting problems or with actual events that we all knew and that as a result were rendered memorable. The same went for the melodies Kaufmann chose for his lyrics – we knew them all … Kaufmann took great pains with the text of his songs. Still today, the reader will find interesting points throughout. Kaufmann was also careful to see that the thoughts sounded well in rhyme.

Mises wrote,

> The private seminar … was and always remained the circle of my – much younger – friends (Hülsmann, 2007: 464).

Being among friends, Mises likely took his fair share of ribbing late into the night. For instance, Kaufman's song 'The Scientist and the Methodologist' pokes fun at Mises.

At a desk in the small room before us,
The scientist sits, wide awake
He's writing with zealous abandon
Playing catch up, his pen starts to shake

His style, it is polished and clever,
And ever more grand are the knots
He's weaving together before him
In the web of his burgeoning thoughts.

He keeps moving forward like Blücher,
That hero from battles of old,
He's used up the bulk of his fodder,
His greatest work yet, all truth told

Fate sneaks up and sits down beside him,
Oh innocent faith, watch your back!
The methodologist chides him
With a song as his plan of attack.

He says to the clever young scientist,
What you've written here's not really clear
After so much reflection and research,
It's dense as the foam on my beer.

I'll not be the cause of your heartache
But experience makes my tongue burn:
Making a priori *assumptions, In the long run*
Will bring no return ... [1]

In a speech honouring Mises, Hayek (1992: 135) said:

> We, his old pupils of the Vienna days, used to regard him as a most brilliant but somewhat severe bachelor, who had organized his life in a most efficient routine, but who in the intensity of intellectual efforts was clearly burning the candle at both ends.

Mises lived with his mother Adele until she died in 1937, despite being financially capable of living on his own (Margit Mises, 1976: 24). She is described as being intelligent, 'with the attitude of a general and a will of iron'. Mises occasionally invited Hayek to his apartment for lunch or dinner. Mises and his mother sat opposite one another at a long table. 'She never spoke a word'. Hayek (1992: 24–25) said, recounting the chilly atmosphere. 'She never participated in the conversation, but one always felt she was there. When the coffee was served she quietly got up and left the dining room'.

Although Mises met his future bride in 1925, at a dinner party at the home of Fritz Kaufmann, and was smitten enough to send a dozen red roses to Margit the next day, the two would not marry until 1938, a year after Mrs von Mises died.

Mises had reservations about marriage in the first place, writing in *Socialism,*

> The ties of marriage become intolerable bonds which the genius tries to cast off or at least to loosen so as to be able to move freely. The married couple must walk side by side amid the rank and file of humanity. Whoever wishes to go his own way must break away from it. Rarely indeed is he granted the happiness of finding a woman willing and able to go with him on his solitary path.

Add to that the fact that Margit was an actress, who in those days were viewed as nothing more than high-class call girls. But the real problem was Ludwig's mother, who had serious reservations about the widow with two children. Then again, Mrs. von Mises had never liked any of her son's girlfriends, but Ludwig deferred to his mother in these matters (Hülsmann, 2008).

During the years the seminar was held, Mises was a bachelor in his 40s and early 50s whose social life appears limited to the seminar, the arts, and his on-and-off-again romance with Margit. Erik von Kuehnelt-Leddihn (forthcoming) describes Mises as 'a great theatergoer, and the other fine arts meant a great deal to him'. According to Kuehnelt-Leddihn,

> Mises needed the arts to counter his growing melancholia mixed with real indignation at the gradual collapse of Western civilization and culture to which he was so deeply attached.

Hayek (1992: 71) described the seminar:

> All ex-university students, discussing I believe predominantly questions of scientific methodology rather than particular problems. Even if we'd start out with a very practical concrete problem of the time, we'd very soon be off with a conflict between the different groups of economics.

However, Hayek, like a number of the other members of the seminar, was not as influenced by Mises as one would expect. 'For these men, Mises was more role model than teacher', writes Hülsmann (2007: 465). Mises dissected problems in social analysis as he had learned from Böhm-Bawerk, but he did not create 'a "school" of disciples advocating his doctrines'. Mises did not attempt to produce followers, 'and in fact had no disciples during his Vienna years'.

Mises was a thoughtful and inspiring teacher, but first and foremost he believed in individualism (Schulak and Unterköfler, 2010: 117). Hülsmann (2007: 465) explains:

> It was more important than any particular creed in religion, politics, or aesthetics. He certainly did not lack firm convictions in politics and science, but in his interactions with students and other people these convictions took only second place to the reverence he paid to the ideal of individualism.

While Mises may not have insisted that his students adopt his views, Hayek (1992; 72) writes that

> Mises was very resentful of any criticism by his pupils and temporarily broke with Machlup and Haberler because they criticized him.

At the same time, Mises accepted Hayek's criticism

silently and even approved the article [1937 article on the economics of knowledge] as if he had not been aware that it was a criticism of his own views.

Hayek has no explanation for why he was treated differently.

In 1926, Mises took over from Wieser as the primary contact of the Rockefeller Foundation in Vienna, providing him with the opportunity to gain favour and power by either providing or withholding material benefits. However, he did neither, never taking advantage of this position to gather sycophants.

Noble as this attitude was, it gave a competitive edge to some of his rivals who did not have the same scruples. (Hülsmann, 2007: 465)

However, Mises' biographer, Guido Hülsmann (2007: 465) believes there was no Misesian school in the 1920s primarily because 'Mises's professional standing was not paramount'. Mises was seen as a monetary expert and the author of a controversial book (*Socialism*), but was not viewed to be as famous or as brilliant as others such as Hans Kelsen, Carl Grünberg, and Othmar Spann, who taught in the law and government sciences departments.

As close as he was to Mises, Hayek would never lose his Wiesarian roots. Mises may have provided the liberalism, but Hayek's analytical construction was framed and remained under the influence of his formal instructor – Friedrich von Wieser. Writes Hülsmann:

All of his life, Hayek perceived himself quite consciously as a member of the Wiesarian branch of the Austrian School.

Writing in 1978, Hayek seems disappointed that the Austrian School had been taken over by Misesians, believing that

he represents only one of the branches into which Menger's teachings had split already among his disciples: the close personal friends and relatives Eugen von Böhm-Bawerk and Friedrich von Wieser.

Hayek goes on to write that Wieser's tradition had gone unfulfilled (Hülsmann, 2007; 475–476).

Hülsmann (2007; 473–474) writes that while Hayek is considered Mises's most famous student, Hayek's intellectual heritage is distinctly Wiesarian. Hayek's doctorial dissertation in economics was on the theory of imputation, based upon Wiesarian price and value theory, in direct conflict with Mises's socialist-calculation argument.

> As a Wieserian value theorist, Hayek could not endorse Mises' argument that a rational socialist economy was impossible because there was no such thing as value imputation.

Peter Klein (1992: 9) sees it differently:

> Undoubtedly, no economist has had a greater impact on Hayek's thinking than Mises – not even Wieser, from whom Hayek learned his craft but who died in 1927 when Hayek was still a young man.

However, Klein quickly undermines his assertion, by quoting Hayek himself.

> Although I owe [Mises] a decisive stimulus at a crucial point of my intellectual development, and continuous inspiration throughout a decade, I have perhaps most profited from his teaching because I was not initially his student at the university, the innocent young man who took his word for gospel, but came to him as a trained economist, trained in a parallel branch of Austrian Economics [the Wieser branch] from which he gradually, but never completely, won me over.

The primary areas of disagreement between Hayek and Mises are the socialist-calculation debate and Mises' 'apriorist' methodology. In 1920 Mises charged that a lack of the price system makes socialism impossible. Hayek (1992: 127) maintained that Mises'

> central thesis was not, as it is sometimes misleadingly put, that socialism is impossible, but that it cannot achieve an efficient utilization of resources.

Hayek's interpretation has been disputed; however Professor Klein (1992: 10) cites the revisionist historian of the calculation debate, Don Lavoie, who writes, central arguments advanced by both Hayek and [Lionel] Robbins did not constitute a retreat from Mises' position, but rather a clarification, redirecting the challenge to the later versions of central planning...Although comments by both Hayek and Robbins about the computational difficulties of the [later version] were responsible for misleading interpretations of their arguments, in fact their main contributions were fully consistent with Mises' challenge.

Hayek (1992: 72) explains that he parted intellectually with Mises beginning with his 1937 article on the economics of knowledge. With this article, Hayek attempted

to persuade Mises himself that when he asserted that the market theory was a priori, he was wrong; that what was a priori was only the logic of individual action, but the moment that you passed from this to the interaction of many people, you entered into the empirical field.

Hayek (1992: 72–73) goes on to write that while Mises's critique of socialism is masterful, it has been ineffective:

Because Mises remained in the end himself a rationalist-utilitarian, and with a rationalist-utilitarianism, the rejection of socialism is irreconcilable.

Mises's view that rational humans can see that socialism is wrong is a mistake, Hayek said. If humans have the intellectual power to rationally arrange things, that notion conflicts with Mises's assertion.

In one place he says we can't do it, another place he argues, being rational people, we must try to do it.

Despite having won a Nobel Prize for his business cycle work, what Hayek is most known for in the current literature and popular press inside and outside the field of economics is his insight concerning spontaneous order. Mises did not share these views, as Hayek wrote,

Mises himself was still much more a child of the rationalist tradition of the Enlightenment and of continental, rather than of English, liberalism...than I am myself (cited by Klein, 1992: 11–12).

Hayek (1992: 146) believed that Mises's statement that liberalism, 'regards all social cooperation as an emanation of rationally recognized utility' is wrong.

> The extreme rationalism of this passage, which as a child of his time he could not escape from, and which he perhaps never fully abandoned, now seems to me factually mistaken.

Hayek believed Mises' extreme rationalism leads to the notion that social institutions not deliberately designed by humans are not beneficial, supporting the socialist idea that markets lack human design and must then be centrally planned by humans to be most beneficial.

So, as close as Hayek and Mises were, ironically each represents an opposing camp in the split within the modern Austrian School: Mises' 'social rationalists' versus Hayek's 'spontaneous order'.

And while these two camps constantly joust in academic journals and in the blogosphere, to those looking from the outside in the debate is much ado about nothing, leaving bystanders to scratch their heads in wonderment over what all the fuss is about.

Perhaps that's apropos. As Klein (1992: 13) writes about the split:

> These differences have not yet been resolved, as the nature of the Mises–Hayek relationship is not fully understood.

While Hayek admits he didn't initially believe Mises' arguments were completely convincing, over time he 'slowly learned that he was mostly right and that, after some reflection, a justification could be found that he had not made explicit'. In later years Hayek (1976: xx) explained their differences by saying that Mises was forced to 'certain exaggerations' to get his point across in a hostile intellectual environment.

While the two scholars had differences of opinion, any supposedly feud is fabrication. For instance, trying to create a rift that never really existed, Hayek scholar Bruce Caldwell believes Hayek's review of the German version of *Human Action* lacked enthusiasm.

> Compared to what others have said about *Human Action*, Hayek's review is extremely favourable. It is lukewarm when we remember Hayek's special relationship with Mises (Klein, 1992: 11).

Whatever the differences of opinion, it is clear that Mises viewed Hayek as his most accomplished student. Writing about Mises' seminar that began at New York University in 1948, Margit von Mises (1976: 135, 48) wrote, 'Lu met every new student encouraged, hopeful that one of them might develop into a second Hayek'. It was Margit's view that Hayek,

> more than any of the others who studied there with Lu, kept his views and writings close to Lu's teachings. As the years passed, Hayek and Lu became very good friends, a natural result of their mutually congenial convictions.

At the same time, Hayek (1976: xx) wrote glowingly about his mentor:

> That they had one of the great thinkers of our time in their midst, the Viennese have never understood.

Hayek may have been a Wiesarian, but his love and respect for his mentor extended to his last days. At the same time, Mises could be stubborn and uncompromising; however his admiration for his most accomplished student never waned.

Modern Austrians should learn not just the tremendous scholarship of these great thinkers, but also the good grace and collegial manners that they treated each other with.

Note

1. http://mises.org/misestributes/misessongs.asp.

Bibliography

Haberler, G. 2000. Between Mises and Keynes: An Interview with Gottfried von Haberler, 1900–1995. *Austrian Economics Newsletter*, Spring, 20 (1), http://mises.org/journals/aen/aen20_1_1.asp.

Hayek, F. A. 1976. Introduction. In Mises *My years with Ludwig von Mises*. Cedar Falls, Iowa: Centre for Futures Education.

Hayek, F. A. 1992. *The Fortunes of Liberalism: Essays on Austrian Economics and the Ideal of Freedom*. Klein, Peter (ed.) Chicago: University of Chicago Press.

Hülsmann, J. G. 2007. *Mises: The Last Knight of Liberalism*. Ludwig von Mises Institute: Auburn, Alabama.

Hülsmann., J. G. 2008. *The Valentine Story of Ludwig and Margit von Mises*. mises.org 4 February 2008. http://mises.org/daily/2875

Kaufmann, F. *Songs of the Mises-Kries*. Translated by Arlene Oost-Zinner.
Kuehnelt-Leddihn, E. von (forthcoming). The Cultural Background of Ludwig von Mises. In *Travelogue: Journeys with Mises*. Arlene Oost-Zinner (ed.) Ludwig von Mises Institute: Auburn, Alabama.
Mises, Margit von. 1976. *My years with Ludwig von Mises*. Cedar Falls, Iowa: Center for Futures Education.
Rothbard, M. 1974. *Human Events,* 16 November: 18.
Schulak, E.-M. and Unterköfler, H. 2010. *The Viennese School of Economics*. Ludwig von Mises Institute: Auburn, Alabama.

7
Hayek in Freiburg

Viktor J. Vanberg

The University of Freiburg is known as home of the ordoliberal Freiburg School (Vanberg, 1998), a research tradition that was founded in the 1930s by a group of economists and jurists[1] who shared the conviction that a properly functioning market order needs to be framed by appropriate rules, that such a framework is not self-generating but needs to be cultivated and enforced by government, and that law and economics are called upon to provide the institutional knowledge required for that purpose. To this research tradition and, specifically, to its principal founder, Walter Eucken, Hayek referred when, on 18 June 1962, in his inaugural lecture at the university of Freiburg he stated:

> Special mention is due to the personal contacts with professional colleagues which have for decades provided for me a connection with this university. ... By far the most important for me was, however, the friendship of many years' standing, based on the closest agreement on scientific as well as on political questions, with the unforgettable Walter Eucken. During the last four years of his life this friendship had led to close collaboration. ... You know better than I what Eucken has achieved in Germany. I need therefore not explain further what it means if I say here today that I shall regard it as one of my chief tasks to resume and continue the tradition which Eucken and his friends have created at Freiburg and in Germany. It is a tradition of the greatest scientific integrity and at the same time of outspoken conviction on the great issues of public life (Hayek, 1967 [1963]: 252f).

93

Hayek and Eucken

As Hayek (1992 [1983]: 188f.) recalls, he came into contact with Walter Eucken through Wilhelm Röpke, with whom he had become acquainted at a meeting of the Verein für Socialpolitik (the professional association of German-speaking economists) in Vienna in 1926, and who introduced him to the Ricardian Group, a network of theoretical economists who opposed the dominance of the German Historical School in the association and to which German liberals like Röpke, Alexander Rüstow and Walter Eucken belonged.[2] About Eucken, whom he met at the 1928 meeting of the Verein für Socialpolitik in Zurich, where they both presented papers on monetary and business cycle theory,[3] Hayek (ibid.: 189) notes in retrospect:

> At that time he was not at all well known, but already had great influence among his closer associates. He was probably the most serious thinker in the realm of social philosophy produced by Germany in the last hundred years. Walter Eucken had published only short studies at that time. Oddly enough, his major work[4] reached me in London during the war. ... It made me realize for the first time what a towering figure Eucken was and to how great an extent Eucken and his circle embodied the great German liberal tradition, which had unfortunately become defunct.

Speaking of Eucken as 'a valuable friend' (ibid.: 190) he reports that in the late 1930s – until the outbreak of WWII made it impossible – he used his trips between Vienna and London for stopovers in Freiburg to visit Eucken,[5] and on these occasions he apparently gave lectures to the ordoliberal group that had formed around Eucken.[6] Unable to maintain direct communication during the war, it was only indirectly, through Röpke – who had left Nazi Germany in 1933 for Turkey and had since 1937 taught at the Geneva Institute for International Studies in Switzerland – that Hayek and Eucken could stay in contact.[7] It was through Röpke that Hayek received Eucken's *Grundlagen der Nationalökonomie* to which he refers in the above quotation and on which he commented in a letter to Röpke: 'It's a very excellent piece of work which has further raised my sincere admiration for our friend. To have retained this independence of thought in this environment!'[8]

Soon after the war ended Eucken resumed his contact with Hayek, writing a letter, dated 12 August 1945, in which he briefly refers to the precarious conditions he had faced under the past 'diabolical system', and then continues:

> About all these things and much else, chiefly scientific questions, we should talk in person. To initiate this is the main purpose of this letter. It is important for those who earnestly refuse to go along the 'Road to Serfdom' to stay not only in contact but in close contact.[9]

In a follow-up letter of 10 November 1945, Eucken stresses again how important he considers it for non-socialist economists to cooperate across borders, a concern to which Hayek responds in his letter of 22 November: 'I have been thinking already for a long time very seriously about the problem of an international organization of all liberals'.[10] It was his exchange with Eucken and others on this idea – about which, as he notes (1994: 133), he had 'thought and talked a good deal' in the years immediately following the war – that led Hayek to organize what was to become the founding meeting of the Mont Pelerin Society at Lake Geneva in 1947.[11] On this meeting and, in particular, on the role that Eucken played at it Hayek (1967 [1963]: 252) has reported in retrospect:

> More than fifteen years ago – less than two years after the end of the war – I had undertaken to call an international conference of some economists, lawyers and historians of the Western world who were passionately concerned about the preservation of personal freedom. ... Eucken ... was the only participant from Germany at the conference on Mont Pèlerin. This made it the more significant that he became the great personal success of the conference and that his moral stature made the most profound impression on all participants. He has thereby contributed much to restore in the West the belief in the existence of liberal thinkers in Germany, and he has further strengthened this impression at a further conference of the Mont Pèlerin [sic] Society[12] and on a visit to London in 1950 from which he was not to return.[13]

Hayek's concluding remark refers to the sad fact that he had invited Eucken to give a series of lectures at the LSE but had already moved to Chicago[14] before this came to be realized (Hayek, 2004 [1979]: 52) and was no longer present when Eucken arrived on 3 March 1950 in London,[15] where he died on March 20 before he could deliver the last of his prepared lectures.[16] In a paper published on occasion of Ludwig von Mises' 70th birthday Hayek (1967 [1951]: 199) noted, in memory of Walter Eucken:

> Today we realize that his sudden death a little over a year ago robbed the liberal revival of one of its really great men. ... It was not until after Germany's collapse that it became apparent how fruitful and beneficial his quiet activities had been during the National Socialist period; for only then was the circle of his friends and students in Germany revealed as the most important bulwark of rational economic thinking.

Hayek and the Ordoliberal Freiburg School

It is difficult to judge to what extent the exchange between them led Hayek and Eucken to mutually adjust their respective views of what a modern revival of the classical liberal tradition, to which they both sought to contribute, requires. The German liberal economists, including Eucken, who belonged to the afore-mentioned Ricardian Group in the Verein für Socialpolitik shared the conviction that 'laissez faire' is not an adequate answer to the question of what providing for and maintaining a free and humane society requires, but that an essential role has to be played by the state as the agency that secures and cultivates the legal–institutional framework within which the free exchange and intercourse among sovereign individuals can evolve to everybody's benefit, a conviction that led them to call themselves 'neo-liberals', in order to dissociate their views from a, in their view, too crude 'laissez-faire liberalism'. As much as they regarded the 'Austrian liberals', Mises and Hayek, as allies in their common opposition to the German Historical School, they had reservations about the particular emphasis of Mises' free-market liberalism,[17] even if to different degrees and for somewhat different reasons. Rüstow was the one among the German neo-liberals who harboured, and expressed, the strongest resentments against the 'Austrians';[18] Röpke took a middle ground, while Eucken's ordoliberal approach came closest to, at least, Hayek's Austrian outlook. Eucken did not share the *interventionist* inclinations that characterize Rüstow's and Röpke's 'sociological neo-liberalism',[19] inclinations that were indeed in conflict with what Mises as well as Hayek considered essential to liberalism. Three months before his untimely death in London, Eucken summarized the essence of his approach in these terms:

The argument today is not ... a matter of conflict about whether the state should interfere only a little or somewhat more. The conflict is a different one. One side, to which I belong, is of the opinion that the state must influence, or even directly establish, the forms and institutional framework within which the economy must work. It should, however, avoid the attempt to steer directly the everyday business of the economy. Others believe that the state must not just establish the framework, but must influence the day-to-day operation of the economy on the basis of central planning.[20]

Where in his friendly exchange with Hayek Eucken voiced disagreement this was not due to irreconcilably conflicting views but rather a matter of differences in emphasis on the role of what the Freiburg School calls *Ordnungspolitik*, the role that government needs to play in providing and securing an adequate institutional framework for a well-working market economy.

In a letter to Hayek of 12 March 1946, in which he comments on his reading of *The Road to Serfdom*,[21] Eucken expresses his essential agreement with Hayek's arguments but also points out that he would like Hayek to adopt a more ordoliberal perspective. Referring to the distinction that Hayek (1972 [1944]: 36) draws between 'laissez faire' and 'making the best possible use of the forces of competition as a means of co-ordinating human efforts', Eucken calls on Hayek to more explicitly elaborate this distinction and to emphasize more strongly how important it is to provide for an appropriate legal-institutional framework – including corporate law, patent law, trade law, taxation law, etc. – in order to secure competition and to prevent a concentration of economic power. That he took Eucken's ordoliberal plea seriously Hayek indicates with his letter of 3 November 1946, in which he explains that his extensive travelling prevented him from responding earlier, and notes:

> By the way, it will be of interest to you that the main purpose of my trip to America has been an attempt to set up in Chicago a major research project on the changes in the legal framework that are necessary for a functioning competitive economy. Unfortunately, the man on whom my plans mostly relied, Henry Simons, suddenly died in the last moment, and I do not yet know if the project can nevertheless be carried on.[22]

It was surely not Eucken's influence alone that led Hayek to pay more attention to government's role in maintaining a legal-institutional framework for markets to operate beneficially. It is noteworthy, though, that this ordoliberal theme plays a much bigger role in Hayek's work from the late 1930s to 1950, that is, during the time he was in contact with Eucken, than before or after. In his 1939 pamphlet *Freedom and the Economic System*, in *The Road to Serfdom* (1972 [1944]), and in a number of chapters, in particular his address at the founding meeting of the Mont Pelerin Society on ' "Free" Enterprise and Competitive Order' (1948b), Hayek emphasized time and again that 'the task of creating a rational framework of law' (1939: 11) should be paid more attention to among liberals, that there is 'all the difference between deliberately creating a system within which competition will work as beneficially as possible and passively accepting institutions as they are' (1972 [1944]: 17), and that 'the fundamental principle of liberalism' calls for 'a policy which deliberately adopts competition, the market, and prices as its ordering principle and uses the legal framework enforced by the state in order to make competition as effective and beneficial as possible' (1948b: 10). In a paper that he presented in 1947 at the European Forum Alpbach,[23] and in which he stressed the same theme, Hayek expressly noted:

> Specifically on this subject a number of very important studies have been published already before the war in Germany, notably inspired by Professor Walter Eucken in Freiburg i.Br. and by Professor Franz Böhm, now in Frankfurt, that I want especially to point out to you. The problem of the 'economic order' in the sense in which these researchers posed it and sought to sketch out its solution, is one of the most important challenges that the human mind can confront today and the solution of which is of immense importance.[24]

When Eucken, together with his colleague Franz Böhm, founded the yearbook *ORDO*[25] which was to become the principal outlet of the ordoliberal circle, he invited Hayek to join the board of editors and to contribute an article to the inaugural volume.[26] Hayek accepted both invitations, contributing a German translation of his essay 'Individualism: True and False' (1948a)[27] to the first volume of *ORDO*[28]; he served as member of the editorial board continuously from 1948 to 1991, contributing over the years numerous chapters to the yearbook.[29] He also maintained close relations with the Walter Eucken Institute that was founded in 1954, with the support of Ludwig Erhard, by friends and students of Walter Eucken, serving, upon invitation of Eucken's widow, from the beginning on its board of trustees.[30]

Although discussing it in more detail would go beyond the scope of this paper, in concluding this section it is worth noting that his affinities to ordoliberal thought have made Hayek the target of harsh criticism from libertarian authors, such as Walter Block (1996: 339), who censures that, measured against the teaching of true advocates of 'free enterprise' and the 'ideal of laissez-faire capitalism',[31] Hayek must be categorized as 'lukewarm, at best, in his support of this system', and that by 'making all sorts of compromises' (ibid.: 340) he has been 'actively supporting its very opposite' (ibid.: 357). It is telling that Hayek (1967 [1949]: 191) found it necessary in 1949 to defend Henry Simons against similar criticisms, noting:

> The most glaring recent example of such condemnation of a somewhat unorthodox liberal work as 'socialist' has been provided by some comments on the late Henry Simons' *Economic Policy for a Free Society* (1948). One need not agree with the whole of this work and one may even regard some of the suggestions made in it as incompatible with a free society, and yet recognize it as one of the most important contributions made in recent times to our problem and as just the kind of work which is required to get discussion started on the fundamental issues. Even those who violently disagree with some of its suggestions should welcome it as a contribution which clearly and courageously raises the central problems of our time.

And it is hardly surprising that advocates of libertarianism always have been and continue to be suspicious of the ordo-version of classical liberalism. As Röpke (1961:10f) reports, at the 1949 meeting of the Mont Pelerin Society in Seelisberg, Switzerland, a somewhat heated dispute erupted between Ludwig von Mises and Walter Eucken, who challenged Mises's claim 'to represent the only authoritative liberalism'. On Röpke's report, which does not provide any more details, I have commented elsewhere (Vanberg, 2001: 18f):

> It is apparent...from his report that Röpke considered the exchange between Eucken and von Mises to be symbolic of a conflict of opinion that, as he notes, repeatedly surfaced within the Mont Pèlerin Society, and it seems obvious to me that it must have been linked to the fact that the two persons, Eucken and von Mises, represented, with their works, distinctly different perspectives on the nature of the liberal market order, perspectives that revolve around different organizing concepts. In the case of von Mises, this is the notion of

the unhampered market; in the case of Eucken, it is the notion of the market as a constitutional order.

Hayek in Freiburg 1962–1969

About his move from Chicago – where he had been a member of the *Committee on Social Thought* since 1950 – to Freiburg Hayek (1994: 131) has noted:

> Much as I enjoyed the intellectual environment that the University of Chicago offered, I never came to feel as much at home in the United States as I had done in England. I also was much concerned about the inadequate provisions for my and my wife's old age which that position offered me: a lump sum at a comparatively early retirement age (65). When I received in the winter of 1961–1962 an unexpected offer of a professorship at the University of Freiburg im Breisgau, which not only was to run three years longer but also secured at least for me a moderate pension for life, I could have no hesitation in accepting the offer and have never regretted the move. The eight years we spent there where in many ways very satisfactory. I had, once again, to become an economist, but was able to concentrate in my teaching on the problems of economic policy, on which I felt I still had something of importance to say.[32] We were very fortunate in finding an attractive apartment and particularly enjoyed the beautiful environment of the Black Forest.

Even if the reasons that motivated him to accept the Freiburg offer were, as Hayek indicates, not least quite earthly ones, considering what I have described in the previous two sections there must have been weighty professional reasons as well that made an appointment as professor of economics at the university at which Walter Eucken had taught and from which the ordoliberal Freiburg School originated an attractive option for Hayek. These reasons Hayek has clearly stated in his inaugural lecture in Freiburg from which the quotation at the beginning of this paper is taken and in which he also noted:

> I do not know to what good star I owe it that for the third time in the course of one life that faculty has honoured me with the offer of a chair which I would have chosen if an absolutely free choice in such things were possible. Not only is the move to this place in the heart of Europe, exactly half-way between Vienna and London,

the two places which have shaped me intellectually, and in addition in *Vorder-Österreich*,[33] ... for me something like coming home. ... I also value particularly the opportunity to teach again in a faculty of law,[34] in the atmosphere to which I owe my own schooling. After one has endeavoured for thirty years to teach economics to students possessing no knowledge of law and the history of legal institutions, one is sometimes tempted to ask whether the separation of legal and economic studies was not perhaps, after all, a mistake (Hayek, 1967 [1963]: 251f).

As natural as the alliance between Hayek and Eucken's former faculty may appear in retrospect,[35] for Hayek to be offered, at the age of 62, the Freiburg chair[36] was quite an extraordinary event made possible only by the concurrence of special circumstances. A necessary but by no means sufficient condition was that the acting Dean of the Freiburg faculty, Hans Besters, was very much in favour of gaining Hayek as a colleague.[37] The most important problem that had to be overcome, though, was Hayek's age. Born in 1899, he was far beyond the age limit up to which someone could normally be appointed as professor within the German academic system, in which universities are under the authority of the respective state within the federal union and in which professorial appointments are made by the state's government, based on proposals submitted by the universities. For the University of Freiburg to propose a candidate of Hayek's age to the government of Baden-Württemberg would have been a hopeless undertaking if it had not been for the fact that the then minister of the interior, and later prime minister of that state, Hans Filbinger, happened to take a particular interest in the case. Filbinger, a graduate of the Freiburg Rechts- und Staatswissenschaftliche Fakultät, who had done his doctoral thesis in law with Hans Großmann-Doerth[38] and had been a student of Walter Eucken, considered the advancement of the Freiburg School tradition of great importance for the intellectual-political development in Germany, and expected Hayek's presence in Freiburg to have in this regard a significant and beneficial impact. Filbinger, who had actually met with Hayek in Chicago in 1961 to explore the possibility of attracting him to Freiburg,[39] exerted his utmost influence with the ministers of cultural affairs and of finance, who both had to agree, to have a special arrangement worked out that circumnavigated the standard provisions and made Hayek's appointment possible.[40] After an extensive correspondence between Hayek (who in the meantime had also received an offer from the University of Vienna),[41] the Freiburg faculty and the ministries in Stuttgart about the terms of the appointment,[42] Hayek finally declared in his letter of 23 April 1962, to Professor Hans Besters, Dean of the Freiburg faculty, that he was going to sign the contract offered him and was preparing to arrive in Freiburg around 15 June.[43]

Leaving New York on 1 June on the Italian ocean liner MS Vulcania, Hayek arrived in Naples on 13 June,[44]travelling on to Freiburg where he held his inaugural lecture 'The Economy, Science and Politics' (Hayek, 1967 [1963]) on 18 June. The way in which, as mentioned before, he emphasized in this lecture his affinity to the Freiburg tradition and his intention 'to resume and continue the tradition which Eucken and his friends have created at Freiburg and in Germany' was a welcome assurance for those among the German ordoliberals who had looked with some suspicion at Hayek's 'Austrian' version of liberalism.[45] In due course, in February of 1963, Hayek was elected to the board of the Walter Eucken Institute as its third member alongside Friedrich A. Lutz, professor at the University of Zurich, and Fritz W. Meyer, professor at the University of Bonn.

By the time Hayek presented his inaugural lecture, the first half of the summer semester had already passed and only the second half remained for him to teach his first two classes in Freiburg, a lecture course on 'Current Issues in Economic Policy' and a pro-seminar on 'Economic Policy'. In the following years, throughout his Freiburg tenure, Hayek continued to offer regular courses on economic policy and he taught, in addition, on such subjects as the history of economic thought, methodological foundations of the social sciences and (jointly with Erich Streißler, his 'Austrian' colleague in Freiburg) on capital and business cycles. Particularly noteworthy is a seminar he held in the summer of 1967 on 'Organisierbare und nicht-organisierbare Interessen' which he used to prepare with his students a German translation of Mancur Olson's *The Logic of Collective Action*.[46] The end-period of his teaching was overshadowed by the student unrests of the time and by the university reforms that they set in motion. In a letter to then Prime Minister Hans Filbinger of 16 February 1968, Hayek stated:

> After having hesitated for a long time I have come to the conclusion that I cannot evade the responsibility to express to you in person my deepest concerns about the University law currently under consideration. My concerns about the consequences that must be expected are so grave that, if I were not already emeritus, I would immediately seek to return to an English or American university. The concessions to the students that the draft law makes must lead

to a politicization of the universities that must cause their rapid ruin.[47]

In retrospect, Hayek (1994: 131) said about the seven years he spent in Freiburg until 1969:

I also was fortunate to preserve almost to the end of the period at Freiburg my full energy and health and working capacity. And though after my seventieth birthday my powers began noticeably to decline...they were on the whole very fruitful years.[48]

Having just recently published *The Constitution of Liberty* (1960), the most important and crowning fruit of his Chicago years, Hayek embarked, as he reports (ibid.), soon after settling down at Freiburg on his next major project that he intended as 'a kind of supplement' to his previous work, namely what was to become the trilogy *Law, Legislation and Liberty*. Even though the three volumes were published only with considerable delay in 1973, 1976 and 1979, Hayek had completed, according to his own account, the bulk of the manuscript when he left Freiburg in 1969.[49] On the occasion of his 70th birthday, 8 May 1969, the *Walter Eucken Institute* published a volume *Freiburger Studien* (Hayek, 1969) that collected the papers that Hayek had authored between June of 1962 and July of 1968, the period he taught at Freiburg University.[50] Many of the chapters in this volume are closely related to the themes that Hayek was to cover in his *Law, Legislation and Liberty* project.

The Salzburg Interlude 1970–1977 and return to Freiburg

In a letter of 19 December 1969, Hayek notified the Dean of the Freiburg faculty of his decision to accept as of the following semester a visiting professorship offered to him by the University of Salzburg, adding: 'I hope you and the colleagues in the faculty will forgive me for leaving you so soon after my retirement. Until a few months ago I had no other plans than to spend my old age in Freiburg in continued personal contact to the faculty'.[51] Not unlike his relocation from Chicago to Freiburg in 1962, Hayek's decision to move in 1970 from Freiburg to Salzburg was motivated not least by financial considerations. As he explained in retrospect,[52] it was because of concerns for his wife's financial security that he felt compelled to accept an unexpected offer from the University of Salzburg to be appointed as guest professor at a full salary until the age of 75, including the offer to purchase his academic library[53] with the provision that it would be kept together and readily accessible for his continued use.[54]

Counter to the hopes that Hayek might have harboured in returning to his native Austria, the years he spent in Salzburg were to become, for several reasons, a rather disappointing experience, even though it was during this time, in 1974, that he was awarded the most visible recognition of his academic achievements, the Nobel Prize in Economic Sciences. Most importantly, from 1969 to 1974 he suffered from health problems – a misdiagnosed heart disturbance and depression (Hayek, 1994: 130; Ebenstein, 2001: 251ff) – that severely limited his working capacity.[55] Finding himself unable to complete the manuscript for *Law, Legislation and Liberty* that he had nearly finished when he left Freiburg, he decided to divide what was originally intended to form a single volume into three parts and to publish the first volume separately in 1973,[56] hoping to be able to complete the remaining parts 'in the near future'.[57] It was, though, only in 1976 that the second volume,[58] and in 1979 the third, were finally published.

A specific local cause for Hayek's disappointment was – as Kurt Leube (1984: xxvii), his research assistant at Salzburg University,[59] reports – 'the fact that at this university economics was taught as a subsidiary to law, and therefore the faculty's and the student's level did not meet his academic expectations'. In an interview in 1975, Hayek responded to a question about whether his work was met with interest at Salzburg: 'It wasn't when I arrived. And even now there is not a great deal of interest outside of the few who have come to my classes'.[60] In the preface to the second volume of *Law, Legislation and Liberty* he complained about having 'no longer that easy access to adequate library facilities which I had when I prepared the first draft of this volume' (Hayek, 1976: xii). Obviously, as Ebenstein (2001: 254) puts it, Hayek was in Salzburg quite generally 'intellectually isolated'. A further factor that contributed to Hayek's dissatisfaction with the Salzburg environment had to do with the political climate that prevailed quite generally in Austria during the era of the socialist chancellor Kreisky and the way that it affected university life in particular.

Hayek's growing dissatisfaction with his life in Salzburg did not go unnoticed in Freiburg. Realizing that there might be a prospect for attracting Hayek back to Freiburg and to the Walter Eucken Institute, Dr. Reinhold Veit and Dr. Alfred Bosch, the institute's research associates, and Professor Erich Hoppmann, Hayek's successor on the Freiburg chair and on the Institute's board, turned for support in this matter to Hans Filbinger.[61] And Filbinger did, indeed, again take an interest in getting Hayek to return to Freiburg, exerting his influence to make it happen. Among the obstacles that had to be overcome was Hayek's desire to return to the same apartment that he and his wife had lived in during their prior residence in Freiburg.

In a letter of 16 June 1975, Filbinger wrote to Hayek:

> The other day I had a talk with Drs. Veit and Bosch of the Walter Eucken Institute, the survival of which is at risk for financial reasons. I want to get the state of Baden-Württemberg to provide the institute with the support needed for it to continue to operate. Especially in our times it seems to me an absolute necessity, to make the broader public aware again of the works of the so-called Freiburg School. I am very concerned, that the trend towards a 'democratic socialism' will become more and more predominant if the ideas of a liberal economic order are not revived. ... In this context it would be of enormous help if you, venerated Professor, were willing to get involved, the ways in which this may happen remaining to be discussed. ... I was told by Drs. Veit and Bosch that you are considering a return to Freiburg. I would exceedingly welcome if this would be realized. If I can be in any way of help, I would of course be most happy to do so. I recall on this occasion my visit with you in 1961 in the Quadrangle Club in Chicago where the idea of your coming to Germany was explored.[62]

Responding to Filbinger's letter, Hayek wrote in reference to the 'possibility of returning to Freiburg':

> I want to confess first that in a sense I always had a bad conscience since I left Freiburg in 1970 after I had been treated so generously by the Ministry. But I had no choice, because I had not the provisions for my wife that the sale of my library to the university here and a five years appointment as guest professor offered. But now that this appointment has come to an end, the news that our former apartment in Freiburg will *probably* be available again is such a great temptation that we would hardly be able to resist if it were to come true.[63]

The efforts made in Freiburg for his return and the bureaucratic annoyances he faced in Salzburg, culminating in a quarrel with the socialist minister of science and research, Hertha Frinberg, about funding for an assistant (Hennecke, 2000: 308f), confirmed Hayek's growing resolution to revise what he in retrospect saw as a wrong decision and to leave Austria, a decision that attracted considerable public attention.[64] In a letter to the editor of the newspaper *Die Presse* he stated:

> People frequently ask why I am leaving Austria. I must confess that I began to have doubts after only a few months. My doubts were reinforced by a circular reminding me of an old ministerial decree, 'University professors must notify the Federal Minister of any foreign travel they undertake'. Over and above this, however, I must mention that the University of Salzburg is not authorized to bestow doctorates.[65] Thus, there are no serious students of economics here. I made a mistake in moving to Salzburg.[66]

Freiburg 1977–1992

It took considerable efforts on part of his supporters in Freiburg to meet Hayek's expectations concerning housing and working conditions at the university, but finally, in early 1977, their previous apartment at Urachstrasse 27 was ready for Hayek and his wife to move in, and Erich Hoppmann, then Dean of the Faculty of Economics, could write to the university administration on 30 March 1977:

> Herewith I can inform you that Professor Dr. F. A. von Hayek has resumed again his affiliation with our faculty on 1 March 1977. He will carry out his research activities and projects within the Institute for General Economic Research and present his research results in publications as well as in seminars.[67]

If there is one aspect of Hayek's second Freiburg tenure that stands out most visibly, it is unquestionably his increasing preoccupation with a project whose laboriously produced outcome was to be his last book, *The Fatal Conceit*. A first indication of Hayek's engagement with this project was a lecture titled 'Drei Quellen der menschlichen Werte' that he held in January 1978 at the Walter Eucken Institute, a kind of trial run for the Hobhouse Lecture on 'The Three Sources of Human Values' which he held a few months later, on 17 May, at the London School of Economics, a lecture which he included as 'Epilogue' in the third volume of *Law, Legislation and Liberty* (Hayek, 1979: 153–176). In the preface to this volume, Hayek (ibid.: xi) commented on his decision to add the epilogue:

Of the last third of the original draft only what was intended to be the last chapter...had not been completed at the time when I discontinued work. But while I believe I have now more or less carried out the original intention, over the long period which has elapsed my ideas have developed further and I was reluctant to send out what inevitably must be my last systematic work without at least indicating in what direction my ideas have been moving. This has had the effect...that I found it necessary to add an Epilogue which expresses more directly the general view of moral and political evolution which has guided me in the whole enterprise.

And the epilogue itself Hayek ended on the somewhat pessimistic note:

In concluding this epilogue I am becoming increasingly aware that it ought not to be that but rather a new beginning. But I hardly dare hope that for me it can be so (ibid.: 176).

Yet, he did in fact embark on this new project,[68] and in his lecture on 'The Flow of Goods and Services' that he held in January of 1981 at the LSE on the occasion of the 50th anniversary of his *Prices and Production* lectures, he remarked:

What I am going to read to you today is essentially a chapter of a book on a much wider subject which I am preparing. For the argument of that book the contention is of critical importance that the coordination of economic activities, to which we owe our ability to maintain the present population of the world, is due to our relying for guidance on prices formed on competitive markets which generate the indispensable signals which tell us what to do. This chapter will be preceded in the book by a more general statement of the process of extension of the economic order into the unknown (Hayek, 2012 [1981]: 3).[69]

One year later, in the preface to the 1982 single-volume edition of *Law, Legislation and Liberty*, Hayek sounded even more confident when in reference to his earlier pessimistic conclusion of the epilogue he stated: 'I am glad to be able to say now that it has turned out to be such and that that Epilogue has become the outline of a new book of which I have now completed a first draft'. (Hayek, 1982: xxi)[70] Yet a long and painful process still had to be endured before the book was actually published in 1988.

The 'first draft' to which Hayek referred became the subject of a Liberty Fund conference, organized by Svetozar Pejovich, that convened at Obergurgl, a small village in the Tyrolean Alps, where Hayek and his wife used to spend their summer vacations. The declared purpose of the conference was to provide Hayek with an opportunity to get feedback for his book project from the other 15 invited participants, including such eminent colleagues of his as Peter Bauer, Karl Brunner, James Buchanan, Ronald Coase and George Stigler.[71] Nobody present at the conference could fail to sense how deeply concerned Hayek was about completing a book that in his mind was to communicate a message that he had not yet stated quite as explicitly in his previous work. Yet, as Buchanan (1992: 133) recalls, there was a generally shared scepticism about the prospects for the existing draft chapters to be developed into a book that would live up to the quality standards one had come to associate with the author's name.

The significance Hayek attributed to his work on *The Fatal Conceit* can be concluded from a short description that he wrote down in May 1985:

> This is to be the final outcome of what I planned about 1938 as *The Abuse and Decline of Reason* and of the conclusions which I published in 1944, the sketch on *The Road to Serfdom*. It is a work for which one has to be an economist but this is not enough.[72]

The Fatal Conceit was to be his definitive refutation of the *pretence of knowledge*, paradigmatically exemplified by socialism that he viewed as a fundamental threat to our evolved civilization, and about which he had said at the end of the *Epilogue*:

> If the Enlightenment has discovered that the role assigned to human reason in intelligent construction had been too small in the past, we are discovering that the task which our age is assigning to the rational construction of new institutions is far too big. ...*Man is not and never will be the master of his fate: his very reason always progresses by leading him into the unknown and unforeseen where he learns new things* (Hayek, 1979: 176).

It was, one must assume, not least in response to the reception his first draft found at the Obergurgl conference that Hayek worked on a thoroughly revised and expanded manuscript over the next few years, hoping to bring the first of the planned three volumes of *The*

Fatal Conceit to completion in 1985. Yet, as his secretary C. E. Cubitt (2006: 73f, 83ff, 134f) reports in her biographical account of Hayek's Freiburg years 1977–1992, his diminishing work capacity frustrated his hopes, and in the summer of 1985 his declining state of health made him realize that he would not be able to complete the project on his own account; after some hesitation, he accepted the offer of William Bartley, his designated biographer and general editor of the *Collected Works of F. A. Hayek*, to assist in getting the existing manu-script ready for publication (ibid.: 157ff).[73] Bartley's assistance was originally meant to be limited to moving to completion the first of the three planned volumes (one chapter of which existed only in frag-ments), and in a letter to Drs. Veit and Bosch at the Walter Eucken Institute of 25 July 1986, he in fact stated '*The Fatal Conceit* is in effect complete'.[74] However, his involvement in the project grew consider-ably and he extensively reworked Hayek's draft version, condensing it finally to a single monograph that was published as volume 1 of the *Collected Works* in 1988. The issue of the extent to which the published version of *The Fatal Conceit* can, in spite of Bartley's editing, be counted among Hayek's authentic works has been repeat-edly commented upon (Ebenstein, 2003: 214f, 219ff; Caldwell, 2004: 316ff; Vanberg, 1994a: 461, fn. 52; Vanberg, 2011a). And indeed, as Cubitt (2006: 238, 244f) reports, Hayek, due to his feeble health, was not able to carefully scrutinize Bartley's revisions, and because of the extensive changes that had been made hesitated for some time before giving his permission for publication (ibid.: 247f, 269). Nevertheless, even if in matters of style and form *The Fatal Conceit* clearly shows Bartley's hand, the substance of the argument it develops is without doubt authentically Hayekian.

After the summer of 1985, Hayek's health condition deteriorated significantly. In greetings he sent in September of 1987 to a meeting of the Mont Pelerin Society he wrote:

After forty years of the existence of the Mont Pèlerin Society it is bitter to resign oneself to the fact that it will have to continue without me. But though I am no longer actually ill, two years sickness have made me an old man. This summer vacation in the Tyrolean mountains is the first time that I have again been able to leave home, and at 88 years of age I can hardly hope that I shall again be able to travel for longer distances. So I must confine myself to send all the partici-pants of the meeting my best wishes for its success and for an effec-tive continuation of the efforts of the Society.[75]

Hayek died on 23 March 1992, in Freiburg. He is buried in Neustift am Walde, Vienna.

Conclusion

The Freiburg connection is not only an important part of Hayek's biography, it is also of paradigmatic significance because of the characteristic mixture of commonalities and differences between the ordoliberal research program of the Freiburg School and the theoretical core of Hayek's own approach (Vanberg, 2003). As I have noted above, in his 1962 inaugural lecture in Freiburg Hayek explicitly stated that he intended to regard it as one of his 'chief tasks to resume and continue the tradition which Eucken and his friends have created at Freiburg and in Germany', but I also pointed out that questions were raised about the extent to which the main thrust of his work was actually compatible with, let alone supportive of, the ordoliberal program. While I sought to show that Hayek did agree with ordoliberals on the need for 'deliberately creating a system within which competition will work as beneficially as possible' (1976 [1944]: 17), I have also noted that this theme is most prominent in his writings between the late 1930s and 1950, but gains much less attention elsewhere. Indeed, even if it is not entirely absent in his later work,[76] Hayek's focus increasingly shifts – most notably so during his second Freiburg period and culminating in *The Fatal Conceit* – towards an evolutionary perspective that puts its emphasis on the role of evolutionary forces in the selection of 'appropriate' rules and a warning against the 'constructivist rationalism' of deliberate institutional design.

Not a few commentators have noted that the evolutionary thrust in Hayek's later work appears to be in conflict with his earlier arguments for a liberal policy of institutional framing and, a fortiori, with the ordoliberalism of the Freiburg School with its emphasis on the need for a liberal order to be cultivated by deliberate *Ordnungspolitik*. There is surely a puzzling tension between those parts of Hayek's work that, in line with the Freiburg *Ordnungspolitik* concept, emphasize liberalism's 'positive task of improving our institutions' (1960: 5), guided by a 'general conception of the social order desired' (ibid.: 114), and some of his later arguments. This applies in particular to statements in *The Fatal Conceit* that seem to border on what I have described elsewhere as 'evolutionary agnosticism' (Vanberg, 1994a) – such as, for example, his assertion that there 'is in fact no reason to expect that the selection by evolution of habitual practices should produce happiness' (1988: 64), and that the evolutionary process to which we owe our civilization 'cannot be guided by and often will not produce what men demand' (ibid.: 74).

Whether – and, if so, how – the apparent tension between the ordoliberal perspective and Hayek's evolutionary approach can be reconciled is an issue that deserves a more careful discussion than is possible in this concluding section. Here a brief summary must suffice of what I have argued on this issue in other contexts (Vanberg, 1994a; 1994b; 2011b). As I have sought to show there, the ordoliberals' emphasis on the role of *Ordnungspolitik* and Hayek's emphasis on evolutionary exploration can – and should – be understood as perspectives that supplement rather than contradict each other. Hayek's focus is on the notion that only by allowing for evolutionary exploration and competition as discovery procedures can we find out what the 'best' solutions to our problems are, in the production of ordinary goods and services no less than in institutional matters. Reversely, the ordoliberal focus is on the notion that evolutionary exploration and competitive discovery cannot be expected to work *per se*, in whatever form and shape they are carried out, to the benefit of the persons involved, but only if they are framed or conditioned by suitable rules of the game. While agreeing with the ordoliberal tenet that an appropriate institutional framework is required in order 'to make the market mechanism operate satisfactorily' (1978: 146), Hayek insists that only by allowing for competition among alternative rules can we find out what 'appropriate' or well-working rules of the game are. Yet, he takes less care than in his comments on market competition to add the qualification that competition at the institutional level must also be framed by 'appropriate' rules if it is to operate to the mutual advantage of the persons involved.[77] Reversely, while entirely agreeing with Hayek's general arguments on competition as a discovery procedure and focusing on the role of *Ordnungspolitik* in framing market competition, the ordoliberals have been less concerned with the issue of how we come to know what an 'appropriate' legal framework is.

Combined with each other, Hayek's evolutionary liberalism and the ordoliberalism of the Freiburg School constitute a coherent liberal view of 'the kind of world in which people want to live' (1960: 114).

Notes

1. The three initial founders were economist Walter Eucken (1891–1950), jurist Franz Böhm (1895–1977), and jurist Hans Großmann-Doerth (1894–1944).
2. For more details see H. Janssen (2009: 42ff).

3. In his *Geldtheorie und Konjunkturtheorie* which includes the two lectures he presented at the Zurich meeting Hayek refers in a footnote (1976 [1929]: 36) to the 'pertinent arguments by W. Eucken in his interesting presentation at the Zurich meeting' (my translation, V.V.).

4. Walter Eucken (1941).

5. Hayek (1992 [1983]: 190): 'Walter Eucken was a valuable friend for me. In the late 1930s, before the outbreak of the war, when I first acquired a car and made the trip from London to Austria by automobile, I regularly made a stopover in Freiburg just to visit Eucken and to keep in touch with him.' Also (ibid.: 188): 'I generally avoided visiting Germany and crossed only the southwest corner of Germany on my frequent trips between London and Vienna, where I regularly paid visits to Walter Eucken.'

6. Introducing a lecture that Hayed presented in 1979 in Freiburg on occasion of the 25th anniversary of the Walter Eucken Institute, Hayek (2004 [1979]: 52) recalled: 'It is now about forty years since a socialism that prefixed itself with the decorative word 'national' brought free movement in Europe to an end and thereby terminated the first series of lectures I presented in the Eucken circle' (my translation, V.V.).

7. W. von Klinckowstroem (2000: 102).

8. The letter is dated 17 August 1941. Quoted from Henneke (2000: 152fn.). – Upon Hayek's initiative Terence W. Hutchison translated in the late 1940s Eucken's book – the English edition was published in 1950 (Eucken, 1950) – as well as a paper that Hayek had invited Eucken to prepare for *Economica* and that was published in 1948 (Eucken, 1948). – In a letter to Eucken, dated 19 February 1948, Hayek notes: 'I shall try to persuade Mr. Hutchison who I hope will translate your book to undertake also the translation of the chapter, and I shall of course go through it carefully before it is published. ... Mr. T. W. Hutchison ... the author of a book on the method of economics which you may know, was at one time a Lektor at one of the German universities, I believe Bonn, and is now lecturer in economics on our staff' (Hoover Institution, Hayek Archives [from now on abbreviated as HIHA], 18–40; the permission by the Estate of F. A. Hayek to quote from the unpublished correspondence is gratefully acknowledged).

9. HIHA 18–40 (my translation, V.V.).

10. HIHA 18–40, my translation, V.V. – In a letter of 24 January 1946, Eucken – as he had done before and did repeatedly in later letters – urged Hayek to come to Freiburg so that they might discuss in person issues of common interest, including 'the problem of an international organization of liberals' (HIHA, 18–40, my translation, V.V.).

11. Hayek (1994: 132f): 'I found that I derived so much instruction by the discussion with similarly minded men in other places – such as Henry Simons and his Chicago group, Wilhelm Röpke at Geneva, and a German group led by Walter Eucken – that the wish grew in me to bring these men together as an international group for a discussion of the problems which their efforts to revive the liberal tradition raised.'

12. Hayek refers here to the second meeting of the Mont Pelerin Society which took place in 1949 in Seelisberg, Switzerland. At this meeting the differences between Eucken's ordoliberalism and Mises' free-market liberalism apparently led to a heated dispute between the two (Vanberg, 1999: 200).

13. In another context Hayek (1992 [1983]: 191) notes on the 1947 meeting: 'I had proposed two Germans as participants. One of them was Walter Eucken. The second one I had in mind was the historian Franz Schnabel. ... Unfortunately I was unable to get Franz Schnabel to come to Switzerland, but Eucken came. ... Eucken was greatly acclaimed at this conference. And I believe that Eucken's success in 1947 – as the only German attending a scholarly international conference – contributed a little, if I may use this term, to the rehabilitation of German scholars on the international scene.'

14. In a letter, dated 8 March 1950, that he sent from Chicago to Eucken at his temporary London address, Hayek states: 'You will probably have heard in London that I have decided to stay here permanently. The reasons for this are problems of a personal nature that date far back and that I hope thereby to bring to an even if painful solution' (HIHA, 18–40; my translation, V.V.). In an earlier letter, dated 18 January 1949, Hayek had already mentioned to Eucken that his life had lately been 'seriously disarranged due to several personal circumstances' (HIHA, 18–40; my translation, V.V.).

15. In a letter to Hayek, dated 2 March 1950, Eucken notes: 'Tomorrow my wife and I will travel to London for the lectures' (HIHA, 18–40; my translation, V.V.).

16. Alan Peacock (2000: 541) recalls: 'Walter Eucken, to our great sorrow, died just before the last of his lecture series at the LSE in 1950 published posthumously as *Unser Zeitalter der Misserfolge* (*This Unsuccessful Age*). It was decided not to cancel his final lecture but, as a tribute to interest in the series and to the man himself, to have it read to the audience. As a young lecturer at LSE, who had studied some of the great man's work in the original, I was given this awesome privilege.'

17. For references see Janssen (2009: 42f).

18. In a letter to Röpke, dated 13 July 1943, Rüstow refers to Ludwig von Mises as 'an old liberal ultra ... who belongs behind glass in a museum,' and he adds, 'Hayek too ... has never been quite transparent to me' (quoted from Nicholls, 1994: 102). See also Rüstow's letter to Röpke of February 21, 1942 (quoted in Janssen, 2009: 43, fn. 59). – Rüstow continued to harbour his resentments, describing in a letter to Wilhelm Krelle of 10 November 1959, Mises and Hayek as 'Palaeoliberals' (Henneke, 2000: 273) and voicing his distaste for Hayek's appointment to the chair at Freiburg University in a letter to Eucken's widow (see Edith Eucken-Erdsiek's letter of 15 June 1962, to Rüstow; Bundesarchiv N 1169/125; references to the Rüstow correspondence used in this paper I owe to Stefan Kolev).

19. Both Röpke and Rüstow shared a conservative-romantic vision of desirable forms of social life (characterized by family farms, small to medium size cities, etc.) and favored interventions that serve to maintain them. – On the differences between Eucken's ordoliberalism and the 'sociological neoliberalism' of Röpke and Rüstow see A. Renner (2002: 217 ff).

20. In a letter that Eucken wrote to a senior official of the post-war economic administration (Verwaltung der Wirtschaft) in the American and British zone (Eucken to Meinhold, 15 Februaury 1950, quoted from Nicholls, 1994: 185).

21. Eucken had read the German translation prepared by Wilhelm Röpke's wife Eva (Hayek, 1945). On this German edition Hayek (1992 [1983]: 190) reports: 'My *Road to Serfdom* was translated into German by Mrs. Röpke shortly after

its publication. The German edition was published in Switzerland, but, as I did not realize immediately, for three years the import of the book into Germany was prohibited, so that it was obtainable only in typescript. An agreement was in effect which obliged the occupying powers to exclude books that took a hostile stand against any one of them. Although this book, which was written at the time that the Russians were our allies, was directed less against communism than against fascism, the Russians instinctively felt that the book was directed against them. They therefore insisted that the occupation authorities ban the import of the book into Germany.'

22. HIHA, 18–40 (my translation, V.V.). –In his posthumously published *Grundsätze der Wirtschaftspolitik* Eucken (1952: 255) refers to Henry Simons' *Economic Policy for a Free Society* (1948) as a work that is in the same spirit as his own work and that of his ordoliberal colleagues. On the affinities between the ordoliberal research programme and Henry Simons' work, see E. Köhler and S. Kolev (2011). See also M. Wegmann (2002: 182ff).

23. The European Forum is an annual event that takes place since 1945 in the Tyrolean village Alpbach. In a letter to Eucken, dated 15 October 1947, Hayek notes: 'I found that summer school in Alpbach in the Tyrol particularly pleasant and attractive, and intend to go again next year. I hope they will act on my suggestion to invite you, and if so I wish you would very seriously consider accepting' (HIHA, 18–40).

24. Hayek (2004 [1948]: 170), my translation, V.V.

25. The yearbook's full title is *ORDO – Jahrbuch für die Ordnung von Wirtschaft und Gesellschaft*.

26. Eucken's letters to Hayek of 11 January and 5 February 1947, HIHA, 18–40.

27. The essay was originally delivered in 1945 as the Twelfth Finlay Lecture, University College, Dublin, and published as *Individualism: True and False*, Dublin and Oxford 1946.

28. 'Wahrer und falscher Individualismus,' *ORDO – Jahrbuch für die Ordnung von Wirtschaft und Gesellschaft*, Vol. 1, 1948, 19–55.

29. Hayek (1967 [1951]: 200): 'The annual *ORDO* which he (Walter Eucken, V.V.) founded continues to be the most important publication of the entire movement.' – See also Hayek (1992 [1983]: 189f).

30. Hayek (2004 [1979]: 52). – Letter from Edith Eucken to Hayek, dated 14 December 1954: 'We would be most pleased if you would be willing to join the board of trustees of our institute, which is to include, among others, a fair number of members of the Mont Pèlerin Society such as Böhm, Einaudi, Lutz, Röpke, Rüstow, Erhard and others' (HIHA, 18–41 ; my translation, V.V.).

31. Block (1996: 339) refers to M.N. Rothbard and H.-H. Hoppe.

32. In reference to Walter Eucken's research program Hayek (1967 [1963]: 263) remarked in his inaugural lecture: 'The chief task of economic policy would thus appear to be the creation of a framework within which the individual not only can freely decide for himself what he wants to do, but in which also this decision based on his particular knowledge will contribute as much as possible to the aggregate output.'

33. To the English version of his inaugural lecture Hayek (1967 [1963]: 251) had added the footnote: 'The Breisgau in which Freiburg is situated and some

connected territories used to be called *Vorder-Österreich* during the centuries when they were part of the domain of the Habsburgs.'

34. As was common in German universities at the time, and as had been the tradition in Austrian universities as well, law and economics were both taught in one faculty, the so-called Rechst- und Staatswissenschaftliche Fakultät.

35. A. Shenfield (1977: 173): 'From 1962 to 1969 he held a Chair at Freiburg i.B., the academic home of the late Professor Eucken and his neo-liberal followers, than which no other place in Germany could have been more congenial to him.'

36. Contrary to what is often asserted (e.g., by Leube [1984: xxiv] and by Hennecke [2000: 283]), Hayek was not offered Walter Eucken's former chair but the chair that had been held by Adolf Lampe who, though not counted among the founders of the Freiburg School, was a close associate of Eucken and, like Eucken, a member of the so-called 'Freiburger Kreise,' three different but overlapping groups of academics, in particular Freiburg economists, who opposed the Nazi regime and, expecting Germany's defeat, secretly worked out plans for a post-war economic and socio-political order. See N. Goldschmidt, ed. (2005).

37. In her letter to Alexander Rüstow of 15 June 1962, Eucken's widow, Edith Eucken, remarks: 'You ask how Hayek came to Freiburg....Certainly the acting dean, Prof. Besters, a determined liberal and very active man, has been a driving force' (Bundesarchiv NL Rüstow/ N 1169/125; my translation, V.V.).

38. See fn. 1 above.

39. In a letter to Hayek, dated June 1975, Filbinger refers to this visit, noting: 'I recall on this occasion my visit with you in 1961 in the Quadrangle Club in Chicago where the idea of your coming to Germany was explored' (HIHA, 19–13; my translation, V.V.).

40. In a letter to Professor Hans Besters, Dean of the Freiburg faculty, of 23 October 1961, Minister Filbinger states: 'The minister of cultural affairs has informed me that his administration is willing to overcome the obstacles and agree to the appointment of Prof. von Hayek, provided that the Ministry of Finance gives its agreement' (Hayek dossier, Economics, Freiburg University [HDEFU]; my translation, V.V.). In his letter of 19 February 1962, minister Filbinger informs dean Besters: 'I am glad to be able to inform you that my interventions with the minister of finance have been successful' (HDEFU; my translation, V.V.).

41. In a letter of 20 January 1962, to Dean Hans Besters, which he sent in copy to Minister Filbinger as well, Hayek states: 'To this is added that a few days ago I received an official inquiry from Vienna under what terms I would be willing to take there a regular (i.e. pensionable) professorship' (HDEFU; my translation, V.V.). – In an accompanying 'personal and confidential' letter to dean Besters, also dated 20 January 1962, Hayek notes: 'I would honestly regret if the possibility in Freiburg should definitely come to nothing. The position has been very attractive for me, even more, which may perhaps surprise you, than the (financially not at all bad) position in Vienna. I would in principle be prepared to accept some sacrifices in order to "buy" Freiburg' (HDEFU; my translation, V.V.).

42. The correspondence is documented in HDEFU.
43. HDEFU.
44. Hayek writes about his forthcoming voyage in a letter of 23 April 1962, to Edith Eucken (HIHA, 18–41).
45. Hayek's favourable comment on the Freiburg tradition seem to have softened, in particular, Alexander Rüstow's resentments (see fn. 18 above). In a letter to Eucken's widow of 23 April 1963, Rüstow notes: 'By far most essential and pleasant is, however, the fact that with his Freiburg inaugural lecture Hayek has unambiguously placed himself within the camp of neoliberalism, while before he equally unambiguously – including in extensive conversation with me – had argued the position of palaeo-liberalism' (Bundesarchiv NL Rüstow/N 1169/125; my translation, V.V.). – In her earlier letter of 22 March 1963, to Rüstow, Edith Eucken had observed: 'I am truly glad that you too were able to convince yourself in the meantime how big an effort Mr. von Hayek makes to carry on the old Freiburg tradition. We all hope for many good things to come out of this in the future' (Bundesarchiv/NL Rüstow/N1169/125; my translation, V.V.). – In a letter to Alfred Müller-Armack of 11 July 1962, Hayek cautioned expectations in the support he was going to lend to the liberal cause in German politics: 'As a newcomer and non-citizen I will be restrained in my comments on all disputes on party politics, but I hope to provide nevertheless by my influence on the young some support to you and Mr. Erhard' (quoted from Hennecke, 2000: 284; my translation, V.V.).
46. In his preface to the German edition of Olson's book (Olson, 1968: x) Hayek notes: 'The book appeared to me so important that I made it the subject of an unusual experiment of which the present translation is the result. It is the outcome of a joint effort in a seminar that I held at the University of Freiburg in the summer term of 1967. Its purpose was to discuss the substantive issues the book raises as well as a practice in English and German scientific language' (my translation, V.V.). As Hayek adds, the draft translations provided by the student participants needed, of course, editing to which Dr. Monika Streissler contributed who came to translate later a number of Hayek's English publications into German. – In the preface of the 1971 edition of *The Logic of Collective Action* (Olson, 1971 [1965]: viii) Olson refers to Hayek's translation project: 'I am also grateful that Professor F.A. von Hayek took the initiative of arranging for the translation of this book into German and in contributing a foreword to the German translation.'
47. HIHA, 19–13; my translation, V.V.
48. Hayek (1994: 131) also mentions that he and his wife 'travelled during these years more than ever before: four visits to Japan (with side trips to Taiwan and Indonesia), and finally, as a return trip from a five-month stay at the University of California at Los Angeles, a flight through the South Pacific (Tahiti, Fiji, New Caledonia, Sydney, and Ceylon).'
49. Hayek (1994: 132): 'Most of what I published during the Freiburg period are offshoots of that work, and when we left Freiburg after eight years, I had completed (except for a concluding chapter) an excessively long manuscript, which I still believe contains some important ideas but which, in its present form, seems to me unsuitable for publication.'

50. Eight of the seventeen chapters included were originally published in English; nine were originally published in German, four of them in the yearbook *ORDO*.

51. Letter, dated 19 December 1969, to Dean J. G. Wolf (HDEFU; my translation, V.V.).

52. In a letter to Prime Minister Filbinger (see fn. 62 below).

53. In his above (fn. 51) cited letter to Dean Wolf Hayek noted that the University of Salzburg had offered to buy his library at a price that allowed him to purchase a 'suitable home' in Salzburg.

54. Correspondence between the President of Freiburg University, B. Boesch, the Faculty and Hayek indicates that when the then Prime Minister of Baden-Württemberg, Hans Filbinger – who, as mentioned above, was in 1962 as Minister of the Interior instrumental in making Hayek's move to Freiburg possible – learned about Hayek's intention to sell his library he encouraged the University of Freiburg to explore the possibility of making a counter-offer. This initiative was, however, to no avail. (President Boesch's letter to Hayek, dated 28 July 1969; Hayek's letter to President Boesch, dated 4 August 1969; President Boesch's letter to the head office of the University Library, dated 12 August 1969; Hayek's letter to President Boesch, dated 19 December 1969; HDEFU).

55. In a letter to Fritz Machlup of 10 May 1972, Hayek complained: 'All attempts to resume the work at my book have failed' (quoted from Hennecke [2000: 304]; my translation, V.V.).

56. In retrospect, in the preface to Vol. 3, Hayek (1979: xi) explained: 'Again unforeseen circumstances have delayed somewhat longer than I had expected the publication of this last volume of a work...(which V.V.) was in fairly finished form as long ago as the end of 1969 when indifferent health forced me to suspend the efforts to complete it. It was then, indeed, doubt whether I would ever succeed in doing so which made me decide to publish separately as Volume 1 the first third of what had been intended to form a single volume, because it was in completely finished form.'

57. In the preface to Volume 1, Hayek (1973: xi) noted: 'Since drafts of these further volumes are in existence I hope to be able to bring them out in the near future. The reader who is curious to know where the argument leads will in the meantime find some indications in a number of preliminary studies published during the long years when this work was in preparation and collected...in my *Freiburger Studien* (Tübingen, 1969).'

58. In the preface to the second volume Hayek (1976: xi, xiii) comments: 'Several circumstances have contributed to delay the publication of the second volume of this work beyond the short time I thought I would need to get a completed draft ready for the printer....Although an almost complete draft of Volume 3 of this work is in existence, I hardly dare again to express the hope that it will appear fairly soon....But I shall do my best to bring the volume concluding this series out as soon as the advance of old age permits.'

59. In a letter (dated 13 August 1975; HIHA 127–22) to the Liberty Foundation and the Relm Foundation Hayek requested funding to employ Leube who, as he noted, 'is not formally my assistant but who, because he is in charge of my library which I sold to the University, has in fact been acting as such. For

some formal reason the authorities believe they cannot continue to employ him and are likely to terminate the contract' (I owe this reference to Robert Lesson).

60. *Reason*, February 1975: 12. Quoted from Ebenstein (2001: 254).
61. Hoppmann letter of 26 June 1975, to Prime Minister Filbinger, HIHA, 19–13.
62. HIHA, 19–13; my translation, V.V.
63. Undated copy of Hayek's letter, HIHA, 19–13; my translation, V.V.
64. Leube (1984: xxviii): 'Somewhat disappointed with Salzburg...Hayek decided to leave his native Austria for Freiburg in early 1977, reluctantly leaving behind his unique library of some 7000 volumes, which he had sold for financial reasons to the University of Salzburg when he assumed the visiting professorship.'
65. It should be noted that Hayek refers here specifically to doctorates in economics.
66. *Die Presse*, 22/23 January 1977; quoted from Ebenstein (2001: 254).
67. Letter, dated 30 March 1977, by E. Hoppmann to the rector's office, HDEFU (my translation, V.V.).
68. As C. C. Cubitt, Hayek's secretary during his second Freiburg tenure, reports, Hayek began actually in 1979 'writing the first draft of what was to become *The Fatal Conceit*'(Cubitt, 2006: 31).
69. I am quoting here from the typescript of the chapter. Prior to its inclusion in Hayek (2012) 'The Flow of Goods and Services' had been published only in a German translation (Hayek, 1983).
70. In a letter to Fritz Machlup of 29 May 1981, Hayek mentioned: 'My book is growing, even if it is not coming much closer to its completion, but it interests me ever more. The other one on the denationalization of money I must therefore postpone' (HIHA, 44–2; quoted from Hennecke, 2000: 367; my translation, V.V.).
71. I had the privilege to be – along with Gernot Gutmann, Erich Hoppmann, Alfred Schüller, Roland Vaubel and Hans Willgerodt – among the participants who had been invited from Germany.
72. Quoted from Caldwell (2004: 319). At the end of the last chapter, before the Epilogue, of the third volume of *Law, Legislation and Liberty* Hayek – after warning that we can 'avoid destroying our civilization' only by shedding 'the illusion that we can deliberately "create the future of mankind" ' – stated in similar terms: 'This is the final conclusion of the forty years which I have devoted to the study of these problems since I became aware of the Abuse and Decline of Reason which has continued throughout that period' (Hayek, 1979: 152). On *The Abuse and Decline of Reason* he commented: 'This was the title I had intended to give to a work I had planned in 1939, in which a part on the "Hubris of Reason" was to be followed by one on "The Nemesis of the Planned Society." Only a fragment of this plan has been carried out and the parts written published first in *Economica* 1941–1945...*The Road to Serfdom* (London and Chicago, 1944) was an advance sketch of what I had intended to make the second part. But it took me forty years to think through the original idea' (ibid.: 196).
73. Designated to be Hayek's as well as K.R. Popper's official biographer, Bartley died in 1990, two years before Hayek died, and four years before Popper.

74. Eucken Institute Archive.
75. Quoted from Ebenstein (2001: 315).
76. In his 1981 LSE lecture on 'The Flow of Goods and Services' Hayek (2012 [1981]: 18) expressed a cautious view on the role of *Ordnungspolitik*: 'I have no doubt that the functioning of the market can still be improved by improving the framework of those rules of law within which it operates. ... It appears to me that at the present time priority must be given to removing the obstacles which, because of lack of understanding of the function of the market, governments have erected or are allowing private agencies to erect. We owe it to the folly of our predecessors that this negative task has become more urgent than positive ones have. Once we have again cleared the road for the more powerful spontaneous forces, we shall be able to return to the slower and more delicate efforts of improving the framework within which the market will function more effectively and beneficially.'
77. To be sure, as statements like the following indicate, Hayek does not entirely ignore the need for institutional competition to be itself governed by rules: 'Government is of necessity the product of intellectual design. If we can give it a shape in which it provides a beneficial framework for the free growth of society, without giving to any one power to control this growth in particular, we may well hope to see the growth of civilization continue' (1979: 152).

Bibliography

Block, Walter 1996: 'Hayek's Road to Serfdom', *Journal of Libertarian Studies* 12:2, 339–365.

Buchanan, James M. 1992: 'I Did Not Call Him "Fritz": Personal Recollections of Professor Friedrich A. v. Hayek', *Constitutional Political Economy* 3, 129–135.

Caldwell, Bruce 2004: *Hayek's Challenge – an Intellectual Biography of F.A. Hayek*, Chicago: The University of Chicago Press.

Cubitt, C.E. 2006: *A Life of Friedrich August von Hayek*, Gamlingay, Sandy, England: Authors OnLine Ltd.

Ebenstein, Alan 2001: *Friedrich Hayek – A Biography*, New York: Palgrave.

Ebenstein, Alan 2003: *Hayek's Journey – The Mind of Friedrich Hayek*, New York: Palgrave.

Eucken, Walter 1941: *Die Grundlagen der Nationalökonomie*, 2nd rev. edition, Jena: Gustav Fischer.

Eucken, Walter 1948: 'On the theory of the centrally administered economy. An analysis of the German experiment', *Economica* 15, 79–100, 173–193.

Eucken, Walter 1950: *The Foundations of Economics. History and Theory in the Analysis of Economic Reality*. Translated by T.W. Hutchison, London: William Hodge & Company.

Eucken, Walter 1952: *Grundsätze der Wirtschaftspolitik*, Tübingen: J.C.B. Mohr (Paul Siebeck).

Goldschmidt, Nils, ed. 2005: *Wirtschaft, Politik und Freiheit – Freiburger Wirtschaftswissenschaftler und der Widerstand*, Tübingen: Mohr Siebeck.

Hayek, F.A. 1939: *Freedom and the Economic System*, Gideonse, H.D. (ed.), Public Policy Pamphlet No. 29, Chicago: The University of Chicago Press.

Hayek, F.A. 1945: *Der Weg zur Knechtschaft*, trans. Eva Röpke, Erlenbach-Zurich: Eugen Rentsch.

Hayek, F.A. 1948a: 'Individualism: True and False', in: F.A. Hayek, *Individualism and Economic Order*, Chicago: The University of Chicago Press, 1–32.

Hayek, F.A. 1948b: ' "Free" Enterprise and Competitive Order, in: F.A. Hayek, *Individualism and Economic Order*, Chicago: The University of Chicago Press, 107–118.

Hayek, F.A. 1960: *The Constitution of Liberty*, Chicago: The University of Chicago Press.

Hayek, F.A. 1967 [1949]: 'The Intellectuals and Socialism', in: F.A. Hayek, *Studies in Philosophy, Politics and Economics*, Chicago: The University of Chicago Press, 178–194.

Hayek, F.A. 1967 [1951]: 'The Transmission of the Ideals of Economic Freedom', in: F.A. Hayek, *Studies in Philosophy, Politics and Economics*, Chicago: The University of Chicago Press, 195–200, (originally published in German in 1951).

Hayek, F.A. 1967 [1963]: 'The Economy, Science, and Politics', in: F.A. Hayek, *Studies in Philosophy, Politics and Economics*, Chicago: The University of Chicago Press, 251–269, (originally published in German in 1963).

Hayek, F.A. 1969: *Freiburger Studien*, Tübingen: J.C.B. Mohr (Paul Siebeck).

Hayek, F.A. 1972 [1944]: *The Road to Serfdom*, Chicago: The University of Chicago Press.

Hayek, F.A. 1973: *Law, Legislation and Liberty*, Vol. 1, *Rules and Order*, London and Henley: Routledge & Kegan Paul.

Hayek, F.A. 1976: *Law, Legislation and Liberty*, Vol. 2, *The Mirage of Social Justice*, London and Henley: Routledge & Kegan Paul.

Hayek, F.A. 1976 [1929]: Geldtheorie und Konjunkturtheorie, 2nd enlarged edition, Salzburg: Wolfgang Neugebauer, (an English translation, prepared by N. Kaldor and H.M. Croome, was published in 1933 as *Monetary Theory and the Trade Cycle* by Sentry Press, New York).

Hayek, F.A. 1978: 'Liberalism', in: *New Studies in Philosophy, Politics, Economics and the History of Ideas*, Chicago: The University of Chicago Press, 119–151.

Hayek, F.A. 1979: *Law, Legislation and Liberty*, Vol. 3, *The Political Order of a Free People*, London and Henley: Routledge & Kegan Paul.

Hayek, F.A. 1982: *Law, Legislation and Liberty*, London: Routledge.

Hayek, F.A. 1983: *Der Strom der Güter und Leistungen*, Vorträge und Aufsätze / Walter Eucken Institut 101, Tübingen: Mohr Siebeck.

Hayek, F.A. 1988: *The Fatal Conceit – The Errors of Socialism*, Chicago: The University of Chicago Press.

Hayek, F.A. 1992 [1983]: 'The Rediscovery of Freedom: Personal Reflections', in: F.A. Hayek, *The Fortunes of Liberalism – Essays on Austrian Economics and the Ideal of Freedom*, The Collected Works of F.A. Hayek, Vol. IV, Chicago: The University of Chicago Press, 185–200, (originally published in German in 1983).

Hayek, F.A. 1994: *Hayek on Hayek – An Autobiographical Dialogue*, ed. by Stephen Kresge and Leif Wenar, London: Routledge.

Hayek, F.A. 2004 [1948]: 'Der Mensch in der Planwirtschaft', in: F.A. Hayek, *Wissenschaft und Sozialismus – Aufsätze zur Sozialismuskritik*, Tübingen: Mohr Siebeck, 153–170, (first published in 1948).

Hayek, F.A. 2004 [1979]: 'Wissenschaft und Sozialismus', in: F.A. Hayek, *Wissenschaft und Sozialismus – Aufsätze zur Sozialismuskritik*, Tübingen: Mohr Siebeck, 52–62, (first published in 1979).

Hayek, F.A. 2012 [1981]: 'The Flow of Goods and Services', in: F.A. Hayek, *Business Cycles: Part II*, The Collected Works of F.A. Hayek, Vol. ?, Chicago: The University of Chicago Press, (previously unpublished lecture, held at the LSE in 1981).

Hennecke, Hans Jörg 2000: *Friedrich August Hayek – Die Tradition der Freiheit*, Düsseldorf: Verlag Wirtschaft und Finanzen.

Janssen, Hauke 2009: *Nationalökonomie und Nationalsozialismus – Die deutsche Wirtschaftslehre in den dreißiger Jahren des 20. Jahrhunderts*, 3rd revised edition, Marburg: Metropolis.

Klinckowstroem, Wendula Gräfin von 2000: 'Walter Eucken: Eine biographische Skizze', in: L. Gerken (ed.), Walter Eucken und sein Werk, Tübingen: Mohr Siebeck, 53–115.

Köhler, Ekkehard and Stefan Kolev 2011: *The conjoint quest for a liberal positive program: 'Old Chicago', Freiburg and Hayek*, Hamburg: Hamburg Institute of International Economics (HWWI), Paper 109.

Leube, Kurt R. 1984: 'Friedrich August von Hayek: A Biographical Introduction', in: Ch. Nishiama and K.R. Leube (eds), *The Essence of Hayek*, Stanford, CA: Hoover Institution Press, xvii–xxxvi.

Nicholls, A.J. 1994: *Freedom with Responsibility. The Social Market Economy in Germany 1918–1963*, Oxford: Clarendon Press.

Olson, Mancur 1968: *Die Logik des kollektiven Handelns*, Tübingen: Mohr Siebeck.

Olson, Mancur 1971 [1965]: *The Logic of Collective Action*, Cambridge, Mass.: Harvard University Press.

Peacock, Alan 2000: 'Some Economics of 'Competitive' Civil Justice', in: B. Külp and V. Vanberg (eds), *Freiheit und wettbewerbliche Ordnung – Gedenkband zur Erinnerung an Walter Eucken*, Freiburg-Berlin-München: Haufe, 541–558.

Renner, Andreas 2002: *Jenseits von Kommunitarismus und Neoliberalismus*, Grafschaft: Vektor-Verlag.

Röpke, Wilhelm 1961: 'Blätter der Erinnerung an Walter Eucken', *ORDO – Jahrbuch für die Ordnung von Wirtschaft und Gesellschaft* 13, 3–19.

Shenfield, Arthur 1977: 'Friedrich A. Hayek: Nobel Prizewinner', in: F. Machlup (ed.), *Essays on Hayek*, London and Henley: Routledge & Kegan Paul, 171–176.

Simons, Henry C. 1948: *Economic Policy for a Free Society*, Chicago: The University of Chicago Press.

Vanberg, Viktor J. 1994a: 'Hayek's Legacy and the Future of Liberal Thought: Rational Liberalism vs. Evolutionary Agnosticism', *Journal des Économistes et des Études Humaines* 5. 451–481 (reprinted in Vanberg 2001: 53ff.).

Vanberg, Viktor J. 1994b: 'Cultural Evolution, Collective Learning and Constitutional Design', in: David Reisman, ed., *Economic Thought and Political Theory*. Boston, Dordrecht, London: Kluwer, 171–204.

Vanberg, Viktor J. 1998: 'Freiburg School of Law and Economics', in: Peter Newman (ed.), *The New Palgrave Dictionary of Economics and the Law*, Vol. 2, London: McMillan, 172–179 (reprinted in Vanberg 2001: 37ff.).

Vanberg, Viktor J. 1999: 'Markets and regulation: the contrast between free-market liberalism and constitutional liberalism', *Constitutional Political Economy* 10, 219–243 (reprinted in Vanberg 2001:17ff.).

Vanberg, Viktor J. 2001: *The Constitution of Markets – Essays in political economy*, London and New York: Routledge.

Vanberg, Viktor J. 2003: 'Friedrich A. Hayek und die Freiburger Schule', *ORDO – Jahrbuch für die Ordnung von Wirtschaft und Gesellschaft* 54, pp.3–20.

Vanberg, Viktor J. 2011a: 'Vorwort des Herausgebers', in: F.A. Hayek, *Die verhängnisvolle Anmaßung – Die Irrtümer des Sozialismus*, Tübingen: Mohr Siebeck.

Vanberg, Viktor J. 2011b: 'Darwinian Paradigm, Cultural Evolution and Human Purposes: On F.A. Hayek's Evolutionary View of the Market', *Papers on Economics and Evolution* #1119, Evolutionary Economics Group, Max Planck Institute of Economics, Jena.

Wegmann, Milène 2002: *Früher Neoliberalismus und europäische Integration*, Baden-Baden. Nomos.

8
Eucken, Hayek and *The Road to Serfdom*

Nils Goldschmidt and Jan-Otmar Hesse

Introduction

Walter Eucken (17 January 1891–20 March 1950) was the leading and most prominent figure of German liberal economics from the 1920s until well after his death. He represented the convergence between the liberalism of the Austrian School of economics' 'third generation' and the liberal tradition in German economics that gained momentum during the 1930s in opposition to the very strong socialist, national socialist and romanticist movements in German economics (Goldschmidt and Wohlgemuth, 2008; Janssen, 2009). Only after the war, when the 'ordo-liberal' School of economic thought was erected at the University of Freiburg, did this strand of German economic reasoning become influential, especially in German economic policy pertaining to the reorganization of the West German economy. Though it was influential after the war, the influence of 'ordoliberalism' in academia faded out after Eucken's death in the 1950s, for many reasons (Hesse, 2010). Therefore, the similarities as well as the differences between the German and the Austrian Schools of liberal thought have remained neglected in the literature.

The differences often appear marginal. They seem to result from the particular historic situation in which they were articulated. But as circumstances evolve over time and fundamental global economic crises return, it is, in our opinion, worth while taking a closer look at the differences between these two strands of liberalism, one having been developed within the totalitarian regime of Nazi Germany and the other one 'in exile'. We think the correspondence between two of the most outstanding figures of the two schools of thought might be a fitting starting point for this approach.

In the following we first want to briefly describe the evolution and the nature of the contact between Eucken and the last Viennese generation of the Austrian School of economics. In a second step, we will analyze the differences between the schools following a close reading of a detailed comment by Eucken on Friedrich A. Hayek's (1944) *The Road to Serfdom*, written in March 1946, a few months after a German translation of the book was published. Our examination begins first with a remark by Eucken criticizing Hayek's neglect of the German liberal tradition. Finally, the third section of the chapter deals with Eucken's observations that highlight the minute yet significant differences between the two approaches of (Neo) Liberalism.

Eucken's position on international liberal economics and his relationship to Hayek

The relationship between the German liberals, later to become the Ordoliberals, and the Austrians, later to become the American Neoliberals, did not actually result from the famous symposium organized by Walter Lippmann in Paris in 1938 – as the story has often been told (Foucault, 2004 [1978]). In fact, the modest reunion of the younger scholars after the 'Methodenstreit' (debate over methods) started much earlier, during the annual meeting of the Verein für Socialpolitik that was held on the question of business cycle theory in Zurich in 1928. (Blümle and Goldschmidt, 2006; Köster, 2011). Then, younger Austrians like Fritz Machlup and Gottfried Haberler met with marginalized younger liberal economists from Germany, scholars such as Eucken, Wilhelm Röpke, L. Albert Hahn and Georg Halm.[1]

It is important to understand that the history of post-war economic liberalism in Europe resulted from the pre-war relationship between the 'Austrians' and the small group of German liberal economists which led to the foundation of the Mont Pelerin Society (MPS) shortly after the war. We are not yet able to date the starting point precisely nor determine the nature of the early contacts between Eucken and Hayek. The earliest letter by Eucken to Hayek that is held by the Hoover Institution dates back to 1939, but was probably not the first one written.[2] Correspondence between Eucken and Machlup, another important figure in the relationship, starts in 1934: Machlup, then a 32-year old Rockefeller Fellow studying in Chicago, had sent a copy of his book on the economic crisis to the then well-established and influential Freiburg Professor of Economics, son of the 1908 Nobel Prize laureate in literature, Rudolf Eucken, and Machlup received a polite thank you note in response.[3] Eucken's early correspondence with Hayek was dedicated to philosophical questions related to Hegel and Marx.

The character of the correspondence changed after the war: remarkably early, only three months after the German surrender, Eucken wrote to Hayek inviting him to Freiburg in order to promote the liberal ideas outlined in *The Road to Serfdom* and to fight against the threat of planning and socialism: 'It is of the utmost importance that those who are determined not to follow the "Road to Serfdom" remain in contact, in close contact. May you come to Freiburg? To give a talk perhaps?'[4] 'We non-socialist economists must cooperate across borders. The helplessness in which practical economics finds itself requires this'.[5] In the correspondence between Eucken and Hayek, the plan to erect an international organization composed of liberal economists and activists was discussed as early as January 1946. And when the MPS was finally established at the famous meeting that took place in April 1947 in Switzerland, Eucken was the only participant from Germany. After Hayek became the first president of the MPS at the first meeting, he always consulted Eucken before inviting any German thinker to join the association. However, Eucken recommended that a rather careful policy be applied in this respect. In the summer of 1947, he suggested inviting only law-professor Franz Böhm, his old faculty colleague Constantin v. Dietze, entrepreneur Walter Bauer, and his two pupils, Karl Friedrich Maier and Bernhard Pfister (later to become professor of economics in Munich).[6] He explicitly advised against inviting Alfred Müller-Armack, then professor of economics in Münster, who coined the term 'Social Market Economy' and later became an influential advisor to the German Minister of Economics, Ludwig Erhard; he suggested including two leading figures from the staff of the Frankfurt administration of economics instead.[7] Eucken apparently served as a kind of gatekeeper in the opening of German liberal circles to international discussion. Even the inclusion of the German Minister of the Economy into the international community of liberal economists and entrepreneurs was discussed with Eucken beforehand.[8]

The early correspondence highlights the fact that Eucken was perceived as an academic authority and respected colleague, not as a victim of National Socialism who needed the help of foreign scholars.[9] It was Hayek who suggested to Eucken to prepare an English translation of his textbook, *Foundation of Economics*, and offered his help in finding a publisher.[10] Most of the letters exchanged dealt with organizational issues, as described above. Therefore, the letter we wish to turn to now is an exception, in that it is a seven-page detailed discussion of Hayek's

The Road to Serfdom. Hayek had asked Eucken for a detailed examination of the work, especially to help him locate quotations from German literature that were difficult to access in English libraries.[11] Though Eucken's answers contain little in that respect, they offer a good opportunity for analyzing the differences between Hayek's and Eucken's approaches to economic policy.

Eucken's idea of a German tradition of liberalism

Eucken introduces his discussion of *The Road to Serfdom* as incomplete, and apologizes for the fact that he did not have the time to think about the book in depth, as he would have liked to. His discussion is divided into seven points. All his comments pertain to the first translation of Hayek's (1945) book by Eva Röpke, published in Switzerland in 1945. Eucken's comments in his last point are different from the preceding six: whereas the other six discuss particular points of Hayek's arguments, the seventh comes as a history of German liberalism that, in Eucken's view, needs to be added to Hayek's story. Furthermore, it allows Eucken to depict his own intellectual tradition. This is why we start by examining the seventh point of Eucken's letter – as well as the persons mentioned in it and the idea of German liberalism as perceived by Eucken – before moving on to a more detailed analysis of the other six points. In our opinion, the fact that Hayek did not mention the German tradition of liberal economics is much more than simple lack of knowledge. It is probably intentional, in that Hayek did not perceive the scholars mentioned by Eucken as liberals. The intellectual traditions of Eucken and Hayek differed significantly, which might explain some of the differences in their approaches.

   Eucken's critique of Hayek's description of the history of German political thought since the late eighteenth century refers to Chapter 12 of *The Road to Serfdom*. Though Hayek (1945: 210) started this chapter by mentioning that some of the 'socialist ideas' that fuelled *The Road to Serfdom* also appeared in English and French political thought, he believed that German authors had been 'leading' in that respect. He started his overview of German literature with Werner Sombart's book *Händler und Helden* (*Traders and Heroes*), a direct attack on the liberal idea of individual freedom. Eucken considered that Hayek had exaggerated Sombart's influence on German political thought. Furthermore, he believed that Hayek overestimated the influence of Johann Plenge, economist at the University of Münster, whom Hayek quotes intensively (Hayek, 1945: 215f). Plenge was, in fact, perceived as an outsider by many serious German economists (see Köster, 2011: 176). Eucken was of the opinion that Othmar Spann had been more influential than Plenge, yet Hayek did not mention him.[12] In general, Eucken supported Hayek's view according to which the idea of a socialist economy – or 'centrally-planned economy' in Eucken's terminology – had gathered momentum in Germany in the 1920s and had been infused with nationalist, and later on racist, ideology in the so-called 'conservative revolution' and in the writing of the *Tatkreis* (literally, Action Circle), which Eucken mentions at the very beginning of his letter. The *Tatkreis* called for an end to capitalism while promoting a neo-mercantilist ideology based on private property, a system that encouraged exports and discouraged imports, promoting German self-sufficiency. The typical economic ideology was to combine the advantages of a market system with the centralized control of all economic action. Though the circle's journal *Die Tat* (*Action*) remained comparatively small in terms of circulation, its ideology was influential, for it was used as a model for the economic reasoning of the Nazis, who then dissolved *Tatkreis* in 1933 (see Barkai, 1988: 92).

Eucken, however, aimed at strengthening another strand of German economic thought that Hayek had broadly ignored. There had always been an opposing strand of intellectual tradition in Germany to counter what Hayek called the 'neo-German' intellectual tradition: 'a classic movement and a romantic movement had developed side by side', as Eucken puts it in his letter to Hayek.[13] Eucken believed that more attention should especially be paid to the liberal strand of economic thought that 'was forced into the catacombs' during the decade of National Socialism. He then briefly mentions some names who in his opinion had been important figures of this tradition: first, the Königsberg professor of economics, Christian Jakob Kraus, was the earliest and most prominent interpreter of Adam Smith in Germany in the late eighteenth century, and became very influential because he trained a whole generation of distinguished Prussian civil servants (Wehler, 2011: 35) who initiated liberal economic reforms in 1809/1811, with the introduction of free markets and the individual freedom of peasantry. The next name that Eucken mentions as a milestone of liberal thought in Germany probably refers to the liberal politician Rudolf von Delbrück (1817–1903), who acted as the head of the Bismarck administration in Imperial Germany and propelled the turn to free trade and liberal economic reforms before he was dismissed during Bismarck's switch to protectionism in 1876.

The Göttingen and Freiburg economist Hans von Mangoldt (1824–1868), whom Eucken mentions as a third figure of German economic liberalism, is probably much better known to historians of economic thought. Although he is generally portrayed as a German 'classical' author, he anticipated 'neoclassical' ideas: Schumpeter's theory of the entrepreneur, Alfred Marshall's partial price analysis, and the graphical representation of supply and demand. Mangoldt remains closely tied to the classical tradition, but he introduced mathematical representations that point in the neoclassical direction. It is remarkable that Mangoldt's contemporaries did not pay much attention to these theoretical developments. Mangoldt's most interesting mathematical ideas were even omitted in the posthumous editions of his principal work. The fourth name given by Eucken is Heinrich Dietzel (1857–1935), professor of economics in Bonn and considered an 'academic loner'. He was neither a follower of the mainstream Historical School, nor did he advocate the tenets of the Austrian Marginalism School – rather, he attempted to follow his very own line, which was based on the roots of classical theory. He 'was a lone epigone of classical economics', as von Mises (1969: 3) puts it. He occupied the middle ground with regard to the theory of value, an issue on which he had fiery debates with Eugen von Böhm-Bawerk. Dietzel tried to unify the objective and subjective theory of value by aiming to prove that utility (*Nützlichkeit*) is the common precondition of marginal utility theory and classical theory. And – of course – he is important because Eucken studied with him during his time in Bonn (Kasprzok, 2005; Goldschmidt, 2002). Eucken wrote to Hayek that when he argued with the promoters of the 'socialist' tradition, Arthur Moeller van den Bruck and Oswald Spengler, these were the people his opponents always quoted as their antagonist thinkers.

Eucken considered himself and a group of colleagues named 'the younger generation' to be part of that tradition and indicated that even under National Socialism he and some colleagues had been able to put forward liberal economic reasoning in official meetings, for example with the Commissioner for Price Regulation in 1941, where Eucken's ideas were supported rather than opposed. In a previous letter to Hayek, Eucken had already described what he calls a 'curious event': one of the members of the Freiburg Circle, the Cologne economist Günter Schmölders, managed to organize a conference on the question of competition in the 'lion's den', namely the administration for price regulation.[14] He also named Heinrich von Stackelberg, Hans Gestrich and August Lösch as part of this group of liberal and market-oriented economists. The existence and the influence of this small group of liberal economists in Germany was broadly confirmed by recent historical research. Hauke Janssen even speaks of 'German Ricardians', a term that appears in the correspondence with Alexander Rüstow but might have been overestimated by Janssen (Janssen, 2009: 38; Köster, 2011: 227). Nevertheless, liberal schools of thought continued to exist in Germany during the 1920s and the 1930s (Ptak, 2004; Nicholls, 1994).[15]

However, the German liberalism that Eucken had in mind was based on more modest – yet essential – concepts than the Anglo-Saxon tradition Hayek reflected upon. German 'liberalism' in the 1930s (and this applies to Eucken as well) did not perceive market competition as a mechanism that would take over when state intervention was absent. To German liberals, state initiative was inevitable since they believed that without it, in some cases, competition would not occur. Furthermore, German liberals (such as Eucken) analyzed the economy with a view to increasing welfare rather than to improving individual freedom, which they believed would mainly strengthen private power. The fact that Eucken and Hayek proceeded based on two opposing premises, though not explicitly mentioned in the letter, might explain why Hayek ignored this German tradition of liberalism, as he would have perceived it as being close to 'collectivism'. Eucken and Hayek clearly had a very different understanding of the relation between freedom and order.

Different approaches to liberalism

When focusing on the differences between Eucken and Hayek's positions, it becomes clear that the seven points of Eucken's letter overlap on several issues, which is why we have reorganized our analysis into three parts: we will first address the issue of social order v. individual freedom, then the conditions and meaning of competition, and finally the relationship between socialism, democracy and liberalism.

Social order v. individual freedom

In his discussion about the principles of economic order in his letter to Hayek, Eucken (1926: 15, our translation) writes: 'But in truth, it is a serious matter that the person who is the most efficient at circumventing the legal order is always the one who fares best'. This statement is fundamental to the understanding of what distinguishes ordoliberalism from the Anglo-Saxon brand of liberalism. In his writings, Eucken focuses not only on the question of a legal order as a prerequisite for competition, but also he connects this idea with his considerations on a 'comprehensive intellectual order of life'. Even though Eucken's (2004 [1952]: 184, our translation) terminology changed later on in his academic life, the objective of his research remained the same and is succinctly summarized in his *Grundsätze der Wirtschaftspolitik*:

> We need to get used to the idea that solemn questions about the intellectual and spiritual existence of Man have to be combined with rather sober and mechanical issues of economic design.

'Order' was Eucken's yardstick for economic policy. Pursuing a venerable tradition, which spans Augustine, the medieval thinkers and the Physiocrats, Eucken (1989 [1940]: 239, our translation) is in search of the order that 'conforms to the reason or nature of Man and things'. While Eucken (2004 [1952]: 347, 373, our translation) abstains from 'immediate derivations from natural law' – a fact which is hardly surprising given his phenomenological methodology (Goldschmidt, 2013) – the competitive order that Eucken strives for is 'in another sense [...] a natural order or *Ordo*'. In this spirit, he details how a competitive order 'brings to the fore those strong tendencies which, in the industrial economy as well, push towards perfect competition. Economic policy, by making these tendencies effective as elements of order, does what corresponds to the nature of things and of Man'.

Thus, the goal is an economic policy guided by principles and corresponding to an ideal order. From this perspective only can one appreciate Eucken's (2004 [1952]: 240: our translation) harsh criticism of the 'experimental economic policy' of the past decade: 'We therefore face the great task of providing this new industrialized economy, with its far-reaching division of labour, with a *functional* and *humane* order of the economy'. Compared with an Anglo-Saxon type of liberalism, the notion of freedom is secondary to the notion of order: freedom plays no fundamental role in Eucken's concept. This is why freedom has no significance in *The Foundations*, first published in 1940; only in the posthumously published *Grundsätze der Wirtschaftspolitik* does it take centre stage. Freedom, for Eucken (2004 [1952]: 370, 179, our translation), is not a value in its own right, and Eucken's call for a 'program of freedom' does not aim at making freedom absolute. Rather, Eucken's *ordo*liberal approach explains his understanding of freedom, which is another way of saying that this notion is important to Eucken because the order that is to be realized must guarantee freedom: 'The crucial question is: what types of order warrant freedom'. Hence, the notion of order is constitutive of the notion of freedom, and that might explain why Eucken emphasizes in his letter to Hayek: 'Indeed, the right way is a third, new way'. Eucken's comments on the different types of competition law may illustrate that difference in a more concrete way.

Conditions and meaning of competition

Competition and concentration of economic power is treated at different points in Eucken's comment. His second remark is concerned with the general process of industrial concentration described by Hayek (1945, Chapter 1). While Hayek (1945: 73ff) emphasizes the role of economic policy in the emergence of big business and concentration, Eucken argues that big business did not necessarily result from the growth of enterprises heading for economies of scale, but from collusion in a broad and general way. Corporate law, taxes and the protection of brands would have fuelled that process according to Eucken. Therefore, state intervention and the failure to regulate contribute to the process of concentration of business. In his third point, Eucken reflects on the role of patent law: in a minor footnote in Chapter 14, Hayek (1945: 252) wrote that in his opinion cases where people resorted to a patent in order to prevent competitors from using the patented innovation without using it themselves were rare occurrences. Eucken, however, believed such cases to be more frequent. Hayek's footnote might sound as though he defends that practice, but Eucken assumes that the reduction of patent law, and especially of its negative effects, would be an important aim for both of them. Eucken also addresses economic power as personal motive in the business elite of private firms in his point 5. He was of the opinion that the erection of a competition-based order (*Wettbewerbsordnung*) would dissolve that negative effect of capitalism as well.

It is on this point that Hayek and Eucken's positions diverge the most, even though the disagreement is not explicit and is to be found in only a few detailed remarks. In Eucken's case, issues relating to cartels and monopoly took on a very concrete dimension when he was asked by the French occupation authorities, at the beginning of 1946, for his expert opinion on legislation aimed at preventing the concentration of economic power as part of the allied demerger and decartelization policy. The principles that he developed in this regard were first published in a summary fashion in the *Ordo Yearbook* of 1949. They were to be the foundation of the German 'Act against Restraints of Competition', which – due to several years of political infighting – was not adopted until 1957. Eucken believed that economic positions of power that interfered with competition should in any case be restricted or forbidden by law. Only in very few cases did he think there were no other means of supply to the population than through a monopoly. In these rare instances of 'unavoidable monopolies', independent oversight bodies should be set up in order to limit the abuse of monopoly power. Though Hayek did not have a definite position regarding antitrust law at the end of the 1940s, after Eucken's death he clearly moved towards the early Chicago Schools' line of thought as well as that of Ludwig von Mises. The latter had openly confronted Eucken during the first meeting of the MPS, arguing against any form of legislation regulating market agreements (Plickert, 2008: 198–206; for a general discussion on Hayek, Chicago and Freiburg see Köhler and Kolev, 2011).

Even though at the beginning of 1946 Eucken agreed with Hayek (1945: 67) about the fact that business concentration was not an automatic outcome of capitalism but instead could be traced back to wrong choices in state intervention, he nonetheless advocated state regulation of economic power and viewed a competition-based order as a solution. Contrary to Hayek, in 1946 he was reluctant to view market imbalances and oligopolies as being the temporary consequences of an adjustment process. Already in 1940, in *The Foundations of Economics*, Eucken (1950 [1940]: 146, 120) had strongly rejected the established terms of 'imperfect competition' or 'monopolistic competition' used to describe these phenomena:

> It is in the interests of economic pressure-groups to confuse the distinction between competition and monopoly. The effect of monopolies are shown to be harmless and the special problems of economic constitutional law which the existence of such powerful private bodies creates, are concealed.[16]

Given that Eucken only marginally addresses the issues of concentration and monopoly facilitation through patent, tax and corporate law in these letters, it is not possible to work out a detailed analysis of the fundamental differences between Hayek and Eucken on these issues at that time, contrary to what could be done based on later publications (Plickert, 2008; Woll, 1989). Rather, these 1946 excerpts highlight a particular aspect revealed by this correspondence: whereas in his *The Road to Serfdom* Hayek focuses mainly on the intellectual history of Liberalism and its opponents, Eucken's comments are already the words of a political advisor dealing with day-to-day operations – a man who, when addressing antitrust law, is no longer thinking in theoretical terms but in view of the concrete problems facing Germany's competitive order.

Relationships between socialism, democracy and liberalism

Eucken's remarks about socialism, democracy and liberalism in his letter to Hayek are, in a way, surprising. On the one hand he criticizes the quote by Tocqueville included by Hayek in his book as being inadequate and not really relevant to the distinction between socialism, democracy and liberalism. In *The Road to Serfdom*, Hayek (1945: 45) quotes the following passage by Tocqueville, addressed by Eucken in his letter:

> Democracy extends the sphere of individual freedom [he said in 1848], socialism restricts it. Democracy attaches all possible value to each man; socialism makes each man a mere agent, a mere number. Democracy and socialism have nothing in common but one word: equality. But notice the difference: while democracy seeks equality in liberty, socialism seeks equality in restraint and servitude.

Eucken responds:

> To sum up, here is how I understand it: socialism and democracy are incompatible. Second, socialism and liberalism are incompatible. Yet liberalism and democracy are not identical. There also exists, as you yourself show, democracy without freedom. Consequently, socialism is incompatible with two different things, namely democracy and liberalism.

On the other hand, Eucken stresses that this latter position is also to be found in Hayek's *The Road to Serfdom*, pointing to the last two pages of the chapter 'Planning and Democracy', in which Hayek describes democracy as a means of safeguarding inner peace and individual freedom. However, according to Hayek the only objective and end to be pursued is liberty. Indeed, although a democratic regime counters dictatorial systems, democracy can also lead to arbitrariness and thus to the annihilation of individual freedom. Therefore, what is needed to prevent arbitrariness and to safeguard individual freedom is not rational democratic choice *per se* but an effective limitation on governmental power.

Against this background, it would seem that there is in fact no disagreement between Eucken and Hayek. Why, then, does Eucken raise this topic in his letter and indicate: 'I should, however, write again in more detail on that subject and particularly tell you of the German experiences'? This sentence alluding to further discussion shows that for Eucken it is about more than just an inadequate quote by Tocqueville. Rather, Eucken's comments reveal an uneasiness that should not be treated as insignificant towards an exaggerated trust in democracy as the necessary counterpart to a liberal order. This scepticism reflects his experience of the Weimar Republic, and it is no coincidence that Eucken did not directly address the question of democracy, even in his posthumously published *Grundsätze der Wirtschaftspolitik*. In the two passages where he discusses democracy, he does so through quotations. He quotes *The Economist* with the following statement: 'If liberal democracy is not compatible with full employment, then it must disappear', a position that Eucken (2004 [1952]: 140, our translation) fully supports. In another passage, he quotes Keynes who, in 'The End of Laissez Faire', mentions the possibility of corporations within a democracy – a concept towards which Eucken (2004 [1952]: 244, our translation) was very critical.

It would, however, be a mistake to describe Eucken and Ordoliberalism as being undemocratic or even antidemocratic on account of this scepticism towards democracy, even though it is a view regularly found in the literature (Kirchgässner, 1988; Haselbach, 1991; Ptak, 2004; Ptak, 2009) and often associated with a concept that Eucken, Böhm and others often referred to, that of a 'strong state'. Eucken's (1932: 308, 303, our translation) reasoning is in fact quite different: ordoliberals oppose 'interventionist state capitalism' (*interventionistischer Wirtschaftsstaat*), a weak set up when it comes to safeguarding the economy against privileges, particular interests and the ideologies they carry with them, thus undermining its own authority. Instead, they advocate a strong state that is able to counter the lobbying of individual groups and allow for a general order that is beneficial to all. This does not mean 'politicizing the economy' but rather establishing a few principles that will then build a framework within which market forces can freely unfold. This concept finds its classical form in the idea of constitutive principles, as outlined by Eucken in *Grundsätze der Wirtschaftspolitik*. It is a matter of establishing a stable economic and social structure that is committed to safeguarding the freedom and dignity of all members of society. A 'strong state' in this sense cannot be equated to a totalitarian state that (as its objective of societal development) increasingly intervenes in the private sphere of its citizens and attempts to guide them; rather, it is an effective state that serves the aims of society (as an instrument). Such an effective state imposes clear and general rules regarding order on the economy in order to safeguard the social function of market competition as a decentralized coordinating process for individuals who enjoy equal rights. Any form of socialism is to be rejected because it ultimately fosters economic and social centralization and leads to a concentration of economic power. The Ordoliberals, however, remain vague as to their position regarding other forms of government, and the role of democracy in safeguarding societal order is considered minor.

Hayek on the other hand has a very different approach: for Hayek (2002 [1965]: 124, our translation) – and this applies to his later writings too – democracy is crucial in its role as a potential barrier against the repression of individual freedom. In his opinion, the threat posed by democracy is not – as Eucken would have it – the fact that it might be impossible to establish a functional and humane economic order, but rather that democracy itself might degenerate if it is not limited by the rule of law:

> All the places where democratic institutions were not kept in check by a vibrant tradition of the rule of law and degenerated quickly into 'totalitarian democracies' or even 'plebiscitary' democracies should make us realize that what is actually at stake here are not particular institutions but certain more profound underlying convictions.

Hayek advocates a constitutionally limited democracy, that is a constitutional liberalism 'that focuses on the need to respect the principle of individual sovereignty at the level of constitutional choice'. (Vanberg, 2011: 3; see also Vanberg, 2008)

To recapitulate: a comparative analysis of political structures as viewed by Eucken and Hayek shows that the heart of the matter is the relationship between freedom and order. Ordoliberals basically conceive a liberal, that is free, society as a society devoid of any concentration of powers, defying both economic and political totalitarianism. In order to achieve this, stable state-run structures are necessary and precede the unfolding of liberty. For Hayek, however, in line with the Anglo-Saxon tradition of liberalism in general, a liberal society is first and foremost characterized by the opportunity to exercise individual freedom. In this perspective, any form of socialism is considered a great evil, whereas democracy can serve this purpose, as long as it is itself bound by general rules.

Conclusion

After the Second World War, Eucken and Hayek were perhaps the two most significant proponents of economic liberalism in Europe. Not only were they both particularly influential in the political debates in their respective countries, but also they were united in their active hostility towards socialist economic policy, which they jointly strove to thwart. To that end, they found ways to start corresponding immediately after the German capitulation, and also cooperated closely in the founding of the MPS in 1947. Though our endeavour in this foregoing discussion has been to emphasize the differences between the intellectual positions of both thinkers, we must not lose sight of the fact that we are addressing nuances between two variants of liberalism, which, given their common stance against socialist thinkers back then, could only be rudimentarily distinguished from one other. To this day, the unifying elements in Eucken and Hayek clearly outweigh the differences, and any statement according to which, had socialism been pushed back, the differences would have emerged more clearly, remains pure speculation.

Moreover, the differences are due to the fact that in 1946, when Eucken discussed *The Road to Serfdom* in his letter to Hayek, the personal circumstances and the lines of thought followed by both thinkers could hardly have been further from one another: while Hayek, through the publication of his book in England and his lecture tours in the USA, had become a public intellectual figure in those countries and mainly concerned himself with the academic issues discussed in this milieu, Eucken was one of the most prominent economic policy advisors in post-war Germany, concentrating on the very concrete political economic problems faced by a 'society in ruins'. This explains why Eucken in his remarks puts forward a more down-to-earth and political argumentation.

Nevertheless, within this framework, we could already recognize in Eucken's detailed remarks – from 1946 – about Hayek's *The Road to Serfdom* some fundamental differences between the two liberal positions. Simply the depiction of his own intellectual path indicated that Eucken, contrary to Hayek, did not trace his brand of liberalism directly back to the British tradition following Adam Smith, but rather perceived it as being the continuation of an idiosyncratic 'German' liberalism. We presented three main points in which we addressed the – sometimes admittedly very subtle – differences found in the 1946 letter:

1. Eucken's conception is based on a representation of societal order that, in his opinion, must prevail over individual freedom.
2. This had a direct impact on his position regarding cartels. He believed that it was necessary to prevent the creation and abuse of power concentration by resorting to state authority. Hayek, on the other hand, tended to reject such intervention in competition and later even publicly opposed a ban on cartels.
3. Eucken's comments repeatedly point to a crucial disagreement, though it is only feebly hinted at in the letter, when dealing with the relationship between political system and economic system: While Eucken assigns to the state the role of organizing competition, Hayek believes that competition is more or less an economic natural state requiring a substantial absence of state intervention.

We believe it is significant that these differences in basic assumptions regarding economic liberalism can already be recognized in the difficult circumstances of 1946, at a time when both parties professed the greatest possible interest in international cooperation between proponents of liberalism. And given the current crisis facing liberal economic policy, these differences are perhaps important enough for them to be addressed once again.

Appendix

Walter Eucken to Friedrich A. Hayek, 12 March 1946, HIA FAH Papers, Box 18, Fo. 40. (Translation from original German).

Professor Walter Eucken
Freiburg i. Br., 12 March 1946
Goethestr. 10

Professor F. A. Hayek
London School of Economics
Houghton Street
Aldwych
London WC 2

Dear Mr. Hayek!

I hope you have by now received the latest edition of my work, The Foundations of Economics, with the letter included. – It is a pity that we can not get together in the next few months. There would not only be plenty to discuss with regards to the situation in Germany and in the world, but there would also be plenty to say concerning many scientific issues. When one, which is our case, has been cut off from the rest of the world for so many years, it is absolutely necessary to quickly re-establish full contact with the intellectual work being pursued outside of our borders. I have here at the moment several scholarly works that are already well advanced, and I also would have liked to discuss them with you. Today, however, I would like to write a few words about your book. Of course these are only preliminary remarks since these past few months I have been caught up in many activities and have not had the peace and quiet I would like to reflect in depth on all this.

As I have already written, I quite agree with your book, and at the same time I have learned a lot reading it. The evidence showing that the English development follows the German one with a certain lag is especially convincing, though it is also depressing. I had already noticed signs pointing to these facts. For instance, Carr's book, which became famous here during the National Socialist era and which is strongly reminiscent of the ideas of the *Tatkreis* ("Action Circle"). But voices apparently coming from the liberal side also sounded worrying. For instance, the fact that the Beveridge Plan was included by the Liberal Party in its platform. Or the position of *The Economist* on the issue of full employment, for example. All this, as well as Keynes' influence, shows a certain ignorance with respect to the formidable risks posed by this development, risks that we experienced first hand in their entirety. (By the way, your book has encouraged me to describe the German experiences, which I have observed very closely, in a systematic way. This also applies to the problem of economic calculation in a centrally-planned economy. The difficulties that had been identified in theory have now appeared in reality and have critically compromised the functioning of central economic planning. Schumpeter should have taken such experiences into account, though we are only acquainted with his book through discussions). Your book, however, is the first to fully depict the tragic situation. In this respect, chapter thirteen is particularly convincing; and one may only hope that this book will help England take stock of the situation and help the English clearly understand that England, especially now, has a historic mission; the English, who are about to renounce this mission.

May I now bring forward a few points for discussion, things that crossed my mind as I was reading:

1. On page 66 you discuss the translation of the necessary planning which is required to make competition a beneficial competition in performance. And on page 37 you underscore the difference between a competition-based order and laissez faire. Wouldn't it be appropriate, however, to mark this difference more strongly. I enclose a few drafts that I wrote in which there is a particular stress on this opposition. (You can also see that in one unpublished report the publisher mentioned your book). Now, after decades of economic policy administered in this way, the process of concentration is so advanced in most industrialized countries that introducing laissez faire would lead to some economic agents gaining too much power, it would lead to monopolistic, partly monopolistic or oligopolistic market forms, to imbalanced markets and to social struggles. Then it would once again be necessary to have state interventions, and in a short period of time centrally-planned interventionist methods would once again dominate economic order. It is therefore critical, from the beginning, to push for a real competition-based order. – Even though the purpose of your book is not to examine in detail the necessary measures to achieve this, one could perhaps nonetheless outline the most fundamental elements in a few pages. Indeed, the right way is a third, new way.

2. On a related note, a few remarks concerning your fourth chapter, especially on the issue of concentration. You rightly argue against the idea according to which there is a technical reason for the rise of monopoly.

Shouldn't one however also note the following: the real process of concentration has nothing to do with the growing size of the company, instead, it has to do with the fact that through the formation of consolidated companies, trusts and cartels, the management of the company, or the market supply, ends up in the hands of one or a few people, who, thus, become monopolists or oligopolists. In this way, a consolidated company, or a trust, or a cartel, usually comprises many, sometimes hundreds, of businesses. Thus, research into the so-called optimal size of a business only marginally deals with the problem of concentration and monopoly. And linked to this, the fact that non-technical causes played a decisive role in industrial concentration; this is also true for modern corporate law, especially with respect to stock companies, for patent law, including licencing law, for the protection of trademarks with the protection of resale price maintenance. It is also true for tax law, for instance the sales tax. This lead to two different things: first to the totally unwarranted centralization of the management of several businesses into the hands of one person, and second, to the fact that ultralarge business sizes were chosen, i.e. business sizes that exceeded the technical requirements. This excess can be observed not only with consolidated companies, but also everywhere with the unions and their quota battles.

I think that it would be appropriate if you dwelled a little more on the true character of the movement of concentration and of monopoly. By the way, there are many very interesting remarks in Haussmann's book on "The economic concentration and its reversal of fortune", [*Die wirtschaftliche Konzentration an ihrer Schicksalswende*] published in 1940, though I may not agree on other points in the book.

3. On a related note, an observation about the remark on page 252. The occasional destruction of wheat etc. can of course not happen in the market form of full competition. But shouldn't one add that this destruction of supplies is a phenomenon that typically occurs in a supply monopoly and – this can easily be shown – can only take place in monopolistic or partly monopolistic market forms?

With respect to the non-utilization of valuable patents, this is something that occurs quite often. We have dealt with these problems extensively, and I hope I will soon be able to send you the work of one of my students on that subject. Current patent law is one of the main culprits for the formation of consolidated companies and monopolies and imperatively needs to be reformed so that an adequate competition-based order can emerge. What I mean is that we should not defend the cases of non-utilization of valuable patents, rather, from these cases, we should draw the conclusion that a definitive reduction of patent protection (which is in its essence monopolistic) is required.

4. About your sixth chapter: we in Germany have experienced how incompatible a planned economy and the rule of law are. Consequently, it might be possible to illustrate this excellent chapter with cases from the German experience.

The fact that the notions of law and justice were already undermined played a decisive role in the elimination of the rule of law. But then, with the expansion of the centrally-planned economy, came the economic policy effects. They were first seen in the fact that with the centrally-planned economy, the administration obtained an unbearable ascendancy over legislation. For instance, in this way, a comprehensive piece of legislation was issued to protect the crafts. But because the central planning agencies needed workers, the craftsmen were simply taken away from their businesses, the businesses closed by agency fiat, and thus, through an administrative act, the legislation was completely hollowed out.

At the same it became clear that in an economic order that was mainly centrally-planned, businesses and households were perpetually led to seek evasions (purchasing on the black market, bypassing price fixing, and so on). Such evasions altogether undermine the foundations of the rule of law. One smiles at first when one hears from them. But in truth, it is a serious matter that the person who is the most efficient at circumventing the legal order is always the one who fares best. Naturally, in addition to this, came an increase in briberies, which blossomed under such an economic order.

In the end, the rule of law in Germany was undermined mainly by the change in working conditions. Earlier, the private employment contract had developed into the collective agreement, but then a crossover to central planning of labour occurred. In this way, the sphere of freedom of workers and employees, and of every single German, was very seriously curtailed. At any time, one could be forced to leave his hometown, his family and his workplace. That is when the crossover to bondage and slavery took place. The role of the employment office was no longer just placement, but giving orders with respect to employment. With this, the rule of law completely disintegrates. The individual's sphere of freedom virtually disappears. One can then see that the centrally-planned economy had precisely the opposite effect of what the many workers among their followers had hoped for. It brought in its wake absolute loyalty, the elimination of their sphere of rights and of their freedom. That is an underlying theme in your book. Germany's experience shows how very real this danger is.

5. About the top of page 185, where you write that private enterprise also emerges through the pursuit of power, I would simply like to add

that for the German experiences this is a very significant issue. There were two types: first, the industrial leaders, who had previously headed a union or a corporate group and that felt quite at ease as directors of central offices of economic planning. They experienced an expansion of their power in that, for instance, unions then took on a mandatory nature and they could issue public law regulations. The second group was formed by young people, who rightly recognized that they could quickly gain power within the framework of central planning. This group also proved to be very dangerous. The situation was such that young people in government departments or in other planning agencies, who were barely 30, continuously made decisions concerning huge investments, or shutdowns, or the relocation of workers, and in this way wielded the power that they had sought through political struggle.

The crucial advantage of a competition-based order, namely that power is so fragmented that it no longer has a harmful effect, is a drawback to the extent that for many, this makes a competition-based order less attractive. I feel that by the way in the moment at numerous negotiations.

6. With respect to the relation between democracy, liberalism and socialism, I indeed have reservations concerning Tocqueville's sentence that you quote on page 45. It might not be entirely correct to establish the opposition between democracy and socialism in this way. You outline all that needs to be said on that subject on p.99. To sum up, here is how I understand it: socialism and democracy are incompatible. Second, socialism and liberalism are incompatible. Yet liberalism and democracy are not identical. There also exists, as you yourself show, democracy without freedom. Consequently, socialism is incompatible with two different things, namely democracy and liberalism.

I should, however, write again in more detail on that subject and particularly tell you of the German experiences.

7. Same thing for Chapter 12. I fundamentally agree with the characterization made in this chapter. I would, however, like to add two things.

First, one can say that there was always another movement challenging the one that you characterize as the "Neo-German movement." This movement was made up of the Germans who were and are defined by Goethe, Humboldt, Kant, etc. But alongside, there always were, and still are, men who dissented for decades. There you find a long tradition, from Krauss through Delbrück, and from Mangoldt to Dietzel, and to us, the younger generation. One should however bear in mind that, for example, Moeller van Bruck (with whom, by the way, I have personally had many discussions) or Spengler spoke of liberals with open hatred; liberals who, though they were unorganised, were actually there. Yet it was quite remarkable that in 1941, during a two-day discussion, the speech that I have enclosed here was hardly critisized by either the representatives of the commissioner in charge of prices, of the ministry of economics, of other central agencies and of the *Reichsbank*; in fact, the speech was largely met with approval, and only a few professors of the Historical School disagreed with it. If one wants to sum up the general intellectual situation here, one could perhaps say that in Germany, a classic and a romantic movement developed side by side. Romanticism has changed a lot under the influence of Nietzsche and Naturalism, and with Jünger it is different from what it used to be. It has become massive and violent. But alongside there has always been another movement, which, as I believe, also represents a facet of the German intellectual life, even though in the past few decades, and especially because of National Socialism, it was forced into the catacombs.

About the description of the details, I would like to note that, in my view, the influence of Sombart is perhaps overemphasized. After all, the entire Historical School has already argued along those lines. Of the most recent proponents, Spann may be more important than Plenge, for instance. This massive confrontation between universalism and individualism has had a strong impact on the younger generation. They call themselves the *Tatkreis* ("Action Circle"). On this topic, Lutz published an excellent article in 1933 in the *Tatwelt,* I am sure you can easily get it from him.

With these words I will conclude. I hope that you receive the version of this letter which contains the documents. About your plans for the coming year, please *especially* consider a visit here.

> With kindest regards,
> Yours faithfully,

Notes

All translations of original German sources by Sigrid Saou. The authors thank Uwe Dathe and Hansjörg Klausinger for their helpful comments and suggestions.

1. Ludwig v. Mises (1978: 102) wrote the following passage about that meeting in his memoirs: 'That these men were no economists we must not hold against them. After all, they were the pupil of Schmoller, Wagner, Bücher and Brentano. They did not know the economic literature, had no conception of economic problems, and suspected every economist as an enemy of

the State, as non-German, and as protagonists of business interests and of free trade. Whenever they examined an economic essay, they were determined to find deficiencies and errors. They were dilettantes in everything they undertook.' But among others, Eucken, Röpke, Hahn and Halm were excluded from that judgement.

2. Eucken to Hayek, 27 June 1939, Hoover Institution Archives (Stanford University Palo Alto, hereafter abbreviated as: 'HIA'), Friedrich A. v. Hayek Papers (hereafter: "FAH papers"), Box 18, Fo. 40.

3. Eucken to Machlup, 25 February 1934, HIA, Fritz Machlup Papers, Box 36, Fo. 16

4. Eucken to Hayek, 12 August 1945, HIA FAH Papers, Box 18, Fo. 40 (our translation).

5. Eucken to Hayek, 10 November 1945, HIA FAH Papers, Box 18, Fo. 40 (our translation).

6. Eucken to Hayek, 26 August 1947, HIA FAH Papers, Box 18, Fo. 40.

7. His former pupil and assistant, Leonhard Miksch, and Heinrich Rittershausen. Eucken to Hayek, 5 April 1948, HIA FAH Papers, Box 18, Fo. 40.

8. Eucken to Hayek, 3 February 1949, HIA FAH Papers, Box 18, Fo. 40.

9. Hayek asked Eucken for help in the denazification-trial of his brother, Heinrich v. Hayek, who had occupied the position of associate professor in medicine at the University of Würzburg during the war. He was suspended in 1946 and had received a call to the University of Freiburg some months later, which was then threatened by the de-nazification committees' decision. (Hayek to Eucken, 1 February 1947, HIA FAH Papers, Box 18, Fo. 40).

10. In his answer Eucken wrote to Hayek that he had given the rights for any English translation of his *Foundations* to his pupil Friedrich A. Lutz in the summer of 1939, when the war broke out. Eucken to Hayek, 22 November 1947, HIA FAH Papers, Box 18, Fo. 40.

11. Hayek to Eucken, 8 February 1946, HIA FAH Papers, Box 18, Fo. 40.

12. Hayek spent three pages on an analysis of Paul Lensch, who played no role in that strand of thought, but Eucken did not comment on that.

13. Eucken to Friedrich A. Hayek, 12 March 1946, HIA FAH Papers, Box 18, Fo. 40, our translation.

14. Eucken to Hayek, 8 February 1946, HIA FAH Papers, Box 18, Fo. 40. The contributions to the conference were later published by Günter Schmölders (1942). In his memoirs, Schmölders (1989: 72) described the organisation of the conference as well as the publication of the volume as an act of opposition against the Nazi regime though 'competition' cannot in itself be treated as anathema to Nazi ideology (see Hesse, 2006). On the resistance of the Freiburg circles in general see Goldschmidt (2011).

15. Perhaps somewhat bold in this respect is David Gerber's (2003: 232) introduction to the contribution of the Freiburg School to the development of international competition law: 'intellectual impulses for the extraordinary reversal of direction in social and political development [...] came not from a traditional liberal bastion such as England, but from the territory of a recent enemy of liberalism: Germany'.

16. Karl Steinbrück, in his 1954 dissertation, supervised by Heinrich Rittershausen, argues that Eucken ignored the international debate.

Ernst Heuss (1986) also links this dissociation to the isolation of German economic sciences during the war. Heinrich von Stackelberg (1940: 266), however, wrote as early as 1940 that 'Eucken did not ignore this distinction [between perfect and imperfect markets]: he expressly rejects it in an argument with Chamberlin and Robinson'.

Bibliography

Barkai, Avrahm. 1988. *Das Wirtschaftssystem des Nationalsozialismus. Ideologie, Theorie, Politik 1933–1945.* Neuauflage, Frankfurt a.m: Fischer.

Blümle, Gerold and Goldschmidt, Nils. 2006. From Economic Stability to Social Order: The Debate About Business Cycle Theory in the 1920's and Its Relevance for the Development of Theories of Social Order by Lowe Hayek and Eucken. *European Journal of the History of Economic Thought*, 13 (4): 543–570.

Eucken, Walter. 1926. Die geistige Krise und der Kapitalismus. In *Die Tatwelt 2*, (alias Kurt Heinrich), pp. 13–16.

Eucken, Walter. 1932. Staatliche Strukturwandlungen und die Krisis des Kapitalismus. *Weltwirtschaftliches Archiv*, 36: 297–323.

Eucken, Walter. 1949. Die Wettbewerbsordnung und ihre Verwirklichung. *Ordo. Jahrbuch für die Ordnung von Wirtschaft und Gesellschaft*, 2: 1–99.

Eucken, Walter. 1926. 1950 [1940]. *The Foundations of Economics. History and Theory of Economic Reality.* London: W. Hodge.

Eucken, Walter. 1989 [1940]. Die Grundlagen der Nationalökonomie. Berlin et al. Springer: Verlag.

Eucken, Walter. 2004 [1952]. *Grundsätze der Wirtschaftspolitik.* Tübingen: Mohr Siebeck.

Foucault, Michel. 2004. *Geschichte Der Gouvernementalität II. die Geburt Der Biopolitik. Vorlesungen am Collège de France 1978–1979.* Frankfurt a.M: Suhrkamp.

Gerber, David, J. 2003 [1998]. *Law and Competition in the Twentieth Century Europe: Protecting Prometheus,* Reprint Oxford: Clarendon Press.

Goldschmidt, Nils. 2002. *Entstehung und Vermächtnis ordoliberalen Denkens. Walter Eucken und die Notwendigkeit Einer kulturellen Ökonomik.* Münster: Lit-Verlag.

Goldschmidt, Nils. 2011. Planning for Freedom. The Repression and Opposition of Economists During the Nazi Regime in Germany on the Example of the Freiburg Circles. In *Subsidiarity and Institutional Polyarchy: Studies of Social Market Economy in Contemporary Democracies.* Yearbook Centro Studi Tocqueville-Acton, www.cattolici-liberali.com/pubblicazioni/Annali/Annale2011.pdf

Goldschmidt, Nils. 2013. Walter Eucken's Place in the History of Ideas. *Review of Austrian Economics*, forthcoming.

Goldschmidt, Nils and Wohlgemuth, Michael. 2008. Social Market Economy: Origins, Meanings and Interpretations. *Constitutional Political Economy*, 19: 261–276.

Haselbach, Dieter. 1991. Autoritärer Liberalismus und soziale Marktwirtschaft. *gesellschaft und politik im Ordoliberalismus.* Baden-Baden: Nomos.

Hayek, Friedrich A. *Der Weg zur Knechtschaft. Herausgegeben u. eingeleitet v. Professor Dr. Wilhelm Röpke*, Übersetzt von Eva Röpke. Erlenbach-Zürich: Rentsch.

Hayek, Friedrich A. 2002 [1965]. *Die Anschauungen der Mehrheit und die zeitgenössische Demokratie*, reprinted in: Hayek, Friedrich A.: Grundsätze einer liberalen Gesellschaftsordnung. Tübingen: Mohr Siebeck.

Hesse, Jan-Otmar. 2006. Zur Semantik von Wirtschaftsordnung und Wettbewerb in nationalökonomischen Lehrbüchern der Zeit des Nationalsozialismus. In Bähr, Johannes and Banken, Ralf (eds) *Wirtschaftssteuerung durch Recht im Nationalsozialismus. Studien Zur Entwicklung des Wirtschaftsrechts im Interventionsstaat Des "Dritten Reiches."* Frankfurt a.M.: Klostermann, 473–508.

Hesse, Jan-Otmar. 2010. *Wirtschaft als Wissenschaft: Die Volkswirtschaftslehre in Der Alten Bundesrepublik*. Frankfurt a.M: Campus.

Janssen, Hauke. 2009. *Nationalökonomie und Nationalsozialismus. Die deutsche Volkswirtschaftslehre in den Dreißiger Jahren*. Marburg: Metropolis.

Kasprzok, Carsten. 2005. *Der Sozialökonom Heinrich Dietzel. Ein deutscher Klassiker*. Marburg: Metropolis.

Köhler, Ekkehard A. and Kolev, Stefan. 2011. The conjoint quest for a liberal positive program: "Old Chicago", Freiburg and Hayek. Hamburg (HWWI Research Paper 109).

Köster, Roman. 2011. *Die Wissenschaft der Außenseiter: die Krise der akademischen Nationalökonomie in der Weimarer Republik 1918–1933*. Göttingen: Vandenhoek & Ruprecht.

Mises, Ludwig von. 1969. *The Historical Setting of the Austrian School of Economics*. New Rochelle: Arlington House.

Mises, Ludwig von. 1978. *Notes and Recollections*. South Holland: Libertarian Press.

Nicholls, Anthony J. 1994. *Freedom with Responsibility. The Social Market Economy in Germany 1918–1963*. Oxford: Oxford University Press.

Plickert, Philip. 2008. *Wandlungen des Neoliberalismus. Eine Studie zu Entwicklung und Ausstrahlung der 'Mont Pèlerin Societiy'*. Stuttgart: Lucius & Lucius.

Ptak, Ralf. 2004. *Vom Ordoliberalismus zur Sozialen Marktwirtschaft: Stationen des Neoliberalismus in Deutschland*. Opladen: Westdeutscher Verlag.

Ptak, Ralf. 2009. Neoliberalism in Germany: Revisiting the Ordoliberal Foundations of the Social Market Economy. In Mirowski, Philip and Plehwe, Dieter (eds) *The Road from Mont Pèlerin. The Making of the Neoliberal Thought Collective*. Cambridge/Mass: Harvard University Press, 98–138.

Schmölders, Günter (ed.). 1942. *Der Wettbewerb als Mittel volkswirtschaftlicher Leistungssteigerung und Leistungsauslese*. Berlin: Duncker & Humblodt.

Schmölders, Günter. 1989. *"Gut durchgekommen?" Lebenserinnerungen*. Berlin: Duncker & Humblodt.

Stackelberg, Heinrich von 1940. Die Grundlagen der Nationalökonomie. *Weltwirtschaftliches Archiv*, 51: 245–286.

Vanberg, Viktor J. 2008. On the complementarity of liberalism and democracy: A reading of F. A. Hayek and J. M. Buchanan. *Journal of Institutional Economics*, 4: 139–161.

Vanberg, Viktor J. 2011. Liberal constitutionalism, constitutional liberalism and democracy. *Constitutional Political Economy*, 22: 1–20.

Wehler, Hans-Ulrich. 2011. Die Deutschen und der Kapitalismus. In Budde, Gunilla (ed.) *Kapitalismus: Historische Annäherungen*, Göttingen: Vandenhoek & Ruprecht, 34–49.

Woll, Artur 1989. Freiheit durch Ordnung. Die gesellschaftspolitische Leitidee im Denken von Walter Eucken und Friedrich A. von Hayek. In *Ordo: Jahrbuch für die Ordnung von Wirtschaft und Gesellschaft*, 40: 87–97.

9
Hayek's Official Biograp
Lost Insights of William Warren
Bartley III

Robert Leeson

Introduction[1]

When Friedrich August Hayek died (1992, age 92) his knowledge had helped undermine the legitimacy of one crusading faith: quasi-religious certainty about the benevolence of government. When his biographer, William Warren Bartley III, died (1990, age 55) his knowledge could also have gone on to perform a similar socially useful function: deconstructing and thus diffusing some of the fratricidal disputes between the 'children of Abraham' or 'the people of the book'.

Bartley attended the Harvard Divinity School and the Episcopal Theological School (1956–1958) before becoming a lapsed Christian and the author of a seminal PhD thesis (published as *The Retreat to Commitment* 1962; second edition 1984). There was no doubt about his professional ability: Karl Popper (his PhD supervisor) described him as the 'most gifted young philosopher I have ever met' (to Ernst Gombrich, 20 March 1961).[2]

Retreat to Commitment (1984: xviii–xix, xxii–xxiii) described the history of Protestantism as a 'kind of battlefield between critical and ideological thought'. As a case study it illustrated 'the *morbidity* of critical thought' and the resulting transformation into a

dogmatically held ideology...the intellectual counterpart of economic protectionism...The book is concerned with how men use ideas to protect ideas from competition, to remove them from the selective process that is the heart of criticism'.

Thus

> a reasonable argument about the limits of reason is used convinc-
> ingly – reasonably – to restrict reason ... This argument transforms
> *whatever* it touches into pseudo-science and ideology. [Bartley's
> emphases]

Bartley (1984: xv, xiii, xiv) saw his work as transcending religion and
Protestant thought: a generalization of Popper's approach to philosophy. He sought to show where all previous attempts to deal with the
'problems of criticism and rationality' had failed by uncovering 'the
common, previously unrecognized "structure" that doomed previous
answers'. He also offered to 'circumvent' this failed structure:

> the whole argument has sweeping ramifications for philosophy of
> science, epistemology, social and political philosophy, of ethics;
> and also for the understanding and interpretation of the history
> of philosophy. For the resolution of such a problem creates a new,
> unprecedented problem-situation within philosophy.

The archival evidence reveals a deep commitment to these fundamental epistemological questions. In a letter to Gombrich, Bartley
(26 March 1964) stated that

> I disagree emphatically with your comment that there is just one
> dominant imperative of rational procedure: namely, 'Thou shalt not
> lie'. And it is also here where my work in 'ethics' connects with my
> work in the 'philosophy of science' ... there is a distinctive *changing*
> moral code of the rationality fraternity, or fraternity of scientists.
> Depending on whether one pays at least lip service to this code
> (which consists, for the most part, of rules of scientific method, or
> of, more generally, 'methodology') one gets various academic prizes
> or has certain sanctions applied against one by the other members
> of the community. This code is, I think, filled with understandable
> but highly incorrect – and at this stage pernicious – dogmas to which
> taboos are attached: e.g. inductivism, essentialism, the justification-
> criticism fusion, the deductibility assumption, the identity principle
> etc. From the beginning, of course, these various rules or imperatives
> of rational procedures were indeed meant to help prevent 'lying'.
> But how to avoid lying and error is a complicated business. Here too,
> we do not know; we can only guess. You might, of course, want to
> reply that you meant 'lying' as a deliberate falsification of the facts.

But even then I am not convinced. 'Lying' often has a lot to do with what is nowadays often called 'self-deception'. [Bartley's emphasis]

In a letter to Imre Lakatos, Bartley (13 December 1963) playfully suggested that

as philosophers we are all passionately, passionately interested in Truth – except when we are interested in jobs.[3]

Humour aside, there are likely to be personal costs incurred when those whose 'truth' is being examined take offence. For various reasons it became privately optimal for him to retreat – somewhat – from his intense commitment to fundamental philosophy and the examination of the dynamics of dogmatism.

In his early twenties, the break with Christianity was apparently accompanied by a personal crisis; in 1965 (age 30), another crisis largely curtailed his career as a creative philosopher. He subsequently focussed on writing biographies: Ludwig Wittgenstein (1973), Werner Erhard (1978) plus Popper (1989, unfinished), Hayek (unfinished) and John Maynard Keynes (unfinished).

Bartley (7 December 1985) appeared to undervalue or miss the contemporary significance of his own philosophical work: he informed Popper that

You are entirely right to say that we had different problem situations and that with the resurgence of terrorism, your problem-situation has become more important again.[4]

Religion-inspired public policy can turn the constraint of Mutually Assured Destruction into a privately optimal, inter-temporal imperative: from the perspective of the twenty-first century it is Bartley-style analysis of faith-based animosity and the irrational roots of social fanaticism that we appear to lack.

Bartley (22 September 1985–29 September 1985) suffered from a long series of ailments: he informed Hayek that he had long been prone to anxiety attacks and in 1980 had experienced a five-month-long depressive episode.[5] He informed Popper (9 January 1980; 11 May 1980; 23 March 1981) that

I returned from hospital yesterday evening. My doctors do not really know what was wrong with me. I had a liver inflammation ... it may have resulted from the course of drugs that I was given in November to treat the amoebic dysentery

He was able to carry on working with the help of 'immense amounts of coffee and tea … I tried to hide my weakness and illness as much as possible'. Later he tried acupuncture.[6]

Bartley (10 October 1980) informed Popper and his wife Hennie that he had 'collapsed' in Alpbach:

It wasn't hepatitis: it was a new mysterious disease I have had since early August … the doctors found nothing … I am hoping for a miraculous recovery.[7]

Bartley was diagnosed with bladder cancer in July 1989 and died at his Oakland home on 5 February 1990.

The fourteen months surrounding Bartley's death (November 1989– January 1991) coincided with the end of one episode of world history (the fall of the Berlin Wall) and the beginning of another – symbolized by an aerial assault on the city most closely associated with the Islamic Golden Age (the bombing of Baghdad). The First Gulf War conjured images of an old biblical crusade. The response (terrorist attacks) and counter-response conjured-up equivalent rhetoric: 'this crusade, this war on terrorism, is going to take a while'.[8]

Seven months before his death, Bartley (1989) recalled that

when a boy in Church School I was taught a doctrine of strict Protestant Stewardship, and frequently admonished, 'You are the only Bible the careless world will read'.

Bartley had been shaped by his family religion – and his struggle to escape. His partner, Stephen Kresge (11 February 1990), wrote to Popper that as death approached

I saw in his face and heard in his voice a quality that had never been there, as long as I had known him (which was 26 years). In some way that I cannot articulate he was becoming transparent to himself, that the carefully forged persona that he had worked so hard to maintain all these years had simply dissolved, and in its place was the simplicity of acceptance of what he had done and what he had not done, how he had lived and not lived and without regret, bitterness, anguish or apology … he seemed to be released from all the feelings of guilt and compulsion which had plagued so much of his life.

Kresge continued:

[Bartley] had long suffered from sleeping difficulties, from bouts of anxiety, even panic. It was clear that he drove himself with sheer will when the basic energy was not there. He had been told by more than one therapist that he did not breathe properly. But he always resisted doing anything about it because he found it required a concentration to correct the problem and he was unwilling to use his mind that way.[9]

Popper was the first to be informed about the cancer: Bartley (21 July 1989) felt that

I am letting everybody down terribly...I want you to know that I shall do my best to finish your biography before I die. That is the one thing that I want to do. My encounter and friendship with you has meant more than to me than anything else that has happened to me.

Popper (25 December 1989) wrote to Bartley: 'we think of you with love. We all wish that each of us could take a piece of your pain and relieve you of it'.[10]

Popper (1990) subsequently informed Kresge that 'I loved Bill very much (in spite of me being completely heterosexual, of course)' adding 'I sometimes felt that he was not absolutely open to me'.[11] This was another aspect to Bartley's complicated personality: referring to blocked computer files, Kresge (5 April 1990) suggested to Popper that 'I fear Bill may have done just this, and there will be secrets of WWB III that we will never know'.[12]

Bartley was ambitious and sought to achieve quality results. For example, he received the 1978–1979 California State University Hayward (CSUH) George & Miriam Philips Outstanding Professor Award. Yet Bartley (1978: 216–217) believed his efforts were being sabotaged by indolent co-workers: he was repeatedly prevented from showing a film to his students by an incompetent projectionist. The expansion of the State protected incompetence: CSUH was set up 'go through the motions and to frustrate attempts to do otherwise...It was not an environment that would tolerate the telling of the truth'.

Bartley attracted controversy. His *Wittgenstein* (1973) led to the implicit accusation – by the Cambridge philosopher Elisabeth Anscombe and others – that he had fabricated evidence in the form of coded diaries and anonymous sources. Bartley (1985: 161–163) reported that he had received a letter informing him that 'you are to be drummed out of the trade and that no academic invitation of any kind will be extended to you from the UK henceforth'. According to Peter Munz (2004: 29), one of Wittgenstein's executors, Rush Rhees, demanded that Bartley 'be prohibited from visiting Britain'.

In 'The Fatal Deceit: Hayek's last words were written by someone else' Alan Ebenstein (2005) accused Bartley of inserting his own philosophy into Hayek's (1988) *Fatal Conceit*.[13] In particular, it appears that book's conclusion may have been written by Bartley:

Perhaps what many people mean in speaking of God is just a person-ification of that tradition of moral values that keeps their commu-nity alive.

In his essay for Popper's 80th birthday Festschrift, *In Pursuit of Truth*, Bartley (1982: 269) stated that *Evidence and Assurance*, Nicholas Nathan's (1980) contribution to the Cambridge Studies in Philosophy series, was guilty of 'garbling' the work on critical rationalism undertaken by himself, Popper and Hans Albert:

Cambridge University Press would be unlikely to publish a work attributing to Einstein a belief in the luminiferous aether, but it publishes a work – no doubt referred and approved by 'experts' from the philosophy profession – attributing to Popper and his followers *precisely those ideas they have spent their lives denying.* [Bartley's emphasis]

Nathan believed that Bartley had misrepresented what he had written about Popper and critical rationalism. Moreover, Bartley attached the word 'incompetent' to his assessment of Nathan's text – which led to the threat of legal action. The British publishers, Harvester Press, declined to issue the book; the editor and the American publisher (Humanities) persuaded a reluctant Bartley to delete the offending word: 'Bartley was less than happy with me' the Festschrift editor Paul Levinson recalled.[14]

Bartley presumably was motivated by devotion to Popper and/or prin-ciple. In addition, after his experiences with *Wittgenstein* (1973), he may have been oversensitive about Cambridge. From a wider perspective, such disputes appear to have been small fry in comparison with the bigger fish that had originally engaged him.

This chapter does not seek to adjudicate between Bartley and his critics. Instead, a narrative and an interpretation of his life and work will be provided. One conclusion emerges: Bartley was suited to writing biographies (the two he completed were readable and contained provocative insights; the Popper and Hayek biographies would probably have fallen into the same category) – yet he was better suited to creative philosophy. From a social perspective, he misdirected his energies in this regard. How he came to do so involves the interaction of Bartley's evolving personality (and associated challenges) with the existing incentive structure.

Sections 2, 3 and 4 are largely biographical: examining aspects of Bartley's childhood through what appears to be an autobiographical account (2); his break with Christianity (3); and his break with Popper and Lakatos (4).

Sections 5–8 relate to Bartley's charismatic biographies. Writing for a wider audience has a different cost–benefit analysis from that faced by those who address only academics. The controversies generated by his biographies were, perhaps, less professionally traumatic than the analytical work associated with the break with Popper. Indeed, through biography he repaired his relationship with Popper and – through Hayek – obtained a high-status Senior Research Fellowship at the Hoover Institution on War, Revolution and Peace. Moreover, Bartley did not abandon fundamental philosophy, as evidenced by his contributions to *Evolutionary Epistemology, Rationality, and the Sociology of Knowledge* (Radnitzky and Bartley, 1987) plus the six Appendices added to the second edition of *Retreat to Commitment* (1984). But in the quarter of a century from 1965 until his death, Bartley devoted most of his professional energies to biographies: Wittgenstein (5); Erhard (6); Popper (7) and Hayek (8). Most of his unfinished work on Popper is not yet in the public domain; section 8 uses material that he collected on Hayek to illustrate the thoroughness with which he worked.

Bartley devoted much of the last five years of his life to preparing for publication Hayek's *Collected Works*. Section 9 outlines some of the difficulties associated with that project. This episode reinforces a general conclusion: Bartley should have remained focused on fundamental philosophy. Concluding comments are provided in Section 10.

Christopher

The *Retreat to Commitment* (dedicated 'To My Mother Elvina Henry Bartley') began with a statement from John Locke (1699):

> There is nobody in the commonwealth of learning who does not profess himself a lover of truth; and there is not a rational creature that would not take it amiss to be thought otherwise of. And yet, for all this, one may truly say, there are very few lovers of truth for truth's sake, even among those who persuade themselves that they are so. How a man may know whether he be so in earnest, is worthy enquiry.

Locke, one of the intellectual progenitors of classical Liberalism and the Enlightenment, was the author of *A Letter Concerning Toleration* which advocated tolerance as an alternative to the religious wars that had ravaged Europe from the Protestant Reformation to the Treaty of Westphalia (1524–1648). From the Salem witch trials (1692) to the United Nations Universal Declaration of Human Rights (1948) and beyond, the expansion of democracy has been generally accompanied by the (uneven) diminution of the intrusive and discriminatory powers of the State. In the face of intense resistance, the Enlightenment facilitated the expansion of civil rights to a variety of groups including Jews, Catholics, women, African–Americans and – towards the end of the twentieth century – homosexuals (at least in part).

Those with a low or 'outside' status became increasingly free to choose: increased social mobility undermined inherited status. Vested interests and prejudice were gradually defeated by a wider sense of justice and collective self-interest. Catholics and homosexuals were – and, by some, still are – denigrated as the 'enemy within'. Yet the 1829 Roman Catholic Relief Act permitted Catholics to sit in the British Houses of Parliament (which in 1605 Catholic terrorists had almost succeeded in blowing up).

Appeals to religion reinforced all sides of these arguments. William Wilberforce's evangelicalism, for example, contributed to the Slave Trade Act (1807) and the Slavery Abolition Act (1833). 'God' was also frequently invoked in defence of the status quo.

Such rules of engagement turn public policy disagreements into conflagrations. In biblical eschatology, 'God coming into history' to take sides in a battle between good and evil precedes 'Armageddon'. The Atlantic slave trade denuded one continent of prime age males: this may have contributed to technological backwardness. As if by nemesis, two and a half centuries after slaves were first brought to the American colonies, the resulting religion-inspired conflict over labour market contracts cost the United States over 20 per cent of its prime age males (1861–1865).

Those who indulge in a taste for discrimination are likely to suffer adverse public policy consequences: pursuing an imaginary 'enemy within' could undermine the ability to contain the 'enemy without'. For example, pre-war persecution encouraged the migration of strategically skilled German Jews into the enemy camp. Self-sabotage was present elsewhere. For example, Alan Turing, OBE, Fellow of the Royal Society, Fellow of King's College, Cambridge, was a pioneer of early computer science and artificial intelligence and devised techniques for breaking wartime German codes when the Allies were near defeat in the Battle of the Atlantic. Sir David Maxwell Fyfe prosecuted German war criminals at the Nuremberg trials; as Conservative Party Home Secretary (1951–1954) Fyfe organized a 'drive against homosexuals' (Annan 1990, 200). In his prime, Turing's (1912–1954) life was ruined.

In 1952, Turing's homosexuality led to prosecution for 'Gross Indecency' under a section of the 1885 Criminal Law Amendment Act. He underwent chemical castration (as an alternative to prison) and died in 1954 from potassium cyanide poisoning, deemed by the coroner to be suicide (Turing, 1959: 117). In the same year, the Diagnostic and Statistical Manual of the American Psychiatric Association began to list homosexuality as a sociopathic personality disorder – a designation that ceased in 1973. Attitudes began to change: Lionel Robbins (1971: 284) is proud of having helped to reform 'the barbarous laws relating to homosexuality'. Half a century after his death, Turing received a posthumous apology.[15]

On the evening of 28 June 1969, persecution of homosexuals culminated in riots outside The Stonewall Inn, Christopher Street, Greenwich Village, New York. With a Preface dated Christmas 1969, Bartley's *Morality and Religion* (1971) was dedicated 'For Stephen Kresge'. Bartley (1971: 61–63) explained how the debate over homosexuality and other contemporary topic issues stemmed

> from a disagreement about what is evil … we are much at the mercy of our projections – that is, in the psychological sense, those interior states which we impose on the external world in the course of interpreting it.

Popper (1968: 90, n1, 99–100) often told Bartley that he disagreed with his 'preoccupation with psychological ideas such as the problem of a man's "identity and integrity"'. Popper was also

> surprised by his remarks on my alleged philosophical development and the influences on it, about which he says things in his lecture which are completely imaginary, though he could easily have tried to check his hunches critically, simply by asking me about them.

In what appears to have relevance to the break with Popper, Bartley (1969: 18, 24, 27, 41) outlined what he believed was an original contribution:

> It is occasionally realized that both Wittgenstein and Popper were school-teachers in and near Vienna during the 1920s. But to my knowledge, no one has ever raised the question whether their activities as schoolteachers might not be relevant to their philosophies. I believe there was a quite important relationship between these two activities...everyone knows that Popper's main formal background was in physics and mathematics. It so happens, however, that what everyone knows is false. In fact, Popper is an amateur physicist and mathematicians, his formal training having been in education and Gestalt psychology under the supervision of Karl Buhler...it is curious that in his later writings he mentions them so rarely...when one views Popper's thought against this background, it is hard, surprising as it may seem to some, to find much of striking novelty in his philosophy.

The answer to the question of

> why the background was allowed to disappear in the first place...would involve a vast program of research – one that I hope will one day be carried out.[16]

Bartley (1969: 34) suggested that it was possible to construe Wittgenstein's latter thought 'as that of an amateur but gifted child psychologist'. In the 'Afterword, 1985' of his biography, Bartley (1985) cited Wittgenstein:

> A man can bare himself before others only out of a particular kind of love. A love which acknowledges, as it were, that we are all wicked children.

In the second edition of *Retreat to Commitment* (1984: xxi) Bartley attached references to *Morality and Religion* (1971) and his Erhard biography (1978) to the statement:

> I do not for a moment believe that man is a rational animal, let alone that men are born with a 'faculty' of reason. Rather, rationality, like consciousness itself is a comparatively late, and still rather rare, and where it exists, a fragile development. Most individuals exist in a troubled, slumbering fantasy world, and, when most awake, are bound by rigid habits and unconscious patterns of behavior. Comparatively few persons enjoy the give-and-take of criticism or think to any purpose other than to dominate.

Despite these limitations, in the previous four centuries science had emerged through a process of 'competition'.

In *Morality and Religion* Bartley (1971: 56–61) stated that 'we have learnt that children inhabit the world of sex'. Using the fictitious name 'Christopher', Bartley provided what appears to be an autobiographical account of a traumatic childhood episode. The eight-year-old Christopher was spanked by his mother for over-sleeping, and in revenge persuaded his five-year-old sister 'Mary' to say that she hated her mother. Christopher then passed this misinformation on to his mother, who then spanked her daughter, Mary.

Eighteen months later, Christopher 'tricked' his father into saying something agnostic about Jesus – which was immediately passed onto his 'devoutly religious' mother as 'Daddy says there wasn't any Jesus'. Bartley noted:

> There followed an extraordinarily heated quarrel between Christopher's parents, one which his father, as was usual, lost ... his father was spanked verbally by his mother and stalked off in despair to the neighbourhood pub ... In this extraordinary way Christopher's religious doubts were laid quietly, but oh so devilishly, to sleep, not to be yanked awake again for nearly a decade, at which time he was thrust into a severe neurosis.

Bartley (1971: 57–58) concluded that Christopher's

> fury expressed itself most crudely, as hate for his mother – and perhaps for all things feminine ... he virtually forced his little sister – only five years old and barely aware of what was happening – to express, to *voice*, the evil sentiment.

Bartley noted that

> one need not hide a certain admiration for the skilful way in which
> he manipulated his social environment. One of the chief reasons
> for this, of course, was its predictability, in particular the predict-
> ability of his mother...Christopher appears to have been able to
> predict, almost to the detail, the sorts of actions she would take in
> response to the information which he fed her. She did not question
> his reports; she did not inquire how these issues...had been raised.
> When her code had been violated she did not pause to make inqui-
> ries; she sought revenge...he could do this only because he knew his
> mother would not *look* at the situation, but would *blindly* defend her
> moral magic. [Bartley's emphases]

The story was repeated in the Erhard biography (1978: 188–189):
Christopher was using family members to commit the crimes he would
have liked to have committed and then 'called on his mother to bring
down God's wrath on the criminal...a puppet using a puppet'. The
adopted position of animosity and manipulation cut off 'experience
and growth'. The resulting shyness 'cut off normal participation in the
classroom' and a 'childish form of faith' was carried into adulthood.

There are three reasons for thinking that Christopher was Bartley.
First, according to the *New York Times* obituary, Bartley had three
siblings ('a brother, Arthur, of Manhattan, and two sisters, Faith, of
Pittsburgh, and Marian [*sic*], of Houston') and was survived by his 'wife,
Elvina'. (Two days later this was corrected: Elvina was 'his mother not
his wife'.[17])

Marion Elvina Bartley was born on 16 September 1937 and died on
3 April 2003.[18] Since William was born in October 1934, his sister Marion
('Mary') would have been five when he was eight. For what it's worth,
having been punished for agreeing to say something she didn't wish to say,
Bartley, possibly in jest, informed Charlotte Cubitt (2006: 122, 265) that he
ended up with a 'disagreeable sister whom he suspected of having links to
the CIA' or the FBI: an allegation 'he repeated...a number of times'.[19]

Secondly, Bartley apparently experienced 'a severe neurosis' about his
'religious doubts' whilst at Harvard. Cubitt (2006: 265) recalled that
Bartley

> did not speak of his mother at all either then or in the future, but
> revealed that the only time he considered killing himself was when
> he was in his last term at university where he had been overworked

as well as having personal problems with people being 'nasty' to him.

Thirdly, what about hate 'for all things feminine'? Bartley informed his later-to-be obituary writer

quite seriously – that he could leave his job as a philosopher if he were offered a job as director of a museum of Chinese art' (Petroni, 1990: 740).

Bartley (1985: 196, n70; 1982: 196) objected to the perceived association between his own preferences and so-called feminine traits:

American children have for years been schooled on the Minnesota Multiphasic Personality Inventory Test, which assigns one a high 'femininity quotient' if one prefers going to the museum or reading a book to playing football or selling brushes door to door. In the circumstances it is hardly surprising that many American professors in the arts live with the not quite irradicable fear that they may be not simply homosexual but downright *queer*. [Bartley's emphasis]

Bartley had 'an aristocratic impatience with compromise' (Petroni, 1990). Democracy has typically advanced through a series of conflicts and compromises. Bartley (23 June 1986) wrote to Rafe Champion that

As to my faith in democracy, I am steeped in 'public choice' literature and the history of the last century. If we could take back the vote from the unpropertied and the women...then maybe it would work [Bartley's "..."]. But would it then be democracy? And why am I asking a question about a word? And who the hell cares? I don't know anything better than democracy but I have no faith in it. Hope perhaps, faith or love, no...you need to have faith in democracy if you are stupid. It makes you feel better.

The break with Christianity

According to Hayek's secretary, Bartley described himself as a 'typical white American' of mixed Irish and German extraction (Cubitt, 2006: 119). He was born on 2 October 1934, in Wilkinsburg, Pennsylvania, which was once known as 'The Holy City' and continues to have a high concentration of churches.[20] On 28 February 1681, Charles II granted a land charter to William Penn in settlement of a debt owed to his father.[21] The new colony attracted religious dissenters, including the 'Pennsylvanian Dutch' (largely of German descent). Its major city, Philadelphia, is a Greek term for 'The City of Brotherly Love'.[22]

According to the city's website, in the inter-war period Wilkinsburg became

> one of Pittsburgh's most outstanding suburbs. Residents were upwardly mobile, and the schools were very good. By 1937, about 85 percent of households had telephones, 95 percent had radios, and 55 percent had automobiles.

Major changes followed: in the post-war period

> the population of Pittsburgh shrank more than 50%... Beginning in the 1970s and 1980s, the steel industry in the region imploded, with massive layoffs and mill closures... The diminished population and depleted tax base of the past several decades brought economic hardships [and] social ills for the borough.

The scholastic performance of Bartley's *alma mater* deteriorated as the socio-economic status of the catchment area fell.[23]

Bartley was an outstanding student: in 1952, he was the Valedictorian at Wilkinsburg High School and the last recipient of the Parshad Scholarship Award (an award sponsored by the United Christian Youth Movement and administered through the National Council of Churches of Christ).[24] He continued to shine academically: A. B. (magna cum lauda) in Philosophy (1956, Harvard College) A. M. in Philosophy (1958, Harvard University) and PhD (1961, the London School of Economics).

Bartley (1978, back page) paid his way through Harvard by working for the night City staff of the *Boston Globe*.[25] He began reporting for the *Harvard Crimson* in early 1953; the *Crimson* (15 December 1954) reported that he had been elected Editorial Chairman[26] and later (10 June 1958) that been awarded 'Income from the Francis Bowen Fund' for his essay 'On Deciding: A Discussion of Some Recent Philosophy of Religion'.[27]

Some of his *Crimson* stories had local significance, such as 'College Replaces Maids Sooner Than Expected At Least Two More Houses Will Be Assigned "Dormitory Crewmen" by Next September' (1 October 1954). [28] In 'Line Tappers Make Calls, Others Get Bills' (25 March 1954) he reported that a spokesperson for the telephone company blamed the university: 'It's not the phone company's fault we can't trace these people', she said. 'It's the fault of the professors. They ought to teach you boys more morals'. [29] Some stories had a wider significance. In 'Harvard Club in Capital To Debate Segregation Younger Members Try For Negro Admission' he noted that 'The move in the Washington Club apparently has stemmed indirectly from the recent Supreme Court measure on segregation in the schools'.[30]

Several stories involved religion. On 9 November 1953, he reported that

> In his first public statement on the place of religion within the college, President Pusey last night said that 'living and practicing religion must supplement the mere studying and reading about it'...Pusey blamed a large part of religious confusion among college students on poor religious background in the home. 'Most students come from backgrounds where religion has no significance as a major part of life. They don't lose religion in college; they have not been well grounded in it to start with, being neither psychologically nor intellectually prepared'.[31]

In 'Religion at Harvard: To Teach or Preach? Renaissance in Pusey Era Produces New Slant on Old College Problem' (17 April 1954), he noted that

> there was and is a 'religious revival' in the nation – brought about, in part, by the appeal of the church in the anxiety of the present world and in part by the increased effort of the churches to appeal to more people in more ways.

Bartley continued:

> But the students of the seventh century and of the 200 years which followed were much like the Harvardmen of today in their dislike of and revolt against petty regulations. As a result the history of religion here during these two centuries is largely a history of revolt. The rise of modern science, with the new knowledge of biology, philosophy, human nature, and the cosmos – although not itself in direct conflict with Religion – had certain implicit assumptions in conflict with the Christian world-view. This resulted in a lack of dynamism in the churches themselves and consequently a lack of emphasis at Harvard as elsewhere. There has been during the past year a wave of organization of new religious groups. The DcMaloy Club, a junior

organization of the Masons, while not specifically religious, has very strong underlying religious principles. It was approved by the Student Council in January. A group which call themselves 'The Saintly Sinners' have organized to 'meet occasionally in Cronin's and talk about religion'. The Harvard Episcopal Society, representing the largest single religious group in the student body was organized last spring to gain for the Episcopal groups the advantages of official University recognition. [32]

According to Leonard and Mark Silk (1980: 11, 27, 42–48), Bartley played a pivotal role in assaulting – and changing – aspects of the *American Establishment*. The origins of the *American Establishment* can be traced back to the Unitarian church in Massachusetts; in 1636 Harvard College was established as an accessory to the 'Puritan religious establishment'. Bartley (28 March 1958) wrote a *Crimson* criticism of the type of 1950s American religious revival that had entered Harvard: a 'button-down' version that was denying Jews the right to be married in Harvard's Memorial Church. *Time* (14 April 1958) reported on the conflict in 'Religion: The Button-Down Hair Shirt'. The *New Republic* printed an edited version of Bartley's essay. In April 1958 a delegation led by J. K. Galbraith and Arthur Schlesinger Jr. protested to the University President, Nathan Pusey, about Harvard's new religiosity. Pusey was a practising Episcopalian; in 1958 Bartley was a second-year graduate student in the Philosophy department and a candidate for the Episcopalian ministry.

According to the Bartley Institute website, in 1958 he 'abandoned both Protestantism and Harvard to study with Karl Popper in London'. Parts of his PhD *Limits of Rationality: A Critical Study of Some Logical Problems of Contemporary Pragmatism and Related Movements* were published as *The Retreat to Commitment* (1962). In his *Encounter* evaluation of Karl Barth, Bartley (1970: 1) proclaimed himself to be 'an atheist and no member of any religious sect'. He also declared that Barth was 'the last great Protestant ... Bankrupt spiritually, the Protestant churches – except in some parts of provincial American suburbia – tend to be physically empty'.

Insomnia and the break with Popper and Lakatos

On 18 September 1958, Popper received a letter from the LSE administration stating that Bartley had arrived, was registered as a Fulbright scholar (under Popper's supervision) and required a first interview.[33]

According to Bartley (1982: 250) attempts were made to replace Popper with 'Professor X', which resulted in the threat to 'return to America on the morrow'.

At Harvard, Bartley had studied under Willard Van Orman Quine (1908–2000). The Duhem–Quine thesis suggests that a collection of theories can be tested but that it is impossible to isolate a single hypothesis in the collection. A single theory cannot therefore be conclusively falsified on empirical grounds. Popper was no doubt delighted to have attracted a defector from a rival school.

By joining Popper's circle, Bartley (1990: 163) regained 'an earlier sense of community and high purpose'. Cubitt (2006: 171) noted that at times Bartley behaved like a 'devoted son' towards Hayek; most of the time, Bartley appeared to have a similar attitude towards Popper. Bartley (9 October 1964) reported to Popper that he doubted that he would ever duplicate the 'quality of my experience in London from 1958–1963'.[34]

Was Bartley seeking to replace the Christian religion of his childhood ('Our Father')? Bartley told Cubitt (2006: 265) that his father was an alcoholic; in contrast, Popper 'neither smoked nor drank' (Bartley, 1990: 163). At age 60, Popper 'used to *run* up the escalators' [Bartley's emphasis]; at age 84 he took up gliding. This led Bartley (7 December 1985) to complain to Popper that his biography would be '*much too interesting*... [readers] will say I made the whole thing up – just as some people still say I made up my Wittgenstein'. [Bartley's emphasis] Bartley described how Christopher's father 'stalked off' to take refuge in alcohol after receiving a verbal spanking from his wife; in contrast, Popper was famous for administered the spankings (mostly verbal, sometimes physical).[35]

In spring 1963, Bartley (1978: xiii–xiv) began to take sleeping pills and tranquillisers to remedy insomnia. He later found that Freudian and Jungian analysis could not cure the insomnia: he was 'desperate' to be free from drug-induced '*pretence*... the theme of my life had become the concealment of my stupor – the appearance, not the reality of alertness'. [Bartley's emphasis] He was hospitalized, reporting to Popper (9 July 1963) that he had been unable to work for two months.[36]

In September 1963, Bartley temporarily left his lecturing position at the Warburg Institute, London, for a one year Visiting Associate Professorship at the University of California at Berkeley where the 'Free Speech Movement' was about to erupt (Cohen and Zelnik, 2002). Bartley reported to Ernst Gombrich, the Warburg Director that he had never been east of Chicago. Bartley (10 September 1963; 7 October 1963) told Lakatos that California was 'astonishingly beautiful... paradise... I am enjoying myself enormously'. He persuaded Lakatos to join him in California.

Bartley sometimes displayed a lack of discretion and tact. Before leaving for Berkeley, he failed to return some Warburg library books (or book) which resulted in a confrontation. Gombrich (8 October 1963) wrote to Bartley about his 'outburst' and censured him for using Warburg funds for personal postage: this was not 'censorship' but

> a bit of a moral problem. All this, as you know, is taxpayers' money... Historically, by the way, you are pretty wrong too, if you identify the Institute with German authoritarian traditions... I don't want to become too personal (to which I have no right), but I think I must suggest to you the possibility, at least, that your rages against restrictiveness are really projections and have very little to do with the objective situation.

Bartley (11 October 1963) replied:

> Why is it that Bartley did not (apparently) project at Harvard and at the London School of Economics, and does not project at Berkeley. Why do Bartley's aggressions and paranoia come out only at the Warburg?

Bartley met a Berkeley graduate (1955) Stephen Kresge (born 1935) 'of the American family of that name' as he later put it (Cubitt, 2006: 330). Kresge became Bartley's life partner and (with Popper's help) inherited the intellectual property rights over Hayek's correspondence and *Collected Works*. Bartley (5 December 1977) informed Popper that he had been 'committed, over the past fourteen years, to living in the Bay Area. Over seven years ago, as the only way to express that commitment, I accepted my present Professorship' at CSUH (now CSU East Bay).[37]

Bartley (14 January 1986) informed Cubitt that after a year at Berkeley he consulted the I Ching and cast a hexagram which recommended that he accept a job offer from the University of California San Diego (then known as UC La Jolla). The UCSD philosophy department was founded in July 1963; in 1964, Bartley (at the rank of Associate Professor) was in the second round of hires.[38]

Popper (23 March 1961) assisted Bartley to obtain jobs at the LSE,[39] Warburg and Gonville and Caius College.[40] Bartley (19 February 1964) informed Popper that he was dismayed by the possibility that on his return to England, his LSE contract might not be renewed: he sent a copy of the letter to Lakatos asking 'What the hell is going on?'[41]

Bartley (1964) was regarded as Popper's favourite student; for Popper's 60th birthday Festschrift, he was given the honour of writing the lead chapter.[42] The following year, Bartley's relationship with Popper and Lakatos turned into a 'bitter rift' beginning at the July 1965 International Colloquium in the Philosophy of Science (Petroni, 1990; see also Gattei, 2002; 2008). Bartley (3 June 1965) wrote to Popper's wife, Hennie, about his conference paper: 'Alas, I am afraid Karl won't like it. We shall see. La Jolla isn't the same without Imre'.[43] Bartley (16 July 1965) then presented a paper in which he intended to 'criticize, as vigorously, as I can Karl Popper's theory of demarcation between science and non-science'.

Scholars produce knowledge; incentives reward those who produce influential knowledge. The 1965 Colloquium appeared to elevate the work of two of Bartley's colleagues (and competitors), Thomas Kuhn and Lakatos. Kuhn (1962; 1970) noted that scholars inhabited paradigm-based communities; Lakatos (1970) suggested that members of a 'scientific research program' would attempt to shield their theoretical core from falsification behind a protective belt of auxiliary hypotheses (a combination of Popperian falsification with the Duhem–Quine thesis: the existence of auxiliary assumptions or auxiliary hypotheses prevent a decisive empirical test of an individual hypothesis). In contrast, Bartley's Colloquium essay appeared to project him onto a different professional trajectory: a classic example of how *not* to launch a paradigm.[44]

Bartley's paper on 'Theories of Demarcation and the History of the Philosophy of Science' was eventually published as 'Theories of Demarcation Between Science and Metaphysics' (1968a) with commentaries by Popper plus three prominent philosophers (with a rejoinder from Bartley). It is intensely analytical – as was *Retreat to Commitment* (1962). Yet Popper (1968: 89) was perhaps understandably offended by Bartley (his protégé) having bitten the hand that fed him: this

criticism came as a shock to me … I was entirely unprepared for this lecture and the criticisms it contains. For I can only describe it as the least valuable kind of criticism – one that misunderstands, misinterprets and even misrepresents the theory it criticizes.

Popper (1968: 101) found Bartley's 'change of mind' between April 1965 and July 1965 'inexplicable'. Bartley (1968b: 114, 115) suspected that the response by Popper and Musgrave to his paper indicated the existence of a 'territorial dispute' which 'bores me'. He also had the 'horrible suspicion that I shall remember Sir Karl Popper's dispute with me'.

Bartley's (1968a: 61–62, 64) re-evaluation amounted to devaluation: 'When, then, it might be asked has Popper done?' Two items were listed: 'Popper destroyed the evaluation of the early logical positivists' and presented 'an excellent resolution of one form of the problem of induction'. His discussion of demarcation was, however, 'obsolete'. The paper ended on a personal note:

> I suggest to Popper that the problem lies not in the demarcation between the scientific and non-scientific but in the demarcation of the rational from the irrational, the critical from the uncritical.

Popper (20 July 1965) informed Bartley that his paper was

> a personal attack on me ... it was not a criticism of my philosophy but an attempt to present me as a dogmatist who cannot be criticized, only attacked. Moreover, it was intellectually on a low level: you said you did not want to present a historical sketch of my development; yet you did, precisely, this; and you did it without respect for the facts – the historical facts ... a complete distortion of the historical facts.[45]

Bartley (1968a: 50, 48) suggested that Popper was

> clearly more positivistic and anti-metaphysical than he is today ... Popper has failed to state explicitly how and why his ideas have changed ... it would be interesting to study the development of Popper's thought from the 1930s to the present.

Popper (20 July 1965) stated that this characterization was "ridiculous'. He accused Bartley of claiming as his 'own discovery ... some criticisms made myself of myself' and provided as evidence some seminar notes: 'Alan [Musgrave] thinks you were present at that seminar'.[46]

Musgrave (1968: 87) detected a 'persistent pattern of 'criticism' in Bartley's paper' which consisted of a strategy: 'use some of Popper's views (without mentioning they are Popper's) to try and criticize some view, or more often alleged view of Popper's'. Bartley (1968a: n50) suggested that Popper was guilty of omitting 'a crucial passage' of a letter – which Musgrave interpreted as an accusation that Popper 'is not to be trusted'. Musgrave asked:

> why does Bartley refer us to *only* to the original version of [Popper's] paper, now out of print, and not also to the revised more accessible version in *Conjectures and Refutations* as he does is *all* similar cases? [Musgrave's emphases]

However, Popper tried to heal the rift: he told Bartley that

> I want to be friends with you, Bill, but not at the expense of not telling you the truth. I do not want to hurt you: I am deeply worried about you, and it is quite clear to me that you do damage to yourself... And now, let me (or us) forget the whole incident, and let us be friends – or if you prefer, part as friends. [Popper's emphasis][47]

Bartley (1 August 1965) – still signing the letter 'Love, Bill' – informed Popper that he would reply shortly from Munich. The following letter – signed 'Yours sincerely' – accepted Popper's offer that 'we part'. Bartley added that he had 'made a long and careful memorandum on [Popper's] letter, and have placed it with my papers'.[48] Bartley (15 December 1965) sent Popper a registered mail suggesting that his inability to obtain the tape of the discussion following his lecture could be interpreted as suppression: 'one implication is that you are attempting to hide something'.[49]

Popper (29 December 1965) asked:

> What has happened to you?...I felt that this letter was not written by you... I cannot recall ever having received one like it before... I am very much hurt by your letters...you *must* know that I have never kept any thoughts from you. Your suddenly changed attitude to me is still incomprehensible to me...if you really have taught yourself to mistrust me, then I am terribly sorry for you. For how will you be able to trust anyone? [Popper's emphasis]

Popper's wife Hennie (4 March 1966) subsequently informed Bartley that only 'friendly' letters would be shown to her husband – his latest letter had not been read.[50]

The matter escalated into a formal investigation by the British Society for the Philosophy of Science whose 'Report' Bartley (13 December 1966) characterized as *HOW TO FALSIFY THE RECORD – AND MAKE IT*

SCIENTIFIC.[51] The Report was co-signed by Richard Bevan Braithwaite – Lakatos' PhD supervisor (Larvor, 1998: 6) – who later played a role in the Hayek biography (section 8, below).

Bartley's focus shifted towards Wittgenstein: in 1968 he asked Popper for comments on his paper on 'Theories of Language and Philosophy of Science as Instruments of Educational Reform: Wittgenstein and Popper as Austrian Schoolteachers'. There are numerous drafts of insulting replies – which Popper may not eventually have sent.[52]

Bartley (1982: 256) recalled that 'Popper is a difficult man...we did not speak for twelve years'. Popper recalled that unexpectedly Bartley asked whether he was 'ready to receive him. I said 'of course, I am very happy' or something like this. And so he came...'[53] The reunion appears to have involved an exchange of letters in 1975.[54] Popper (11 October 1978) explained to Bartley that he wanted to resume their friendship but 'could not do anything towards it, believing you thought I was a liar (and perhaps a plagiarist)'. Popper was 'deeply sorry to have contributed to your unhappiness'. Bartley (23 October 1978) replied:

> *of course* I never thought *you* a liar or a plagiarist. What I did think – and we can discuss it sometime – is that my work on theory of rationality was never properly acknowledged *by anyone*. And at the time that annoyed me very much. [Bartley's emphases][55]

Bartley (11 May 1980) explained to Popper that

> I still feel a little inhibited in touching on those old incidents of 1965. I think there are still some other matters that you may not know about in connection with that old discussion, and I promise to fill you in – so that you will know the 'logic of the situation' as it were – when we next meet.[56]

According to the Bartley Institute website, Lakatos was the culprit:

> Also to arrive as a visiting professor at UCSD was Imre Lakatos, whose mischief-making caused a rift between Bartley and Popper.

According to the archival evidence, Lakatos viewed 'history as an apocalyptic struggle between angels and devils'; according to Brendon Larvor (1998: 7) he sometimes told his friends and colleagues that their views were so dangerous that they 'ought to be shot'. Bartley (19 November 1965) informed Lakatos that

I suppose, as a result of your activities during the past several years the history of the Popper school will be written as a series of heresies, schisms, and excommunications. Fortunately, we are not living in your Hungary; you cannot have me shot.[57]

In his Open Letter, Bartley (26 February 1966) also stated that it was 'impossible for me in integrity to consider being associated with Dr Imre Lakatos in any publication venture'.[58] They didn't speak again (Bartley, 1976: 37); although shortly before Lakatos' death (2 February 1974) – as controversy over *Wittgenstein* (1973) was about to erupt – Bartley (24 July 1973) wrote with an apparently conciliatory gesture (asking for a bibliography of Lakatos' publications).

Bartley's relationship with Lakatos had initially been close, but complicated: letters to him (like those to Popper) were usually signed 'Love, Bill'. Bartley (27 January 1964) playfully told Lakatos that

I hate you as much as ever ... I hate you only *intellectually* because of all your false, wicked and absolutely corrupting ideas. Nonetheless, as Karl has taught us, one false idea can have much greater truth content than another; and I believe your crazy ideas to have more truth content than their rivals. *Personally*, of course, I adore you as usual. [Bartley's emphases][59]

Bartley (2 November 1963) informed Lakatos that

I am now convinced that all my friends are Communist spies – probably Karl too. And I am the only one not so far recruited into the ranks of the elect?[60]

Also (presumably playfully) Bartley (2 June 1965) forwarded a note to Lakatos headed with a swastika:

ACHTUNG! The Martin Heidegger Post #333 of the American Nazi Party is hereby making it known that Imre Lakatos is going to receive some visitors one dark night very soon. Pass the word.

Bartley stated that that he had found the note in a book adding 'This is not a joke. Love Bill' [Bartley's emphasis].[61]

As the International Colloquium approached, Bartley (20 June 1965) addressed Lakatos as 'Dear Unfriend ... unlove to all Hungarians'. Lakatos scribbled all over Bartley's letter: 'slander against my financial reliability ... defamation of the conference ... slander against my personal behaviour ... effort to fire me ... suicidal tendencies'.[62] Lakatos (11 May 1966) explained to John Watkins that almost everybody believed that Bartley suffered from 'persecution mania'.[63]

Popper (29 December 1965) referred to this 'unsavoury quarrel' including Bartley's accusation that Lakatos had been 'spreading vicious and damaging rumours about you'.[64] Bartley (10 September 1965; 19 November 1965) informed Lakatos that 'I do not regard your criminal slander of me as a joke and shall take all steps to protect myself'.[65] After Bartley was informed that 'you had been denouncing me as a vicious homosexual, I realized I could have nothing further to do with you'.[66]

The rift became a vendetta. In 1969, Lakatos wrote to Paul Feyerabend about a clientele for anti-Lakatos letters: 'I am sure Bill Bartley will give you his address list'. In a 'STRICTLY PRIVATE AND CONFIDENTIAL' letter, Lakatos informed Feyerabend that he had just given a lecture on George Joachim Rheticus, sixteenth scentury astronomer who was obliged to flee Leipzig after allegations of a homosexual encounter with one of his students, and that he had compared Rheticus 'with Bartley, a homosexual' (Lakatos and Feyerabend, 1999: 174, 290).[67]

Lakatos apparently left instructions that Bartley was to be denied access to his archives. Thanks to Popper, the lack of access was addressed by the LSE Director:

> Please give Bill Bartley my love ... and tell him that [Ralf] Dahrendorf will try to give him access to the LSE library, to the Lakatos letters and MSS! He was surprised that Bill had no access to these papers (Popper to Hayek 11 February 1984).[68]

Bartley was not the first complicated academic. Philosophers (or at least those in the Popper circle) appear to be oversensitive and – to put it mildly – undiplomatic. Bartley (13 October 1961), for example, wrote to Josef Agassi to tell him that he could 'go to hell' – and sent Popper a copy. Bartley (9 July 1963) then told Popper that Agassi was staying in his London flat: 'one feels more alive when he is here'.[69] The following year, Agassi asked Popper for criticism, and when it was received he replied to Popper with a 'farewell letter'.[70] Bartley (17 December 1982) later commented 'I have often over the years thought that you were unfair to Agassi. I now see that I was a naive fool, and I apologize for my incorrect judgement'.[71]

These tensions led Bartley to 'put my lawyers onto' various people including former friends such as Agassi[72] and Lakatos. He also considered suing his current employer, CSUH, to prevent the proposed Proposition 9 tax-payer-revolt budget cuts impacting on him.[73]

This oversensitivity appears to have been partly caused by professional rivalry: Bartley (1976) stated that Lakatos had named his 'acclaimed' notion of the 'scientific research programme' by taking Popper's 'metaphysical research programme' and substituting the word 'scientific' in order to remove a 'public relations obstacle'. Lakatos's 'rational reconstructions' of the history of science – his theory of history – grossly pervert history'. Lakatos developed the 'methodology of scientific research programs' as a generalization of Popper. Bartley believed himself to be the appropriate wearer of the generalization crown. As he explained to Rafe Champion (24 May 1986):

I do think that my old work on rationality revolutionizes epistemology and theory of rationality and does generalize Popper's work in an exceptionally important way. I'd love more recognition for that, and I'd like it if my work eventually had some more impact and made the areas it touches more interesting.

As Bartley was dying, he sought to complete *Unfathomed Knowledge, Unmeasured Wealth: On Universities and the Wealth of Nations* (1990); Stephen Kresge's Preface was dated a few days after his death. Beyond the grave – so to speak – Bartley was still reflecting about his relative lack of influence: Chapter 6 was entitled 'An End Run: Why Do Professors Like Kuhn So Much? Or – Why is Kuhn a Sociologist of Knowledge and not an Economist of Knowledge?'

Charismatic biography: Wittgenstein

Some aspects of Bartley's career are difficult to unravel: the UCSD episode (1964–1966) may require access to intelligence files; most of his employment files at Gonville and Caius College, Cambridge (1966–1967), the University of Pittsburgh (1967–1973) and CSUH (1970–1990) have apparently been destroyed.[74]

Herbert Marcuse, the author of *Eros and Civilization: a philosophical inquiry into Freud* (1966) and *One Dimensional Man* (1964) was the first UCSD Philosophy Department non-foundation hire. In its first two years, the Department sponsored 'a campus-wide symposium on Marxism'. In July 1967, Marcuse told students in Berlin that 'We have to develop the political implications of the moral, intellectual and sexual rebellion of the youth'. This brought the unwanted attention of the Ku

Klux Klan, who threatened to kill him: 'You are a very dirty communist dog. You have 72 hours to live [*sic*] the United States. 72 hours and then we will kill you Marcuse'.[75]

According to the chronology on the Bartley Institute website

> So began Bartley's time of troubles. He became involved with Erica Sherover (later to be Mrs. Herbert Marcuse) who came to study with Marcuse at La Jolla. This connection brought the unwanted attention of government security agencies. Every hero must spend a sojourn in the wilderness, conquering demons. The wilderness turned out to be his home town, Pittsburgh, where Bartley accepted a professorship in the philosophy department at the University of Pittsburgh (1967–1973).

He was recruited to Pittsburgh by Adolf Grünbaum (one of Popper's critics) as an Associate Professor and was promoted to Full Professor in 1969. At the time, the Pittsburgh Philosophy Department was highly ranked and rising. His return to Pittsburgh may have also been associated with what he believed to be his mother's fragile health following his father's death in 1967 (she outlived her husband by over 45 years).

It also appears that in 1969 he decided to return to California for life-style reasons. He was appointed as a Full Professor at CSUH in fall of 1970 and was awarded tenure in July 1972. This represented a considerable loss of academic status. However, Bartley remained employed by Pittsburgh for three years.

Four years after the 1969 Stonewall riots in Christopher Street, Bartley was obliged to resign from the University of Pittsburgh: he informed his friends and colleagues that he had been sacked when they discovered he was homosexual (an illegal activity in Pennsylvania at that time).[76]

1969 appears to have been a decisive year in Bartley's life in other ways. The autobiographical account of Christopher first appeared in *Morality and Religion* (Preface dated Christmas 1969). In 1969, Bartley began researching the 'lost' years of Wittgenstein's life. Bartley (21 March 1964) had previously believed that Walter Kaufmann's review of his *Retreat to Commitment* amounted to a charge of plagiarism.[77] Kaufmann (1985 [1973]: 9) subsequently commissioned Bartley to write the Wittgenstein biography.[78] This led to his involvement with the International Conference on the Unity of the Sciences (ICUS) network, funded by the Moonies. Bartley (4 September 1983) informed Hayek that Kaufmann recruited him to join the ICUS network in 1977 (Bartley joined the ICUS Advisory Board in 1979).

Bartley (1985: 17) referred to the 1918–1929 period as Wittgenstein's 'dark decade'. The second edition of Bartley's (1985: 12) *Wittgenstein* referred to a larger planned volume on Wittgenstein in addition to the biographies of Popper and Hayek. All three were born '1889–1902' and were 'centrally – and very differently – concerned with fundamental questions of the scope and limitations of rationality'. The book was dedicated to the memory of one of their contemporaries: Bartley's father (1895–1967).

As a village school teacher, Wittgenstein's use of corporal punishment became the 'talk of the town'. He caned the boys (and apparently at least one girl also) and would 'box their ears', and he 'slapped their cheeks for minor offenses'. Wittgenstein apparently always punished dishonesty: 'one way to avoid punishment was to confess honestly'. In 1926, Wittgenstein was formally charged with sadistic punishment – which ended his career as a school teacher. This encounter with corporal punishment resulted in a 'deep transition in his life' and he considered becoming a monk (Bartley, 1985: 107–112, 116).

In 1969, Bartley (1985: 18–20) went to a part of Austria where 'the peasants are sometimes suspicious and taciturn'. His first two encounters – apparently accidental – uncovered a talkative 'old peasant woman' who had known Wittgenstein, the 'teacher', in 1926; plus a grocery store owner who had been one of Wittgenstein's students (1920–1922) and with whom Wittgenstein later lodged. Bartley had stopped to buy bananas; almost half a century earlier Wittgenstein had provided this student (the future store owner) with his first banana.

Bartley made some sensational claims about the details of Wittgenstein's homosexuality. His anonymous sources became the subject of controversy. Bartley (1985: 22, 23, 201) frequented 'homosexual bars in Vienna and London in search of those who knew Wittgenstein in another way; and I was successful in that search'. Bartley's walked 'alone and rather apprehensively through the Prater late at night' and chatted about Wittgenstein with

> some aging homosexual in his own special pub…any reader of the first chapter will understand without further ado why a few persons (to whom I am deeply indebted) asked that their names not be revealed.

These informants 'for reasons of their own do not wish to be mentioned'.

Bartley (1969: 22) noted that Wittgenstein's career as a school reformer came to an end after complaints about his 'rough disciplining of certain students'. Bartley (1985: 26, 25, 29, 40) concluded that Wittgenstein 'was tormented by intense guilt and suffering over his sexual desires and activities'. He sought 'the company of tough boys in London pubs...rough blunt homosexual youths'. Chapter 1 ('The Magic Carpet') begins where Christopher's trauma began: with Wittgenstein asleep (and dreaming of a prayer rug which looked like 'an erect penis'). In his second dream Wittgenstein 'was a priest'.

Bartley (1985: 193) dismissed his critics:

> This entire attack on my book, and on my own bona fides, has been based on bluff, on projection and on plain naïveté...The documents confirming Wittgenstein's homosexuality – his own coded diaries – have been in the possession of the Wittgenstein literary estate all along.

Bartley refused to reveal his sources to Ray Monk (1990; 584), the author of *Ludwig Wittgenstein: The Duty of Genius* on the grounds that it would be dishonourable. His first biography appeared to further alienate him from the philosophy community.

Charismatic biography: Erhard

His second biography – *Werner Erhard: the transformation of a man, the founding of est* (1978) – compounded the alienation. In March 1972, Bartley (1978: xiii) was referred to *est* (Erhard Seminars Training) by a physician as an alternative to another decade (and more) of sleeping pills. The *est* (quasi-religious?) experience temporarily cured his insomnia ('I no longer take pills of any kind') and led to him being commissioned to write the biography which rapidly jumped to 8th on the *TIME* magazine list of non-fiction best-sellers.[79]

Erhard did not attend university;[80] but later breached what Bartley (1978: 94) described as the 'split in American intellectual life between the ideology and the university and the ideology of the American market place'. Erhard organized and led Harvard seminars and training sessions in association with Michael Jensen, Professor of Business Administration Emeritus at Harvard Business School who co-founded the *Journal of Financial Economics* and was the recipient of the 2009 Morgan Stanley-American Finance Association Award for Excellence in Financial Economics.

There were distinct similarities between Bartley (1978: xvi, 4, 5, 31, 60, 25, 115, 116) and Erhard: almost the same age, they had both spent their childhoods in Pennsylvania. Both carried heavy parental burdens: 'III' for Bartley; the name 'Jack Rosenberg' after his dead uncle for Erhard. Erhard needed *'a winning self-image'*; Bartley cultivated a Harvard-style aristocratic image. Both were 'hard driven'.

Both had Episcopalian mothers. Erhard believed that he had become his mother: 'How can someone who is Dorothy escape from Dorothy?' Christopher experienced 'hate for his mother – and perhaps for all things feminine'. Both attended Episcopalian churches and had highly religious childhoods; both had spent their childhoods in towns with names heavy with religious significance: Plymouth Meeting for Erhard; Wilkinsburg ('The Holy City') for Bartley. Both had experienced parental violence as a result of over-sleeping. Both were 'TWICE BORN' – first as 'homo religious' and then as 'homo philosophicus'.

Erhard (1978: xii) provided a Foreword:

I truly did need to be educated. And God did take me and educate me – unconventionally and *very* privately: for a long time no one including myself knew that anything was happening. This is what did happen. [Erhard's emphasis]

Bartley (1978: xx) observed that 'American Will and *Oriental* Intellect' had fused:

Erhard is the very embodiment of American Will. Intrusive and aggressively enterprising...a liar, an impostor, and a wife-deserter [Bartley's emphasis].

Bartley (1978: xx, 145, 156) provided some insightful comments about the origins of religions: unknown quantities are 'mysteries. Where there is mystery there is fantasy; and where there is fantasy there is belief'. Hence the struggle between 'competing beliefs'. Erhard provided a 'universal story of the search for true identity and for Self'. In his search for a new religion – or healing experience – Erhard provided a 'respectful hearing to sentimentalists, wizards, cranks, quacks, and impostors – for it is hard to draw the line'. In turn, Bartley sympathetically examined L. Ron Hubbard's ideas despite the fact that the founder of Scientology had 'made exaggerated claims about his past and his scientific qualifications'.

New religions and groups were part of the 'counter-culture' of the period: for example, the *New York Review of Books* (19 April 1979) contained a discussion of four books on the Jim Jones People's Temple, the Bay Area cult that resulted in mass suicide in Guyana. It was inevitable that *est* would be labelled by critics as a dangerous cult (e.g. Pressman, 1993). The *New York Review of Books* (5 April 1979) contained a review of Bartley's book, 'Est is Est' by Jonathon Lieberson, which was followed by an angry exchange of letters (31 May 1979).

In defence of his book, Bartley explained that he had asked himself

Was I the victim of mass hypnosis? Did this man's power lie in my own naïveté?...Is this fraud?...Was he a charlatan?...What a combination! Can any of it be taken seriously?

He concluded that *est* was a

rampant restless sea of metaphor...I think that *est* theory, even at its weakest, is provocative, useful, wise, even deep...My account of Werner Erhard is favourable.

In contrast, Lieberson referred to *est* as an 'abusive and upsetting training together with a handful of sterile generalities about Perfection and the Self'.

Lieberson added that

it seems that Bartley leaves behind his philosophical equipment when addressing problems that challenge the very coherence or worth of *est*. I found this uncritical and disturbing...I would suggest that if blowing our minds is not to be a worthless spasm, it seems advisable to have a good and specific reason for doing it and at least a thumbnail sketch of how intelligent reconstruction is to proceed.

He speculated that Bartley had 'fallen' for *est* because of the 'malicious' influence of his teacher, Popper. Bartley regarded this accusation as 'outrageous and irresponsible.[81]

Other personal experiences led to further offers to write charismatic biographies. Bartley (13 December 1985) informed Rafe Champion that

I knew Feldenkreis and Rolf, and have been Rolfed at least a hundred times. Although I suspect that it contributed to an abdominal hernia that was brought on six months ago as I worked at my rowing machine, I have nothing but good to say about it. And my Rolfer tried various Feldnenkreis techniques on me too, leading me to think I had been Feldencreased. Ida Rolf rang me up the week she died to ask me to do her biography, but I did not have the time – nor did she.

Charismatic biography: Popper

Bartley wrote hundreds of pages on 1919 alone but finished only one chapter of his Popper biography. In a section on 'An event invested with significance', Bartley (1989: 49, 50, 64, 67) suggested that the young Popper's brief flirtation with communism and his observation of bloodshed in an attempted coup in 1919 took on a 'grand, symbolic and even mythic character' despite the fact that Popper's recollections were 'understated and misleading'. These were the 'seedbed of a number of problems and contradictions that Popper was not fully to work through for decades'. In 1919 Popper was in a 'tangle' which came into play in his rejection of Marxism and in his momentary acceptance of irrationality ... Karl just turned seventeen, appears to have been confused'.

Bartley (1989: 14–15, n23) cited Popper as stating that 'the inner circle of Schonberg's group was 'like a communist cell' full of conspiracy' and added:

> This raises an important historical question for which I have been able to find no answer. Just who was putting pressure on Schonberg to adopt the views he did ... ?

Bartley (1989: 62, n106) endowed Popper with foresight powers with respect to divining spies:

> Popper was invited several times by Carew-Hunt [the author of the *Theory and Practice of Communism* (1950)] to give talks on communism at British foreign service staff weekends near Oxford. On the last of these occasions, when there was extensive discussion with the audience, Popper identified the 'moles' Burgess and MacLean as communists (by their manner of argumentation) and reported to Carew-Hunt, that 'those two men sitting at the window are communists'. They had not said much, but their terminology, he said, 'was so well known to me from those old days in 1919'. Some months later, he opened his newspaper, on the train to London, to find

their photograph and the newspaper report of their defection to Russia.

Bartley (1989: 52) used a graphic analogy to illustrate Popper's (1974: 33) rejection of communism:

> the shootings in the Horlgrasse seem to have given him a glimpse of his own backside, of the demon that crept inside. Horrified at his behaviour, he drew back, and began to think. To tame any further temptation to violence, he eventually became a sort of Kantian in ethics.

The collaboration between biographer and subject can be hazardous. Bartley (6 September 1986) told his research assistant Jeffrey Friedman that Hayek 'repeatedly suggests that I entitle his biography *Against the Stream'*. On the other hand, the biographer-as-collaborator can also unearth memories that would otherwise be lost. In 1908, Vienna was the sixth largest city in the world with a population of two millions (Hamann, 1999: 277). Yet Bartley (1989: 44, 46) uncovered a remarkable coincidence: on 17 April 1919, Popper observed a group which included Hayek (who he didn't meet for another seventeen years) 'ducking the crossfire, sprawl [*sic*] on the street near the Café Landmann'.

Charismatic biography: Hayek

Bartley's correspondence with Hayek appears to have started in September 1962.[82] They both contributed to Popper's 60th birthday Festschrift; Bartley wrote the biographical material for 'von' Hayek and the other contributors (Bunge, 1964; Preface). He was highly recommended: Popper (23 October 1964) told Hayek that he 'was very glad that you were impressed by Bill Bartley'.[83] In addition to the Austrian (Popper and Wittgenstein) connection, Bartley served as seminar leader (summers 1961, 1965, 1980 and 1985) and plenary lecturer (summers 1975 and 1982) at the Alpbach summer school to which Hayek also contributed.[84] Bartley (15 June 1974) invited Hayek to join the Editorial Board of *California Studies in Philosophy, Politics and Economics*. He asked him to review Stephen Kresge's 'treatise' on monetary theory which 'seems brilliant to me'. Hayek duly sent comments.[85] When Hayek won the Nobel Prize, Bartley (9 October 1974) with 'very sincere congratulations' informed him it was 'so richly deserved'. [86]

They could have first met in difficult circumstances: Lakatos (24 January 1964; 21 December 1964) invited Hayek to attend the July 1965 International Colloquium. Although Hayek declined, Lakatos (9 July 1965) persisted and sent Hayek a conference program.[87]

Initially, Hayek appears to have formed an adverse impression of Bartley as a result of *Wittgenstein* (1973). Bartley (1973) claimed that Wittgenstein pleaded with his cousin not to reveal his Jewish identity – an allegation Hayek (another of Wittgenstein's cousins) regarded as 'absurd'.[88] Hayek expressed similar sentiments about Bartley's (1973) account of Wittgenstein's homosexual promiscuity.[89]

Moreover, Hayek had been invited to review Bartley's *Wittgenstein* by the *New York Review of Books* and had been forwarded a letter (3 April 1973) to Bartley from solicitors acting for 'Major John J. Stonborough (Nephew of Wittgenstein) and Professor Rush Rhees (Senior Executor)' demanding that all copies be withdrawn on grounds of defamation and breach of copyright.[90]

Hayek then received a series of letters from Stonborough (15, 20 and 27 February 1974) referring to Bartley's 'petty bourgeois mentality'.[91] Bartley was 'writing pornography for gain' and Hayek was invited to expose him and his publisher as 'scientific frauds'. Austrians, Hayek was told, 'despite some charm loathe foreigners' especially 'silly professors' from – presumably referring to CSUH – 'cow colleges'.[92]

Stonborough informed Hayek that the US Attorney General had informed him (via the Chief of Internal Security Division, Criminal Branch) that he would appreciate receiving any information about Bartley.[93] If this was accurate, Stonborough must have been referring to William Saxby (4 January 1974–2 February 1975) or his predecessor, Robert Bork, whose term began with the firing of Watergate Special Prosecutor Archibald Cox (a failed attempt to suppress the White House tapes – Richard Nixon's 1973 Saturday Night Massacre) and whose Supreme Court nomination was later rejected by the Senate.[94]

When Bartley and Hayek finally met (23 June 1977), the conversation involved Wittgenstein. Later that day Bartley wrote to Hayek:

I feel that I may have been unwittingly rude to you at one point in our conversation and write to apologize. The episode to which you allude was a quite painful one for me – what with the outrageous behavior of Stonborough and Anscombe – and I was reluctant to deal with that material again. There is, however, really no reason why I cannot give in confidence a complete circumstantial account of what I know about Wittgenstein and how I came to know it. I cannot give you the names of my informants, for I gave my word I would not do that.[95]

Bartley (28 April 1978) then informed Hayek that

some diaries of Wittgenstein have now turned up, in the possession of G. H. von Wright. They confirm completely, so J. Hintikka reports to me, what I had stated in my book about Wittgenstein's homosexuality. I hope to have more details soon.[96]

Later in 1978, Bork was one of Hayek's UCLA oral history interviewers.

The draft of Hayek's *New York Review of Books* essay on Bartley's *Wittgenstein* breaks off mid-sentence just after Hayek refers to the biographical revelations. However, Hayek noted that given their ages, Bartley sources had been accessed just in time.[97]

Bartley (5 February 1983) wrote to Hayek about 'your magnificent proposal that I might write your biography'. Bartley promised his publishers that he would rewrite and double in length his biography of Wittgenstein. This, combined with the 'two volume' Hayek biography plus the 'several volumes' of the Popper biography, could become

a major intellectual (and social) history of our century, focusing on three of its greatest thinkers. All three would begin in Vienna and would reflect, mirror and contrast with one another in all sorts of wonderful ways that would lead to a certain drama and interest and which would help tie the whole into a coherent statement of problems, difficulties and creative resolutions ... Preparatory work on your biography should begin without any delay.[98]

Bartley complained to Popper (4 May 1982) and Hayek (24 April 1983) that he was being forced to teach on three days a week (Monday, Wednesday and Friday), and that his teaching load had increased to 16 hours per week.[99] Hayek (15 May 1983) provided a glowing reference to assist the process of leaving CSUH: 'Any academic institution should regard itself as fortunate to be able to enjoy him as a fellow worker as well as a personal companion'.[100]

Bartley (6 December 1983) reported to Hayek that the Hoover Institution had offered him a Senior Research Fellowship plus a two-term-out-of-three-buy-out from CSUH. After extensive negotiations, Bartley's contract was apparently finalized on 14 March 1985, for an initial period of four years.[101] Hayek (29 March 1985) stressed to Glenn Campbell, the Hoover Institution Director, that

It has become even more important and helpful for me now I know I find Bartley there whom I can thus assist with him on his work on my Biography as well as the collection of my writings. He is a man whom I learn to esteem ever more highly and sometimes wonder whether he is not wasting energies which has [*sic*] better be devoted to original work.[102]

Hayek added:

Since I only gradually discovered the extraordinarily varied development he has gone through I asked him to describe his development in a letter to me which I now enclose, together with some other material he gave me with it.[103]

In a 'PRIVATE AND CONFIDENTIAL' letter Hayek (3 December 1984) informed Campbell that Bartley's continued employment at Hoover was effectively a pre-condition for Hoover receiving his archives:

I am now giving, and wish him to have in the future, full access to my papers. Now if I could assume that he would remain at the Hoover Institution that would make the solution quite simple: I would leave all my scientific papers and professional correspondence to the Hoover Institution. I do not wish to appear to bring any pressure on you on this point, but I believe that I can honestly say that the better I come to know Bartley the more suitable he appears to me for such a position ... in the year of close collaboration I have not only learnt to esteem him ever more highly but he has also become [*sic*] close friend whom I fully trust. If I knew that he was at least likely to stay at Hoover my problem would be solved in the most satisfactory manner: I could leave all my papers to Hoover.[104]

Bartley and Hayek had many overlapping interests. In the 1950s, the *Boston Post* often referred to Harvard as 'the Kremlin on the Charles' (Silk and Silk, 1980: 29). In 'McCarthy v. Harvard' *Time* 25 (January 1954) concluded that 'By week's end McCarthy's critics could accurately say that he had again failed to dig up any evidence of actual espionage'. Bartley reported in the *Harvard Crimson* (19 November 1954) that 'an independent group of students here has begun a national "students for McCarthy Censure" movement'.[105] In 'Charge of the Right Brigade' (27 November 1954), he reported that one pro-McCarthy Harvard student complained that 'Fifth Amendment Communists' were opposed to 'the greatest blessing sent to America by God since Theodore Roosevelt'.[106]

Bartley painted a sympathetic picture of the

> Red Decade... Seven million college-age young people were unemployed. Teachers were being fired; low salaries were being cut still further. Capitalism seemed on the rocks. And it appeared that only the Communist party was ready to adjust its program to the opportunity which presented itself. So, in a way, it was inevitable that the dissenters of the 1920's should become the communists of the 1930's. The new goal was not a chicken in every pot, but anything at all in the pot – in a word; economic security. Communism offered this'.

This sympathetic picture contrasted with Bartley's description of anti-communists: 'A European liberal was causing a stir in Cambridge. Harold J. Laski, later famed as an economist at London University's School of Economics' had been 'represented as the worst of Bolsheviks – morally and politically... In its own words, the [Harvard magazine] *Lampoon* 'dipped its pen in vitriol', and castigated Mr. Laski'.[107]

Laski was associated with both Hayek and Popper. Hayek (28 September 1943) enlisted Laski in his efforts to find a publisher for Popper's (1945) *The Open Society and its Enemies*. Hayek (12 November 1943) then reported to Popper that Laski had written a very enthusiastic review for Nelson Publishers.[108]

Bartley (7 October 1978) requested Hayek's support for a Stanford University Fellowship to work on the Postscript to Popper's *Logic of Scientific Discovery*. Hayek (24 October 1978) enthusiastically supported Bartley's application:

> I agree with Sir Karl that Professor Bartley is the most suitable and perhaps the only person capable of performing his [sic] task adequately. He is, however, able to undertake it only if he is for an appropriate period relieved of his teaching duties at Hayward. I know Professor Bartley as an unusually educated widely interested and personally very pleasant person who should be a valuable addition to any group of scholars.[109]

A few days later, in an interview with Leo Rosten, Hayek stated that Laski had become a propagandist, very unstable in his opinions...Curiously enough, Laski and I had a good deal of contact because we are both passionate book collectors. It was only that way. And he was frightfully offended by my The Road to Serfdom. He was very egocentric and believed it was a book written especially against him.

Rosten responded 'Really? He didn't know economics?' To which Hayek replied:

No, not at all...he was wholly unreliable, both his stories and his theoretical views. I was present one evening in August 1939, when he held forth for half an hour on the marvels of Communist achievement. Then we listened to the news, and the story of the Hitler–Stalin Pact came through. And when we finished the news, he turned against Communism and denounced them as though he had never said a word in their favour before.

Rosten (1908–1997), an LSE graduate, responded: 'That's amazing'.[110] Hayek (1994: 85) and Robbins (1971: 139–141) successfully opposed William Beveridge's attempt to relocate the Marxist-orientated Frankfurt Institute for Social Sciences to the LSE as part of a rescue operation of eminent scholars from Nazi persecution. Decades later, Hayek remained 'full of venom about the Frankfurt Institute and its possible move to the LSE' (Dahrendorf, 1995: 291). In early 1979, a favourable reference to the Frankfurt Institute was 'more than he could endure' (Cubitt, 2006: 31). Yet Hayek appeared to be unconcerned about (or ignorant of) Bartley's connections with Marcuse (1898–1979), a leading member of the Frankfurt School and the 'father' of the New Left, and his wife Erica Sherover-Marcuse (1938–1988).

Marcuse incensed other Austrians. When Hitler came to power, the Jewish Marcuse escaped to the New York Institute of Social Research where he published 'The Struggle Against Liberalism in the Totalitarian View of the State'. Liberalism, Marcuse (1968 [1934]: 3, 11–12) argued, was a front for the 'total-authoritarian state...In order to get behind the usual camouflage and distortion and arrive at a true image of the liberalist economic and social system, it suffices to turn to von Mises' portrayal of liberalism'. Mario Raico (1996: 4, 5, n13) accused Marcuse and other Marxist writers of 'outright dishonesty' and of providing a 'venomous' critique of Mises.

Marcuse incensed Glenn Campbell. When Marcuse's contract at UCSD was renewed, the San Diego Chapter of the Association of the US Army complained that he had been destroying 'the moral fibre of our youth' and that his dismissal would restore 'public confidence in our educational system'. Assemblyman John Stull of the 80th District insisted that UCSD Chancellor William McGill be immediately dismissed. Campbell (21 February 1969) moved that the UC Board of Regents (of which he was one) disapprove Marcuse's reappointment. When that failed, he moved that the Regents should disassociate themselves from McGill's action. The employment at UCLA of Marcuse's student, Angela Davis, became an even more incendiary issue.[111]

Shortly after the September 1984 Mont Pelerin Society (MPS) meeting, Hayek had lunch at the Reform Club with Donald McCormick (aka Richard Deacon), the author of *The British Connection: Russia's Manipulation of British Individuals and Institutions* (1979). Indeed, a significant part of 1984 was taken up by investigating 'Deacon' McCormick's claim that Arthur Cecil Pigou, Hayek's wartime Cambridge colleague, was a Bolshevik spy. The interaction illustrates how diligent Bartley was in tracking down potential biographical material.

Referring to Popper, Bartley stated that 'the world would be a greatly richer place intellectually had a tape-recorder been running at his side for the past seventy years'.[112] Bartley began tape-recording conversations with Hayek – which subsequently formed the basis of *Hayek on Hayek: an Autobiographical Dialogue* (1994). Referring to Pigou, Hayek (1994: 121) recalled that

> We were both at Cambridge during the War... But it was only when I looked at a certain book by Richard Deacon, which is a pseudonym, that it occurred to me why Pigovu suddenly got interested in me. Deacon suggests that Pigou was interested in people who could cross frontiers'.

Bartley (28 February 1984) began: 'I have a couple of questions for you. There is a fun one. Did you happen to know that Pigou was a KGB agent? He was an agent for the Russians?' Hayek responded: 'That must have been something I missed, because I have recently noticed that there is a reticence on the part of my friends to talk about him'.

Bartley continued: 'That may be it. The thing that will interest you is that he took his recruits rock climbing and mountain climbing so he may have been trying to recruit you'. Hayek responded: 'This comes as such a surprise. Although of course I am becoming more and more aware that in that circle I was uncomprehending about what was going on'.

The transcripts state that 'Mrs Cubitt gives information'. Hayek apparently read a section of photocopied page from the *British Connection* and noted that Pigou 'was the sort of person who had most enthusiastic young followers, partly in connection with his interest in ** [apparently a symbol meaning unclear transcript]. Let me see; this seems a great deal different from what had occurred to me before. So much so that I even wondered whether the carefulness was what kept me out of anything; I was playing chess with Pigou'.

Bartley replied: 'They may well have known, yes. You went to the Lake District with him?' Hayek replied: 'I spent one holiday during the war in the Lake District. I ** with him there... he was so exclusive in his contacts. Which may of course have been in general cover for his activities. It was extremely difficult to get access to him... he welcomed me; was very friendly; we played chess together and climbed together on one occasion'.

Hayek may have been about to repeat a favourite story about Pigou: 'You know this story I love to tell about Pigou's American visitor' which elsewhere continued 'You know, I am almost inclined to give the famous answer which Pigou once gave to an inquiring American professor: "I am not in the habit of reading my own books."') – but Bartley interrupted and refocused Hayek: 'But it's exactly that technique that would serve to keep people from bringing up awkward questions, yes'.

In 1923, while Hayek was in New York, Adolf Hitler and Rudolf Hess attempted a beer hall putsch in Munich as a prelude to the capture of Germany; they used their subsequent imprisonment to write *Mein Kampf*. Hayek reflected that the 'papers on Hess will not be made available until 2010'. Bartley asked 'Is this a Russian initiative on the papers?' Hayek replied: 'That he is kept is due to the Russians'. Bartley asked again: 'Yes, but are the Russians involved in the papers?' Hayek replied: 'That I can't imagine, but it may be the reputation of some other people in the connection which are actually being protected'.

A decade before, Hayek had been informed by John Stonborough that Bartley was under investigation at the highest levels of the US Government.[113] Bartley informed Hayek that in the United States there was

something called the Freedom of Information Act, according to which you can get your own FBI files and CIA files. Takes a while, apparently; I've not done it in my case. But you can get a lot of static from the government, they can put you through delay after delay, but eventually they will turn it over to you. So if you are willing to spend a year and a half or so haggling, you can eventually get this kind of material.

Bartley asked Hayek about 'the Gestapo speech in which [British Labour Party leader Clement] Attlee attacked you. Can you tell me anything about that?' Hayek then began to ponder whether wartime books had arrived uncensored because he had been targeted for special (manipulative?) treatment by the Nazis.

Referring to Pigou, Bartley asked 'Did you know about his universal socialism? He talks in there about how he considered himself a universal socialist and did not use the word communism...But the published work doesn't echo this kind of thing at all, does it?' Hayek replied: 'No, no...the foundation of modern welfare economics is Pigou'. Hayek (or the transcripts) got the date of publication wrong: 'I am surprised it is 78 already. I am surprised it hasn't attracted more attention among the welfare economists of which he used to be a hero'. Bartley replied: 'I want to get that book. I have a pile of things I want to bring up with you and this just surfaced. Let me get a copy of this for you'. Hayek responded: 'I am more and more puzzled; what an extraordinary thing'. Bartley added 'There are so many. Did you know Anthony Blunt?'

Presumably referring to Julian Mitchell's play, *Another Country*, based on the life of the spy Guy Burgess, Bartley stated that this was an 'excellent play, on the way this kind of conversion took place. Beginning in boy's school and working up and showing how they...' Hayek interrupted: 'You know I have been through one experience like this before. As I told you, I was unaware of the homosexual character of this group. I wonder, for instance, about Rylands. He may well have been a communist'.

Hayek told Bartley that he had felt rejected by the King's scholar Dadie (George) Rylands, who according to his *Independent* Obituary was often 'pink shirted', referred to as 'darling' and specialized in taking leading female roles in Elizabethan drama. When it came to comedy, Rylands

> was aided and abetted by his contemporary and colleague at King's, the talented comedian Donald Beves. The two of them ran a double act, putting on a Greek or Jacobean tragedy one week, parodying it the next (Cribb, 1999; see also Wilkinson, 1980: 94–95).

Beves was wrongly suspected of being 'The Fourth Man' – a hoax first aired in public on 15 June 1977 by Peter Hennessey, the *Times*

Whitehall correspondent, who later became Professor of History at London University (Penrose and Freeman, 1986: 513–4). The hoax was almost immediately exposed by *Private Eye* (24 June 1977; 8 July 1977). According to L.P. Wilkinson (1980: 174, n21) both Hennessy and *The Times* printed a retraction and an apology. Hayek was apparently unaware that it was a hoax: 'Beves ** I have heard one occasion; no evidence, I believe. But he has been under suspicion'.

Bartley (19 May 1984) wrote to Hayek from Woking, Surrey:

> I have finally tracked down the book about Pigou's work as a spy, and am enclosing copies of the pages on which Pigou is mentioned.

Hayek (19 May 1984) replied:

> This I want to follow up, because it is almost incredible that such an account (pretendedly [*sic*] based on a diary of Pigou) should have remained so unnoticed. If I were at London this spring I would at once consult the publishers and try to trace the author to find out what happened. Reading this, as it happens, together with the idyllic description of King's College in L. P. Wilkinson's *A Century of King's [1873–1972]*, is almost comic.[114]

On the basis of these photocopied pages, Hayek inferred that there had been a conspiracy to protect Pigou:

> Since none of the people I asked about it in London knew anything about it, some masterpiece of suppression must have been done.

Hayek (19 May 1984) considered writing about the issue:

> I am playing with the idea of using the standing offer to print an article of mine on the chief page of The Times for an essay on the Vanished Book!

Hayek's diary records planned additional visits from Bartley on 2–3 April and 7–13 June 1984.[115] Bartley (6 June 1983) informed Hayek that he would write four parallel biographies of Hayek, Popper, Wittgenstein and Keynes:

> The dramatic, literary, and historical possibilities (God knows how it will turn out) are wonderful.

Two specific topics were mentioned: 'the whole story of later attitudes to you in England' and for 'dramatic effect...the wonderful love story of your life, relating to your cousin and later wife'. [116] Bartley (11 June 1984) outlined what was apparently the third part of his biography:

> the presentation of your ideas and background, which is the opposition, Keynes and his dominance and the, what I call the 'fool's paradise' (I think that's also one of your terms)[117]

Hayek (9 June 1984) informed William Deedes, the editor of the *Daily Telegraph*, that the accusations about Pigou must be either refuted or made widely public. Hayek inferred that the book might have been silenced not just because of a libel action but also to protect the reputation of Cambridge University: 'It seems to me there is great public interest in clearing up this matter'.[118]

Bartley (30 June 1984) alerted Hayek to his further efforts:

> If the Daily Telegraph editor sends you any information about Pigou or the Deacon book, I'd be very interested to hear about it. Graham Hutton told me Pigou was mentioned in connection with Blunt.

Bartley (4 July 1984) informed Hayek that

> I also still have made no real progress with the Pigou story: [John] Hicks says it must certainly be false; Graham Hutton says everyone knows it to be true. I would like to have (or see) some real evidence, and intend to write at length to Deacon himself on my return to California.[119]

Hayek (12 July 1984) duly received the information:

> From the Daily Telegraph I did indeed get in addition of all the stuff requested, which essentially confirmed merely what we knew already a review of the book by Rebecca West(!) in the *D.T.* without a date given on the Xerox copy and the mention in the report on the suit that Deacon is a pseudonym of Donald MacCormack [*sic*] and that the wrongly accused physicist was Sir Rudolf Peierls...For the moment I have put the whole matter aside until I can take it up systematically in London after [the MPS meeting in] Cambridge.[120]

Bartley (30 June 1984) had previously informed Hayek that he had spoken to [Nicholas] Kaldor on the 'phone the day that your [Companion of Honour] was announced, and the poor man was obviously miffed by it.

Referring to his planned biography of Hayek, Bartley (15 July 1984) reported that

Kaldor was very little help – mostly just 'wisecracks' and negative feelings. But he did tell me something that may bear on the Pigou question. He told me that Pigou could not have been an agent.[121]

Bartley continued:

the origin of the story stems from a British document about Burgess and MacLean in which a third name is crossed out. One can tell from the document that the name which has been deleted had five letters, and that it began with a 'B' or a 'P'. The first guess was Beves. The second guess was Pigou – and thus the story. But it turned out to be Blunt. This is interesting, but it doesn't explain Deacon's claims to evidence, diaries of Pigou etc. More later!

Hayek presumably knew that the spy, Guy Burgess, was a fellow Reform Club member: perhaps he also knew that one of the last telephone calls that Burgess made (to Goronwy Rees) before he disappeared was made from the Reform Club (Cecil, 1998: 138). A chapter by Robert Cecil (1984) on 'The Cambridge Comintern' was published in *The Missing Dimension* (Andrews and Dilks, 1984). Hayek (19 July 1984) wrote to Cubitt explaining that he had seen an announcement of Cecil's (1988) forthcoming book – presumably *A divided life: a personal portrait of the spy Donald Maclean*. This 'together with news from Bartley has very much reactivated my curiosity about the Pigou affair which I meant to put aside until I got to England'. The following day, Hayek (20 July 1984) asked Cubitt to obtain a copy of the essay on Pigou in the *Dictionary of National Biography*.[122] Hayek told Cubitt (2006: 123) that he could not understand why 'such a story had remained unknown unless the book had been suppressed'.

Bartley (4 August 1984) informed Hayek that he looked 'forward to seeing you [at the MPS meeting] in Cambridge and to hearing about what the Daily Telegraph people have told you about Pigou'.

In response to a letter which is not in the Hoover archive, Bartley (13 August 1984) wrote:

Many thanks for your latest note about Deacon. I was particularly interested to hear of your trip in 1939 to see relatives in Austria – was it in Carinthias – and must remember to ask you about this adventure when we meet in Cambridge...My very best regards to Mrs Hayek.[123]

Hayek's (2 September 1984) diary records 'MONT PELERIN MEETING CAMBRIDGE TALK TO SOMEONE AT KING'S ABOUT PIGOU'. Above 'KING'S' Hayek wrote the name 'BRAITHWAITE'.[124] This presumably refers to the philosopher, Richard Bevan Braithwaite, Fellow of King's (1924–1990) in whose rooms Wittgenstein reportedly waved a poker in the direction of Popper during a legendary confrontation at the Moral Sciences Club meeting (Popper, 1974: 140–142; Munz, 2004; Edmunds and Eidinow, 2001).[125] There was a sizeable Quaker community at King's; like Pigou, Braithwaite served with the Friends Ambulance Unit during World War One (Wilkinson, 1980: 30; Trevelyan, 1919: 201; Young, 1953: 319). [126] Hayek (13 August 1943) informed Popper that he had 'come to know Dr. Braithwaite rather well'.[127] Bartley (1 October 1984) wrote to Hayek: 'I hope you had a good talk with Braithwaite'.[128]

Shortly after the close of the MPS meeting, Hayek telephoned the publishers of *British Connection* (Hamish Hamilton). While unable to speak to the Managing Director, Christopher Sinclair-Stevenson, he took notes from a telephone conversation with his secretary: 'former foreign...of Sunday Times'. Hayek made drew up a list of other 'Deacon' McCormick books including *The Private Life of Mr Gladstone* (1965).[129]

Hayek (23 September 1984) then wrote two letters. One was to Sinclair-Stevenson asking about the *British Connection*: 'For some time rumours had been reaching me that he had been alleged to have been a communist spy'. Hayek stated that he had been provided with these pages by 'one of my former students (I taught at the L.S.E. from 1931 to 1950)'.[130] Hayek explained that he had 'spent a considerable amount of time following up the matter'. The importance of the matter was that

for almost forty years Pigou was, according to all accounts, the most influential person guiding the elections of Fellows to King's College, a fact of some real importance. If it turns out to be correct, some of the equally alarming stories contained in the book certainly ought to become generally known, even if in the case of Professor Peirels Mr. McCormack [*sic*] made an unfortunate mistake.

The *British Connection* had been withdrawn after four days after Rudolf Peirels sued both 'Deacon' McCormick and Hamish Hamilton.

Sinclair-Stevenson (27 September 1984) replied to Hayek that his memories were 'inevitably slightly bitter'. Hayek suggested lunch at the Reform Club at 1pm on 24 October (overlapping with 'Deacon' McCormick); Sinclair-Stevenson (10 October 1984) suggested 3.30 p.m. instead.[131]

The second letter was to 'Deacon' McCormick (which Sinclair-Stevenson was asked to forward):

> Having long been intrigued by the to me at first unbelievable stories that the late Professor A.C. Pigou was a Russian spy and having at last succeeded in obtaining a copy of your book The British Connection, I am at last more or less persuaded that you must be right. I not only knew Pigou probably better than any other person still living and not only had been staying with him in College, sharing lectures with him (while I was with the LSE evacuated to Cambridge during the war) played chess with him and even climbed with him in the Lake district, but as I now realize, was subject by him to exactly the tests which you described... Also, characteristically, he dropped me as suddenly when he discovered that my political views made me wholly unsuitable for the purpose he had evidently in mind.

Hayek asked:

> could I have an opportunity to talk to you about the whole affair of the suppression of your book when I am next in London. The next occasion will be fairly soon, since I am to be at the Palace to receive a decoration on October 25, and if you could possibly see me, perhaps at my club, the Reform, either then or on the preceding or the following day, I should be very grateful.

Hayek (23 September 1984) added a handwritten ps:

> What I have in mind is an article on Suppression of Information for *Encounter*, using Pigou as an illustration because I know the case well.

In reply, 'Deacon' McCormick (28 September 1984) explained why he was 'delighted' to receive the letter:

> though not an economist, I am not only a fervent admirer of what you preach, but probably in my enthusiasm for your code and rules that I almost go beyond it. I believe (1) that we awakened too late to the insidious, if seemingly plausible doctrines of Keynes, and that

he spelt the doom of 19th century Radical Liberal free trade, free market economics, even ruining the Liberal Party of any credence in the process; (2) that my motto is 'Less than enough is a means to an end'. This is not meant to be reactionary, but simply that today people are abnormally greedy because they have been conditioned to be greedy.

The *British Connection* was published in the same year as Andrew Boyle's (1979) *Climate of Treason* exposed the 'fourth man' via the pseudonym 'Maurice' – after E. M. Forster's (1971) posthumously published novel about homosexuals. 'Deacon' McCormick's book ended in lawsuits; Boyle's book led Mrs Thatcher (16 November 1979) to name Blunt as the 'fourth man'. 'Deacon' McCormick (28 September 1984) appeared to claim Blunt's exposure as almost his own:

> there were other attempts to stop publication as well, and I was very angry when, after agreeing that they would re-issue it, they decided against this. Andrew Boyle's book on Blunt came out after mine, and curiously bore out many of the points I made. I even suggested that a revised book might cover the USA as well, making the new title THE ANGLO AMERICAN CONNECTION. But this was not followed up. There is much I could talk about on the theme of suppression.

'Deacon' McCormick asserted that the

> organization, or even organizations, to which [Pigou] passed information, or actively supported in any way, was (or were) entirely separate from the Soviet Intelligence Service. Certainly, the USSR had his information passed on to them, but the actual organizations with which he kept in touch were anti-fascist bodies who served the USSR independently ... I am myself convinced that Pigou was a voluntary agent for the USSR.

'Deacon' McCormick informed Hayek that 'I cannot disclose the identity of my informant 'ROGER' as yet, mainly because he could be at risk from the KGB'. 'Deacon' McCormick was more forthcoming with other evidence: 'I can let you have photocopies of the Pigou diaries in code'. Lunch on 24 October would be 'splendid'. Hayek recorded in his diary (24 October) '12.50 McCormick 3.30 Sinclair-Stevenson' and (25 October) 'Queen' (to be made a Companion of Honour).[132]

Hayek was intensely busy with the *The Fatal Conceit*: he wrote to Jacques Schatz withdrawing his offer to write a book Preface on the grounds that he had to 'firmly resist all distractions' (4 October 1984).[133] On the same day Hayek replied to 'Deacon' McCormick:

I will now only explain that my chief aim is to do an essay on the sort of suppression of information which the withdrawal of your book illustrates, and my picking out Pigou as an examply [*sic*] is merely due to me knowing a good deal about him which made the story at first incredible and then quite plausible.

'Deacon' McCormick (10 October 1984) replied that in *The British Connection* he had

tried to show that people can also be manipulated by the USSR without knowing it. I do not put Pigou in quite the same category as Blunt, or [Kim] Philby, but he was an agent of influence, directly or indirectly, over very many years, and what was important was to show how this started in pre-revolutionary days.

Hayek (15 October 1984) replied:

What you say about Pigou agrees very much with my impression of the man, who would wish to help a fascinating experiment, but not directly harm his country harm. Nevertheless it is historically important because representative of intellectual, particularly Cambridge opinion of the time'.

After lunch 'Deacon' McCormick (27 October 1984) wrote to Hayek:

I was so glad that we were able to cover so much ground in so short a time. If I can help further in any way, or send you any information, or copies of notes, documents etc., do please let me know. It is, as you say, the suppression of information which creates more dangers and problems than it prevents, and it is one reason why the KGB finds it easier to plant disinformation in such a psychological climate. When information is suppressed, false information can so easily be fed into the vacuum, and thus exploited among those eager for information, but not getting it.

In *The British Connection*, 'Deacon' McCormick (1979: 90) implicated Wittgenstein in the left wing ... class struggle ... David Haden Guest ... stressed the fact that one of the prime influences in Cambridge in that year [1929] was the Viennese philosopher, Ludwig Wittgenstein, who had just arrived at the university.

'Deacon' McCormick then cited the following words from M. T. Parker:

[Wittgenstein] proceeded to tear all our preconceived ideas to pieces. He taught us that no proposition had meaning unless one could demonstrate what experiences would demonstrate it.

After a gap, 'Deacon' McCormick continued the quote:

We were all left wing in the sense that we believed in the necessity of the class struggle and were highly critical of the 1929 Labour Government and of the right wing leaders.

Turning to his forthcoming *The Cambridge Apostles: a History of Cambridge University's Elite Intellectual Secret Society* (1985) 'Deacon' McCormick (27 October 1984) asked:

Your cousin, Ludwig Wittgenstein, was an Apostle in the years prior to World War I, and in my book I need to refer to him occasionally. But I have the feeling that he has not been fully interpreted in this country, that much of what has been written about him has not is not altogether accurate, or even helpful. Would it be asking too much, I wonder, if you could, please, in a very few sentences sum up what in your opinion were his outstanding qualities and what he had to tell us. Praise or criticism, or a mixture of both, would be welcome. But I feel I need some outside guidance, as I am not at all happy with some of the comment made about him. I feel he has sometimes been misinterpreted ... Do please let me know if you do this article for ENCOUNTER. Meanwhile I hope you will let me know when you next come to this country, as my wife and I would very much like to see you. With all good wishes, yours sincerely, Donald McCormick.

In a letter that 'Deacon' McCormick (1985: 91) later cited in *The Cambridge Apostles* Hayek (28 January 1985) replied:

Please forgive me for my long delay in replying to your letter of October 27. Various events have led me once more to concentrate entirely on my main task, the finishing of a long delayed book and made me put everything not absolutely urgent aside. As a result I have got no further with the intended article for Encounter and also forgotten the other questions you raised in your letter. It is difficult for me to express an opinion on Wittgenstein's philosophy. I have of course known him longer than any one person still living and was sixty ago very much impressed with his first book. But his latter work meant little to me and I have never quite understood the enormous admiration he has gained in Oxford. Crudely expressed, he always seemed to me the maddest member of a highly gifted but somewhat neurotic family, always on the verge of actual madness and not to be taken too seriously. These may be my limitations but I just do not find it worth-while to spend too much time on them – they certainly do not fit into my system of thought.

Hayek's diary (11 November 1984) records a visit from Bartley.[134] Bartley asked Hayek: 'This man Deacon (or … I can't remember his name offhand) do you think he would see me some time to talk about these things?' Hayek replied that 'Deacon' McCormick was: 'a very nice man. He would probably welcome it. He's retired now, I think. He was very willing to talk and a very pleasant conversationalist'. Bartley asked: 'So he seemed quite genuine; he wasn't making these things up?' to which Hayek replied: 'Oh, I've no question about that'.

Bartley continued: 'What about these documents?' to which Hayek replied: 'The only relevant document he has – is supposed to have – is the 1905 [diary]'. Bartley responded: 'That's the one I was going to ask you about. That refers to Stalin'. Hayek replied: 'At that time – well that exists. He was prepared, I didn't see him a second time; for some reason these documents are not deposited with the Weiner Library, so he could not produce them'. Hayek then added 'He may be sometime [*sic*] making things up. I suppose his exactitude is not that of a scholar, but of a journalist. But entirely honourable'. Bartley replied: 'That's very interesting, yes'.

Hayek referred to his planned essay on Pigou: 'I myself in contemplating this ** – but most of this seems to have been dealt with in other books, so that the whole story … ' Bartley added: 'Still, that is the centrepiece of the whole book, the Cambridge connection'. Hayek replied: 'The Cambridge connection, yes. I think someone ought to do a book on the Cambridge connection. There's much more to be said about it. I am not the person to write about this I'm almost ashamed to have remained living among the group. Without even having become aware of any [*sic*]. Have I told you the story of how when I was there Rylands carefully kept me out – I had no idea why I didn't fit in'.

Hayek's collected works

Bartley was especially suited to edit the first volume of Hayek's *Collected Works: Fatal Conceit the Errors of Socialism* (1988) – he was an acknowledged authority on the epistemological foundations of religion. Hayek acknowledged his weakness in this area. When asked 'What area do you receive questions about on a most frequent basis that you feel is categorically beyond your professional area of competence?' Hayek replied, 'Religion. I just lack the ear for it. Quite frankly, at a very early stage when I tried [to get] people to explain to me what they meant by the word God, and nobody could, I lost access to the whole field. I still don't know what people mean by God. I am in a curious conflict because I have very strong positive feelings on the need of an 'un-understood' moral tradition, but all the factual assertions of religion, which are crude because they all believe in ghosts of some kind, have become completely unintelligible to me. I can never sympathize with it, still less explain it ... In spite of these strong views I have, I've never publicly argued against religion because I agree that probably most people need it. It's probably the only way in which certain things, certain traditions, can be maintained which are essential'.[135]

Hayek abandoned his Roman Catholic family 'tradition' at an early age: 'I don't believe a word of it. ... I must have been thirteen or fourteen – when I began pestering all the priests I knew to explain to me what they meant by the word God. None of them could. That was the end of it for me'.[136] Bartley abandoned Christianity at a slightly later age – but subsequently devoted much of his early professional life to exploring his own personal religious crisis. Bartley (4 September 1983) informed Hayek that 'I need not tell you that I myself am an unbeliever, a complete naturalist. I don't like Christianity at all – in any form – although I do have some sympathy with Buddhism'.[137] Hayek concurred: 'So far as I do feel hostile to religion, it's against monotheistic religions, because they are so frightfully intolerant. All monotheistic religions are intolerant and try to enforce their particular creed'.[138]

Political philosophers from Plato through Machiavelli to Leo Strauss have propagated 'noble lies' supposedly to assist the process of maintaining social order (Hayek, 1988: 137–138). Hayek denied that his 'extended order' benefited in this respect: 'there is no reason to suppose that the support derived from religion usually was deliberately culti-vated ...' *The Fatal Conceit* can be interpreted as Hayek's attempt – with Bartley's assistance – to build a bulwark against the perceived societal crisis associated with the breakdown of 'superstition' or 'symbolic truths'.

In his September 1984 MPS closing address, Hayek stated that the Society should be concerned with 'changing opinion ... Its intellectuals who have really created socialism ... who have spread socialism out of the best intentions'. Hayek emphasized the

> moral inheritance which is an explanation of the dominance of the western world, a moral inheritance which consists essentially in the belief in property, honesty and the family, all things which we could not and never have been able adequately to justify intellectually. We have to recognize that we owe our civilization to beliefs which I have sometimes have offended some people by calling 'superstitions' and which I now prefer to call 'symbolic truths' ... We must return to a world in which not only reason, but reason and morals, as equal partners, must govern our lives, where the truth of morals is simply one moral tradition, that of the Christian west, which has created morals in modern civilization.

Bartley was not the first biographer that Hayek agreed to assist. For three decades, Sudha Shenoy included on her list of publications at the University of Newcastle, Australia, that she was in the process of writing such a biography – not a single page of which has ever surfaced. At the 1984 MPS meeting another biographer apparently emerged: Kurt Leube.

Bartley (2 February 1985–15 March 1985) reported to Hayek that the Anthony Fisher-initiated Pacific Institute for Public Policy Research via its President, David Theroux, and Senior Economist (and CSUH Associate Professor) Gregory Christainsen, might be able to provide a $1 million funding-donor for the *Collected Works* project.

'Dr. Kurt R. Leube' attended the September 1984 MPS conference as a member; Bartley, Theroux, Christainsen and another CSUH economist, Charles Baird, attended as guests.[139] In August 1984 Fisher proposed 'with enthusiasm' that Theroux be awarded MPS membership; Milton Friedman seconded the proposal.[140] Bartley (10 April 1985) subse-quently invited Christainsen for lunch at which, as well as discussing the *Collected Works* project, he promised to deliver 'my little lecture on British nobility – which we'll need for the project'.

A dispute then arose over the royalties. Theroux suggested to Bartley that the Pacific Institute should (with Hayek's permission) share the royalties. Bartley (31 May 1985) then claimed that Hayek's royalties were being claimed by the Pacific Institute – and complained to Theroux. Since their discussion of this matter was largely verbal, misunderstandings could have arisen. Theroux (4 June 1985) wrote to Bartley:

> As for royalties, I only raised the question to explore whether Professor Hayek might agree to let Pacific share in them in proportion to our promotional activities. But again, this matter is up to his approval. There exist many other possible arrangements which we could explore with the publishers wherein his heirs would receive 100% of the royalties.

What is certain is that the misunderstanding – or change of mind – rapidly escalated. A prospectus had been circulated in which Shenoy was listed as 'the proposed editor' of multiple volumes. Bartley's version of events was that this was circulated without his approval. Theroux replied (4 June 1985):

> May I first indicate that the prospectus I drew up was only intended to be a tentative outline of how the program could be put together. All those I have contacted understand this to be the case. The prospectus was also primarily drawn from your memos to [Hoover Deputy Director] John Moore. Before proceeding with it, I received your approval on the content. You may recall that I also discussed the budget at our luncheon at the Hyatt, with your agreeing to my utilizing the figures in your memos plus the added costs of production, promotion, etc. ... As I believe I have stated, *no* aspect of the program would or should proceed without the *complete* approval of you and Professor Hayek. ... [W]e believe that a very worth-while division of labour exists between you as director of the scholarly series and Pacific Institute in handling the production, trafficking, promotion, and other logistics necessary. In fact, we would not be interested in the *Collected Works* if it were not for *your* taking full responsibility for directing the project. Hence, in no way was I attempting to appoint Greg [Christainsen] to a position with the series. On the contrary, it had been my understanding that you had already agreed to his editorial participation and I simply sought to provide the *least* authoritative and *least*

binding label imaginable which would still lend respectability to the series for prospective supporters. Furthermore, I assure you that I have no intention to appoint volume editors, advisors, or any other scholarly positions for the series. I may have suggestions for your consideration as will many other individuals but all final scholarly decisions are yours as project director. [Theroux's emphases]

In reply, Bartley (7 June 1985) sent Theroux what appeared to be a conciliatory letter in which stated that he, Bartley, must retain control of promotion, budget and personnel. Two weeks later, Bartley (22 June 1985) telephoned Hayek and sent a telegram plus follow-up letter:

I began to smell a rat three weeks ago...[the Pacific Institute] were abusing the situation...they had (again without consulting us) appointed an 'associate editor' (Kurt [Leube]'s friend Greg Christainsen) and 'co-editors' for the individual volumes.[141]

Shenoy was one of the proposed co-editors.
Bartley (20 July 1985) inferred that Leube was involved:

the net effect of his proposal (which I gather has independently been conveyed to you via an 'envoy' – I presume K.L.) is – although not expressed explicitly – to put Theroux in entire control of your literary estate...If this were, as he has indicated to me, really your wish as conveyed by your 'envoy' I should of course lay down this responsibility.

Hayek's diary (14 July 1985) records a scheduled visit from Leube and his wife;[142] according to Cubitt (2006: 166), Bartley's inference was correct.
Hayek (26 July 1985) replied from Obergurgl:

you need not be alarmed. I smelled a rat as soon as Leube presented me with Theroux's elaborate proposals and not only refused to sign anything but even to study it in detail or express any opinion but told Leube explicitly that they just not do anything without your approval.

Bartley (2 August 1985) subsequently reported that he had

discussed the matter with Leube; and although there are inconsisten-
cies in his story, he says he was duped by Theroux and Christainsen,
and he has apologized.[143]

In the 1960s, Bartley had been traumatized by being (in his view)
outmanoeuvred and marginalized by Lakatos, which had severed his
relationship with Popper; Bartley may have felt he was being victim-
ized again. Meanwhile, Theroux (23 July 1985) tried to rescue matters
by proposing to Hayek that 'The Hayek Centre in Political Economy'
be established with Theroux as Director, Christainsen and Leube as
Managing Editors and Bartley as General Editor.[144] Shortly afterwards,
Theroux was dismissed by the Pacific Institute and replaced by William
H. Mellor III (1986–1991).

Hayek then 'descended into a massive depression'. Referring to 'Leube's
treachery' Cubitt (2006: 157, 167–169) 'wondered whether these events
had not been responsible for Hayek's breakdown: he must surely have
felt betrayed'. Hayek's eyes were so red that Cubitt thought he must
have been crying; she and Mrs. Hayek put Hayek on a suicide watch.[145]
Mrs. Hayek was unable to mention Leube to her husband because 'the
very mention of his name excited him extremely'.

Bartley (30 June 1986) received a list of Hayek's books published
by Philosophia Verlag plus the information that 'Dr' Kurt Leube was
receiving half the royalties. The copy of this letter in the Hayek archives
was annotated '?' – presumably by Hayek.[146] Cubitt (30 July 1988)
subsequently informed Bartley that she couldn't find any evidence to
support this royalty splitting arrangements except a letter that Leube
had written which 'irritated [Hayek] enough to overline with a yellow
marker'.[147] This letter is not apparently in the Hayek archives.

Bartley (6 September 1989) drafted for Hayek a list of people who
must at all costs be excluded from the *Collected Works* project: including
'Leube D.L.E. (Salzburg)', Christainsen, Thoreaux, Hannes Gissurarson
and Larry White. The letter was posthumously delivered on 9 February
1990, four days after Bartley's death.[148]

According to Cubitt (2006: 321, 329, 334–5, 356, 358, 372, 237, 207,
236) Hayek's physical decline opened a 'Pandora's Box of greed and
hypocrisy, the betrayal of Hayek by persons he had been fond of and
whom he trusted, even by his peers'. With the exception of Herbert
Furth, all sought to 'press their claims and further their own ends'.
Henceforth Hayek would 'distrust ... his personal bogeyman, Leube'.

Mrs Hayek told Cubitt that 'Leube had telephoned and warned her
to prevent Hayek from signing any agreement in connection with the

Collected Works project because he wanted to do the job himself!' Despite visits and further calls, Hayek was 'so annoyed', and told Leube 'Was geht Sie das den an [What has that to do with you]?' Mrs Hayek called Leube a 'cheat and a liar'. After initially allowing contact to be resumed, Hayek 'dropped [Leube] completely'. Mrs Leube, however, continued to telephone and obtained information (Cubitt, 2006: 206). It was such information that provided Leube with his 'Hayek insider' status.

Leube complained that Kresge was 'not qualified for or capable of' continuing the Hayek project that Bartley had initiated. Cubitt (2006: 340–342) suggested to Shenoy that she could have access to her diaries for her own biography: 'I also asked her not to mention the project until I had returned to Freiburg and consulted Hayek'. Shenoy immediately mentioned this to Leube, who informed Mrs Hayek, who became was 'very cross' with Cubitt. Leube and Shenoy 'caused an uproar' at the Munich MPS meeting by sending a fax about Cubitt's proposed biography.

Ralph Harris (6 September 1990) informed Hayek that Shenoy had provided him reports which indicated that 'serious scholars' – which presumably meant Shenoy and Leube – could be denied access to the archives and that taped interviews could be misused. Two days later (8 September 1990) Leube and Shenoy followed Hayek to Obergurgl and pressured him into signing the 'ObergurglDocument' which transferred the literary executorship away from Kresge in favour of Harris (Cubitt, 2006: 342).[149]

Referring to 'Mr.' Leube, Kresge (9 November 1990) wrote to Hayek about the 'intrusion of your peace' at Obergurgl. He then sent Shenoy what appears to be a lawyer-drafted letter (27 November 1990). Shortly afterwards (15 December 1991), this acrimonious dispute was resolved in Kresge's favour – four months before Hayek's death.

As noted above, this chapter does not seek to adjudicate between Bartley and his critics; Bartley's account of the dispute with the Pacific Institute must be juxtaposed with Theroux's account. From the perspective taken in this chapter, Bartley had assumed a time-consuming task that prevented him from pursuing fundamental philosophy. Bartley (20 July 1985) informed Hayek that

> I curse the day that I ever let [Theroux] cross the door of my home ... I have had to put out one fire after another; gossip and malicious attacks and petty conspiracies, for he works by stirring up and dividing. I am a scholar and a writer and have no gumption for such behaviour.[150]

By any standards, Bartley was a world-class scholar; Shenoy and Leube were not. One of the reasons that Shenoy was unable to undertake Hayek's biography was that she failed to learn German. She digitized the *Fatal Conceit* and Hayek's (pre-Bartley) *Law, Legislation and Liberty*, and asked her University of Newcastle colleague John Burrows to undertake a comparative stylistic analysis in order to delineate Bartley's influence. Shenoy provided Bruce Caldwell (2004: 317, n34) with an alleged empirical discovery:

> Shenoy summarizes Burrows's findings as follows: 'The results showed a definite divergence, i.e. some other hand definitely played a clear part in the published text of FC'.

In reality, Burrows and his research assistant have confirmed that they 'conducted no tests for her [Shenoy] and reached no findings, tentative or otherwise'.[151]

Concluding Remarks

Milton Friedman reflected adversely on the academic process that turns 'so many promising intellectuals into second-rate, pedantic, unenterprising faculty' (Friedman and Friedman, 1996: 93). Bartley proceeded down a different path. By any standards, his published output was impressive; yet he failed to fulfil his initial intention of making a major impact on fundamental research.

Bartley alchemized a personal crisis into *Retreat to Commitment* (1964); the clash with Popper and Lakatos left him 'shattered': it 'altered permanently my attitude to my fellow professionals in philosophy' (Bartley, 1976: 37). He had previously regarded Lakatos as 'the most immoral person I had ever met...I often saw Lakatos lie when it suited his purposes'. He subsequently came to realize that

> Lakatos merely talked openly and appreciatively – with a certain connoisseurship – of the sort of behavior that is widespread and almost universally *covert*. I can now appreciate the merits of his practice...he was remarkably without *self*-deception and quite without cant. In this regard he was morally my superior and moral light years ahead of some of our friends and colleagues at the London School of Economics. [Bartley's emphases]

In the 15 years or so after *Retreat to Commitment* (1964), organized religion and the State appeared to continue along separated trajectories – as an almost teleological mandate of the Enlightenment. Yet in the late 1970s, there were renewed Islamic and Christian attempts to re-capture the State. But by then, Bartley had found a niche as a biographer. The interaction of his 'demons' with the intensely competitive and oversensitive world of Popperian philosophy isolated him somewhat within his profession; likewise, his subsequent embrace of the Hayek community has not exactly been reciprocated.

Apparently secular communities often share dynamics with their religious equivalents. Bartley was intensely involved with at least five evangelical communities – moulded respectively by Martin Luther, Popper, Wittgenstein, Werner Erhard and Hayek. It would be most useful to have a Bartley-style comparative analysis of such communities – perhaps among his papers will be found the beginnings of such a work.

Bartley was a complicated and outspoken character. He informed his research assistant Jeffrey Friedman that

> without any magisterial tone of voice: when I was young I found that most of my contemporaries were full of shit. This point of view has not changed with the passing of the years: I still view my contemporaries in the same way – and I have certainly not become enamoured of the 'young people'. My own contemporaries may have been full of shit, but at least they were relatively literate and numerate; whereas the young people of today represent a national educational and economic disaster, the fruit of the lowering of standards of the 'sixties and 'seventies. Young people – like most people follow fashions. And the less they know, the more they are susceptible to fashion. I am not interested in following fashion any more than Hayek is ... (6 September 1986).

Bartley (23 June 1986) also informed Rafe Champion that

> I know rather few academics who listen to arguments or who have the slightest interest in doing so. Each goes to hell in their own way, and God bless.

He offered what he described as 'ad hominem' remarks about a variety of scholars, and then finished with:

> I have been nasty enough for one day. I am now going to do something rational – just for spite (which relieves stress)!

His obituary writer stated that *Wittgenstein* was a 'splendid example of Bartley's capacity to join his interest in ideas with his interest in lives' (Petroni, 1990: 740). Bartley (6 November 1983) informed Rafe Champion that

> I sometimes think of calling these books, together with my biography of Wittgenstein, 'Tales from the Vienna Woods'.

Most scholars are capable of writing biographies; a much smaller proportion have the capacity to successfully undertake fundamental research. The Hayek and Popper biographies would have been major contributions – yet they incurred an opportunity cost. Likewise, *The Collected Works of F.A. Hayek* provided social benefits (by reducing search costs) – yet it further diverted Bartley from his comparative advantage.

In 1963–1964, Bartley and Kuhn overlapped at Berkeley. Kuhn's (1962) *The Structure of Scientific Revolution* transformed the understanding of scientific communities. Bartley could have performed a similar task with respect to religious communities: *The Structure of Religion*, perhaps. Equally, *Retreat to Commitment* could have been developed into *The General Theory of Religion* or *The Structure of Belief.*

Notes

1. I am grateful (a) for comments and information provided by Josef Agassi, Bruce Caldwell, Rafe Champion, Steve Dimmick, Stefano Gattei, Adolf Grünbaum, Stephen Kresge, David Laidler, Gerry Massey, Greg Moore, Ray Monk, Alan Musgrave and Nicholas Nathan; (b) to Jeffrey Friedman and Rafe Champion for providing me with letters from Bartley; and to (c) the Hayek estate for permission to cite from the material contained in the Hayek archives; to Stephen Kresge for permission to quote from his own correspondence and also from William Bartley's archival material; to Leonie Gombrich for permission to quote from the correspondence of E.H. Gombrich; to John Worrall for permission to quote from Imre Lakatos' archival material; to the University of Klagenfurt/Karl Popper Library for permission to quote from Karl Popper's archival material; to Ian Sayer for permission to quote from Donald McCormick's correspondence; to Christopher Sinclair-Stephenson for permission to quote from his correspondence; and to Mike Fisher for permission to quote from Ralph Harris' correspondence.
2. Warburg Archives, Bartley file.
3. Lakatos Papers 13/54 64.
4. Popper Papers Box 272.9.
5. Hayek Papers Box 125.16.
6. To Popper. Popper Papers Boxes 272.9 and 528.19. See also letter to Popper (6 February 1980). Popper Papers Box 528.20.

7. Popper Papers Box 272.9.
8. President George W. Bush, 16 September 2001 (Dietrich, 2005: 41).
9. Popper Papers Box 547.5.
10. Popper Papers Box 528.21.
11. Popper Papers Box 547.5.
12. Popper Papers Box 547.5.
13. http://www.catallaxia.org/wiki/Friedrich_A._Hayek:The_Fatal_Deceit
14. http://organizationsandmarkets.com/2010/02/25/quote-of-the-day-bartley-on-the-marketplace-of-ideas/
15. http://news.bbc.co.uk/2/hi/technology/8249792.stm
16. Popper (1971: 69) later confirmed that 'In physics I was only an amateur, never a professional'.
17. http://www.nytimes.com/1990/02/22/obituaries/william-w-bartley-3d-research-fellow-55.html
18. Faith was born in 1944; Arthur in 1941.
19. Cubitt didn't indicate which sister was disagreeable.
20. According to the city's website, the initial village was named after William Wilkins, one of the founders and the first president of the Bank of Pittsburgh and subsequently Minister to Russia and then Secretary of War in President Tyler's administration.
21. Charles II was famous for his mistresses; in 1936, another playboy monarch, Edward VIII, chose abdication so as to marry a Pennsylvanian divorcee, Wallis Simpson.
22. The University of Pittsburgh Philosophy Department is housed in the 'Cathedral of Learning'.
23. http://www.wilkinsburgpa.gov/about/History.aspx
24. According to the NCCCC Reference Archivist, 'Alfred and Ethel Avery, of Malden, Massachusetts, created the Parshad Holding Corporation in 1929. Parshad is a Hindu word meaning Gift of God. Because of the Avery's interest in Christian youth and education, they instituted the Parshad Scholarship Award in 1945'.
25. The oral tradition at Hoover is that he also paid his way through Harvard by performing as a magician (at children's parties etc).
26. http://www.thecrimson.com/article/1954/12/15/crimson-elects-thompson-iselin-to-head/
27. http://www.thecrimson.com/article/1958/6/10/prizes-awarded-psargent-kennedy-28-secretary/
28. http://www.thecrimson.com/article/1954/10/1/college-replaces-maids-sooner-than-expected/
29. http://www.thecrimson.com/article/1954/3/25/line-tappers-make-calls-others-get/
30. http://www.thecrimson.com/article/1954/6/2/harvard-club-in-capital-to-debate/
31. http://www.thecrimson.com/writer/3148/William_W._Bartley%20iii/page/4/
32. http://www.thecrimson.com/article/1954/4/17/religion-at-harvard-to-teach-or/
33. Popper Papers Box 271.23.
34. Popper Papers Box 272.2.

35. Bartley recounted how Popper physically removed one student from his class.
36. Popper Papers Box 271.25.
37. Popper Papers Box 272.6.
38. http://ucsd-phil-dept-history.blogspot.com.au/p/chronology.html
39. Popper to LSE Director. Popper Papers Box 271.24.
40. Notification dated 21 May 1965. He wrote to Popper 'will try to delay until '66'7 when I could certainly come'. Popper Papers Box 272.2.
41. Lakatos Papers 13/54 88.
42. This may also have been purely coincidental.
43. Popper Papers Box 277.2.
44. Richard Popkin, the founding Chair of the UCSD Department of Philosophy, attended the conference. Bartley's behaviour may have led to adverse consequences for him at UCSD.
45. Popper Papers Box 528.19.
46. Popper Papers Box 528.19.
47. Popper Papers Box 528.19.
48. Popper Papers Box 272.2.
49. Popper Papers Box 272.2.
50. Popper Papers Box 272.2.
51. Popper Papers Box 277.3.
52. Popper Papers Box 272.2.
53. Popper (1990) to Kresge. Popper Papers Box 547.5.
54. Popper Papers Box 272.5.
55. Popper Papers Box 272.7.
56. Popper Papers Box 272.9.
57. Popper Papers Box 272.2.
58. In an Open Letter to members of the International Colloquium in the Philosophy of Science. Popper Papers Box 271.22.
59. Lakatos Papers 13/54 77.
60. Lakatos Papers 13/54 58.
61. Lakatos Papers 13/54 149.
62. Lakatos Papers 13/54 170.
63. Lakatos Papers 13/54 250.
64. Popper Papers Box 272.2.
65. Lakatos Papers 13/54 202.
66. Lakatos Papers 13/54 216.
67. Popper informed Hayek that 'Feyerabend has lost his head completely and has become a leftist Scharfmacher who tells the Negro students to develop Negro magic instead of western science, and such nonsense. I think he is just bursting with ambition; he was always a bit mad'. Hayek Papers Box 42.2.
68. Hayek Papers Box 40.2.
69. Popper Papers Box 271.25.
70. Popper to Bartley (31 May 1964). Popper Papers Box 272.2.
71. Popper Papers Box 273.2.
72. To Popper (17 December 1982). Popper Papers Box 273.2.
73. 'The rules have never been tested; and it may all be illegal. But that is not much comfort: even if the State allowed you to sue it may take years for a resolution' (to Popper, 11 March 1980). Popper Papers Box 272.9.

74. The University of Pittsburgh allege that the Bartley files were inadvertently destroyed around 1975 (the only surviving documents are copies of articles that Bartley sent to the University President).
75. http://ucsd-phil-dept-history.blogspot.com.au/search/label/Herbert%20 Marcuse
76. Email correspondence to the author from Joseph Agassi (14 May 2012) and Ian Harvey (27 April 2012).
77. To Agassi. Popper Papers Box 272.2.
78. Bartley saw an analogy between the Hayeks and the Kaufmanns. Walter Kaufmann (1921–1980) 'hated his wife Hazel so much that he wrote poetry in which he spoke of her loathing for her and his love of a younger woman. He had made Bartley his legal executor but his son turned his mother into a sick woman by revealing all. Mrs. Kaufmann now hated Bartley because she saw in him the perpetrator of all evil that had befallen her. He thought that Mrs. Hayek could pose a similar threat' Cubitt (2006: 140).
79. http://www.time.com/time/magazine/article/0,9171,948354,00.html
80. Erhard initially talked of winning a scholarship to MIT but his grades declined (Bartley, 1978: 25).
81. http://www.nybooks.com/articles/archives/1979/may/31/deep-est/
82. Hayek Papers Box 125.16.
83. Hayek Papers Box 44.2.
84. Hayek attended Alpbach in 1969. Hayek Papers Boxes 43.13 and 94.6.
85. Hayek Papers Box 125.16.
86. Hayek Papers Box 40.37.
87. Lakatos informed Hayek that after leaving prison in 1955 he read Hayek's *Counter-Revolution of Science* (1952): 'that afternoon was roughly the end of my fifteen years' Marxist period'. In reply, Hayek confessed that he was 'always anxious to find [a special pretext] for a visit to England' but would have to 'deny myself the pleasure'. Hayek Papers Box 32.3.
88. To B.P. McGuiness (21 February 1974). Hayek Papers Box 61.18.
89. To B.P. McGuiness (21 February 1974). Hayek Papers Box 61.18.
90. Hayek Papers Box 40.9.
91. 'Kleinbürgerliche cow college Mentalitaet des Bartley'.
92. Hayek Papers Box 61.22.
93. Hayek Papers Box 61.22.
94. Coincidentally, in 1975 Hayek was interviewed by Leonard Silk of the *New York Times* who later co-authored the *American Establishment* in which Bartley played a significant role (Silk and Silk, 1980: 11, 27, 42–48). Hayek Papers Box 95.5.
95. Hayek Papers Box 125.15.
96. Hayek Papers Box 125.16.
97. Hayek Papers Box 129.23.
98. Hayek Papers Box 125.16.
99. Popper Papers Box 273.2.
100. Hayek Papers Box 125.16.
101. Bartley to Hayek (15 March 1985). Hayek Papers Box 125.16.
102. Hayek Papers Box 25.24.
103. I have been unable to locate these 'Bartley development' documents in the Hayek Papers.

104. Hayek Papers Box 25.24.
105. http://www.thecrimson.com/article/1954/11/19/group-begins-national-pro-censure-maneuver-pan/
106. http://www.thecrimson.com/article/1954/11/27/charge-of-the-right-brigade-pthey/
107. http://www.thecrimson.com/article/1955/4/22/its-effects-on-a-few-have/
108. Hayek Papers Box 44.2.
109. Hayek Papers Box 65.12.
110. 1978 UCLA oral history interview.
111. Campbell Papers Box 69.
112. http://www.criticalrationalism.net/2010/04/10/bartley-on-lakatos-and-popper/
113. Hayek Papers Box 61.22.
114. 'I was much interested in the brief enclosure (from Scharfstein) with your earlier letter, but extremely so in those from the book about Pigou'.
115. Hayek Papers Box 123.7.
116. Hayek Papers Box 125.16.
117. Hayek Papers Box 125.16.
118. Hayek Papers Box 97.20.
119. Hayek Papers Box 126.1.
120. Hayek Papers Box 125.16.
121. Hayek Papers Box 125.16.
122. To Cubitt (12 July 1985–16 July 1985). Hayek Papers Box 128.5.
123. Hayek Papers Box 125.16.
124. Hayek Papers Box 123.7.
125. The incident is reported in the second paragraph of the King's Philosophy prospectus.   http://www.kings.cam.ac.uk/study/undergraduate/subjects/philosophy.html
126. His father, William Charles Braithwaite, was an historian of the Quakers and was Honorary Treasurer of the Committee of the Friends' Ambulance Unit, 1914–19 (Tatham and Miles, 1919, appendix). John Bevan Braithwaite also drove for the Friends Ambulance Unit at the battle of Caporetto and elsewhere (Trevelyan, 1919: 201; Young, 1953: 319). Together with Pigou, John Braithwaite assisted Philip Noel-Baker (1972: 10) with the production of *The Private Manufacture of Armaments*.
127. Popper Papers Box 541.1.
128. Hayek Papers Box 126.1.
129. Hayek Papers Box 170.
130. Hayek Papers Box 170.
131. Hayek Papers Box 94.6.
132. Hayek Papers Box 123.7.
133. Hayek Papers Box 48.13.
134. Hayek Papers Box 123.7.
135. 1978 UCLA oral history interviews with Robert Chitester.
136. 1978 UCLA oral history interviews with Robert Chitester.
137. Hayek Papers Box 125.16.
138. 1978 UCLA oral history interviews with Robert Chitester.
139. Hayek Papers Box 47.3.
140. Hayek Papers Box 89.9.

141. Hayek Papers Box 43.13.
142. Hayek Papers Box 128.5.
143. Hayek Papers Box 126.2.
144. Hayek Papers Box 42.13.
145. Mrs Hayek instructed Cubitt (2006: 168) not to let her husband near the parapet of their balcony.
146. Hayek Papers Box 127.34.
147. Hayek Papers Box 127.50.
148. Hayek Papers Box 126.6.
149. Hayek Papers Box 127.5.
150. Hayek Papers Box 125.16.
151. 'We have both been members of the Centre for Literary and Linguistic Computing in the University of Newcastle, Australia, since its inception in 1989. Emeritus Professor Burrows was the Foundation Director and Dr Antonia has been the Centre's principal Research Assistant throughout these years. As the recognition of the Centre has increased, especially in the field of authorship attribution, we have become accustomed to being asked to consider problems brought to us by scholars from within Australia and from overseas. Some of these projects lapse but the number of published articles and book chapters resulting from such approaches runs well into double figures. Dr Shenoy approached us to discuss whether we could assist her with her inquiry into the putative joint authorship of Hayek's Fatal Conceit. Her original approach was to Antonia, who saw her on a number of occasions. Burrows met her only once or twice. We gave her the same information that we give all our prospective clients – that much laborious preparatory work is entailed; that, in general, we expect them to supply the e-texts that are required before analysis can commence; and that we prefer not to be told their opinions on the matter at hand until we have offered them our find-ings. In this case, Antonia assisted Dr Shenoy to prepare some e-texts. After that, we do not know whether she did further work on the preparation of e-texts or what tests, if any, she herself may have made. We conducted no tests for her and reached no findings, tentative or otherwise. Our memories of all this are in complete accord. So far as we are aware, no other member of our Centre had any part in Dr Shenoy's project. We know almost nothing of Hayek's work, have never read any of his writings, and still have no opinion whatever on the question Dr Shenoy brought to us. Yours sincerely, John Burrows and Alexis Antonia' (email to Leeson, 10 May 2012).

Bibliography

Andrews, C. and Dilks, D. 1984. (eds) *The Missing Dimension: Governments and Intelligence Communities in the Twentieth Century* (London: Macmillan).
Annan, N. 2000. The Cult of Homosexuality in England 1850–1950. *Biography*, 13 (3): 189–202.
Ascherson, N. 1980. What Sort of Traitors? *London Review of Books*, 2 (2) (7 February): 6–7.
Bartley, W. W. 1962. *The Retreat to Commitment* (New York: Alfred A. Knopf, Inc.)

Bartley, W. W. 1964. Rationality and the Theory of Rationality. In Bunge M. A. (ed.) *Critical Approaches to Science and Philosophy* (New York: The Free Press)

Bartley, W. W. 1968a. Theories of Demarcation Between Science and Metaphysics. In Lakatos, I. and Musgrave, A. (eds) *Problems in the Philosophy of Science* (Amsterdam: North Holland) Vol. 3, 40–64.

Bartley, W. W. 1968b. Reply. In Lakatos, I. and Musgrave, A. (eds) *Problems in the Philosophy of Science* (Amsterdam: North Holland) Vol. 3, 102–119.

Bartley, W. W. 1969. Theories of language and Philosophy of Science as Instruments of Educational Reform: Wittgenstein and Popper as Austrian School Teachers (Mimeo).

Bartley, W. W. 1970. Karl Barth. *Encounter* 1 –4.

Bartley, W. W. 1971. *Morality and Religion* (London: Macmillan).

Bartley, W. W. 1973. *Wittgenstein* (New York: Lippincott Co).

Bartley, W. W. 1976. On Imre Lakatos. In Cohen, R. S. (ed.) *Essays in Memory of Imre Lakatos* (Reidel: Dordrecht, Holland).

Bartley, W. W. 1978. *Werner Erhard: The Transformation of a Man, the Founding of Est* (New York: Clarkson N. Porter).

Bartley, W. W. 1982. A Popperian Harvest. In Levinson, P. (ed.) *In Pursuit of Truth: Essays in Honour of Karl Popper's 80th Birthday* (Atlantic Highlands, NJ: Humanities Press).

Bartley, W. W. 1984. *Retreat to Commitment* (La Salle, Ill.: Open Court). 2nd edn.

Bartley, W. W. 1985. *Wittgenstein* (London: Century Hutchison). 2nd edn.

Bartley, W. W. 1989. Rehearsing a Revolution – Karl Popper: A Life (Mimeo).

Bartley, W. W. 1990. *Unfathomed Knowledge, Unmeasured Wealth: On Universities and the Wealth of Nations* (La Salle, Ill.: Open Court).

Boyle, A. 1979. *The Climate of Treason* (London: Hutchison)

Bunge, M. A. 1964. (ed.) *Critical Approaches to Science and Philosophy* (New York: The Free Press).

Caldwell, B. 2004. *Hayek's Journey: an Intellectual Biography of F. A. Hayek* (Chicago: University of Chicago Press).

Carew-Hunt, R. N. 1950. *The Theory and Practice of Communism* (Middlesex, England: Penguin).

Cecil, R. 1984. The Cambridge Comintern. In Andrews and Dilks (eds) *The Missing Dimension: Governments and IntelligenceCommunities in the Twentieth Century* (London: Macmillan).

Cecil, R. 1988. *A Divided Life: A Personal Portrait of the Spy Donald Maclean* (London: Bodley Head). Foreword by Noel Annan.

Cohen, R. and Zelnick, R. E. 2002. (eds) *Free Speech Movement: Reflections on Berkeley in the 1960s* (Berkeley: University of California Press).

Cohen, R. S. 1976. (ed.) *Essays in Memory of Imre Lakatos* (Reidel: Dordrecht, Holland).

Cribb, T. J. 1999. Obituary: George Rylands. *Independent* (20 January).

Cubitt, C. 2006. *A Life of August von Hayek*. Authors on line: Bedford, England.

Dahrendorf, R. 1995. *LSE: A History of the London School of Economics and Political Science 1895–1995* (Oxford: Oxford University Press).

Deacon, R. 1965. *The Private Life of Mr Gladstone* (London: Muller).

Deacon, R. 1979. *The British Connection: Russia's Manipulation of British Individuals and Institutions* (London: Hamish Hamilton).

Deacon, R. 1985. *The Cambridge Apostles: A History of Cambridge University's Elite Intellectual Secret Society* (R. Royce: London).

Dietrich, J. W. 2005. (ed.) *The George W. Bush Foreign Policy Reader: Presidential Speeches and Commentary* (London: M.E. Sharpe).

Edmunds, D and Eidinow, J. 2001. *Wittgenstein's Poker: The Story of a Ten-Minute Argument Between Two Great Philosophers* (Faber and Faber Ltd: London).

Erhard, W. 1978. Foreword. In Bartley. (ed.) *Werner Erhard: The Transformation of a Man, The Founding of Est* (New York: Clarkson N. Porter).

Forster, E. M. 1971. *Maurice* (London: Edward Arnold).

French Smith, W. 1991. *Law and Justice in the Reagan Administration: The Memoirs of an Attorney General* (Stanford, California: Hoover Press).

Friedman, M. and Friedman, R. 1996. *Two Lucky People* (Chicago: University of Chicago Press).

Gattei, S. 2002. The Ethical Nature of Karl Popper's Solution to the Problem of Rationality. *Philosophy of the Social Sciences*, 32 (2) (June): 240–266.

Gattei, S. 2008. *Thomas Kuhn's 'Linguistic Turn' and the Legacy of Logical Empiricism: Incommensurability, Rationality and the Search for Truth* (Ashgate: Aldershot England).

Gattei, S. 2010. Imre Lakatos, the man who would be philosopher-king. In Marletti, C. (ed.) *First Pias Colloquium in Logic, Language and Epistemology* (Pisa: ETS)

Hamann, B. 1999. *Hitler's Vienna: A Dictator's Apprenticeship* (New York: Oxford University Press).

Hayek, F. A. 1952. *The Counter-Revolution of Science: Studies on the Abuse of Reason* (Glencoe, Ill.: Free Press).

Hayek, F. A. 1988. *The Fatal Conceit: The Errors of Socialism* (Chicago: University of Chicago Press).

Hayek, F. A. 1994. *Hayek on Hayek: An Autobiographical Dialogue* (Chicago: University of Chicago Press).

Kaufmann, W. 1985 [1973]. Foreword. In Bartley *Wittgenstein* (London: Century Hutchison). 2nd edition.

Kuhn, T. 1962. *The Structure of Scientific Revolution* (Chicago: University of Chicago Press).

Kuhn, T. 1970. Logic of Discovery or Psychology of Research. In Lakatos and Musgrave (eds) *Criticism and the Growth of Knowledge* (Cambridge: Cambridge University Press).

Lakatos, I. 1970. Falsification and the Methodology of Scientific Research Programs. In Lakatos and Musgrave (eds) *Criticism and the Growth of Knowledge* (Cambridge: Cambridge University Press), 91–196.

Lakatos, I. and Musgrave, A. 1968. (eds) *Problems in the Philosophy of Science* (Amsterdam: North Holland). Vol. 3.

Lakatos, I. and Musgrave, A. (eds) 1970. *Criticism and the Growth of Knowledge* (Cambridge: Cambridge University Press).

Lakatos, I. and Feyerabend, P. 1999. *For and Against Method* (Chicago: University of Chicago Press). Edited by Motterlini, M.

Larvor, B. 1998. *Lakatos: An Introduction* (London: Routledge).

Levinson, P. 1982. (ed.) *In Pursuit of Truth: Essays in Honour of Karl Popper's 80th Birthday* (Atlantic Highlands, NJ: Humanities Press).

Magee, B. 1971. *Modern British Philosophy* (London: Martin, Secker and Warburg).

Marcuse, H. 1964. *One Dimensional Man* (Boston: Beacon Press).

Marcuse, H. 1966. *Eros and Civilization: A Philosophical Inquiry into Freud* (Boston: Beacon Press).

Marcuse, H. 1968. *Negations Essays in Critical Theory* (Boston: Beacon).

Marletti, C. 2010. (ed.) *First Pias Colloquium in Logic, Language and Epistemology* (Pisa: ETS).

Monk, R. 1990. *Ludwig Wittgenstein: The Duty of Genius* (New York: Penguin Books).

Munz, P. 2004. *Beyond Wittgenstein's Poker: New Light on Popper and Wittgenstein* (Ashgate: England).

Musgrave, A. 1968. On a Demarcation Dispute. In Lakatos, I. and Musgrave, A. (eds) *Problems in the Philosophy of Science* (Amsterdam: North Holland) Vol. 3 78–88.

Nathan, N. 1980. *Evidence and Assurance* (Cambridge: Cambridge University Press).

Noel-Baker, P. 1972. *The Private Manufacture of Armaments* (New York: Dover). 2nd edn.

Penrose, B. and Freedman, S. 1987. *Conspiracy of Silence: The Secret Life of Anthony Blunt* (London: Vintage).

Petroni, A. 1990. William Warren Bartley III. *Critical Review*, 4 (4): 737–741.

Popper, K. 1945. *The Open Society and Its Enemies* (London: Routledge). 1st edn.

Popper, K. 1961. *The Open Society and Its Enemies* (London: Routledge). 4th edn.

Popper, K. R. 1968. Remarks on the Problem of Demarcation and of Rationality. In Lakatos, I. and Musgrave, A. (eds) *Problems in the Philosophy of Science* (Amsterdam: North Holland) Vol. 3, 88–102.

Popper, K. R. 1971. Conversation with Karl Popper. In Magee, B. (ed.) *Modern British Philosophy* (London: Martin, Secker and Warburg)

Popper, K. R. 1974. *Unended Quest: An Intellectual Autobiography* (London: Routledge).

Popper, K. R. 1982/3. *Logic of Scientific Discovery* (London: Hutchison).

Popper, K. R. 2002. *Unended Quest: An Intellectual Autobiography* (Routledge: London).

Pressman S. 1993. *Outrageous Betrayal: The Dark Journey of Werner Erhard from Est to Exile* (London: St Martin's Press).

Radnitzky, G. and Bartley, W. W. 1987. (eds) *Evolutionary Epistemology, Rationality, and the Sociology of Knowledge* (LaSalle, Ill: Open Court).

Raico, R. 1996. Mises on Fascism, Democracy and Other Questions. *Journal of Libertarian Studies* (Spring) 12 (1): 1–27.

Robbins, L. 1971. *Autobiography of an Economist* (London: Macmillan).

Silk, L. and Silk, M. 1980. *The American Establishment* (New York: Basic Books).

Tatham, M. and Miles, J. E. 1919. (eds) *The Friends' Ambulance Unit, 1914–1919: A Record* (Swarthmore Press: London).

Turing, S. 1959. *Alan M. Turing* (W. Heffer and Sons: Cambridge).

Trevelyan, G. M. 1919. *Scenes from Italy's War* (London: TC and EC Jack).

Wilkinson, L. P. 1980. *A Century of King's: 1873–1972* (King's College: Cambridge).

Young, G. W. 1953. *The Grace of Forgetting* (Country Life: London).

10
Hayek, Bartley and Popper: Justificationism and the Abuse of Reason

Rafe Champion

William Warren Bartley III had three strings to his bow: original philosopher, biographer and editor. This paper takes up his major philosophical contribution which Friedrich Hayek (1988) used in *The Fatal Conceit* to support his critique of constructivist rationalism. This is the concept of 'justificationism' which Bartley identified as a major and pervasive philosophical error, following Karl Popper's criticism of the authoritarian strand in Western epistemology and political theory.

Popper (1963: 25) argued that 'The traditional systems of epistemology may be said to result from yes-answers or no-answers to questions about the sources of our knowledge. *They never challenge these questions, or dispute their legitimacy*; the questions are taken as perfectly natural, and nobody seems to see any harm in them. This is quite interesting, for these questions are clearly authoritarian in spirit. They can be compared with that traditional question of political theory, 'Who should rule?', which begs for an authoritarian answer such as 'the best', or 'the wisest', or 'the people' or 'the majority'. (It suggests, incidentally, such silly alternatives as 'Who should be our rulers: the capitalists or the workers?' analogous to 'What is the ultimate source of knowledge: the intellect or the senses?') This political question is wrongly put and the answers which it elicits are paradoxical (as I have tried to show in Chapter 7 of my *Open Society*). It should be replaced by a completely different question such as 'How can we organize our political institutions so that bad or incompetent rulers (whom we should try not to get, but whom we so easily might get all the same) cannot do too much damage?' I believe that only by changing our question in this way can we hope to proceed towards a reasonable theory of political institutions'.

The key point in the passage is 'these questions are clearly authoritarian in spirit'. Popper and Bartley used the term 'justificationism' to describe the philosophical quest for 'justified true beliefs', based on the appropriate authority. They argued that this quest is misplaced because foundationalist justification cannot be achieved, although it is possible to justify a *preference* for a particular position in the light of evidence and arguments produced to date, on the understanding that the preference can change in the light of new evidence and arguments.

The first section of this chapter notes the damaging effect of moral relativism and the subversion of traditional values by the constructivist rationalists who Hayek subjected to protracted criticism in his 'abuse of reason' project. The second section examines the failure in the market of ideas which creates problems for classical liberalism, sketches the core problem of rationality, that is, the dilemma of the infinite regress versus dogmatism, and introduces Bartley's proposal for a solution.

The third section sketches the various responses to the dilemma and the way that classical liberalism has suffered from the 'justified belief' framework. It notes that academic philosophy and the 'true belief' religions tend to propagate the framework of justificationism and the 'true belief' mindset. The fourth section shows how the non-justificationist approach resolves some tensions in the treatment of rationality and criticism in the work of Popper and Hayek. The final sections signal Jan Lester's application of Bartley's ideas in political economy and a rejoinder to the deconstructionists in literary theory.

A land mine in Western thought

The Fatal Conceit (1988: 67–70) contains a section on 'The Justification and Revision of Traditional Morals' where Hayek explained that the demands for justification of traditional mores cannot be provided in the way demanded by a theory of rationality, based on constructivism, scientism and positivism. The result is a persistent and radical assault on traditional values which is intellectually incoherent but it is no less destructive for that reason. Closely related to this is the problem that Paul Craig Roberts (1992) described as 'a land mine at the very basis of Western thought': 'The eighteenth century Enlightenment had two results that combined to produce a destructive formula. On the one hand, Christian moral fervor was secularized, which produced demands for the moral perfectibility of society. On the other hand, modern science called into question the reality of moral motives'.

These tendencies might appear to be contradictory, but they have not balanced each other; instead they have produced an explosive mixture of moral indignation and moral relativism or scepticism. The first leads to attacks on traditional mores and institutions, while the second pre-empts any defences that might be offered. This is no small matter, as demonstrated by Deirdre McClosky's (2010) work on 'the bourgeoise virtues' and Popper's (1963: 351) reference to the all-important moral framework of society.[1]

Hayek (1988: 68) turned to Bartley's critique of 'justificationism' for additional philosophical support. This appears to be the first use of this concept in his published work: 'No matter what rules we follow, we will not be able to justify them as demanded; so no argument about morals – or science, or law, or language – can legitimately turn on the issue of justification (see Bartley, 1962/1984; 1964; 1982) ... The issue of justification is indeed a red herring, owing in part to mistaken and inconsistent assumptions arising within our main epistemological and methodological traditions, which in some cases go back to antiquity'.

If the issue of justification is a red herring, the question has to be asked; 'What is the defensible position for a critical rationalist to adopt towards traditional values and mores?' The answer is that we can form 'critical preferences' for particular theories or traditions by comparison with rival theories and traditions. Traditions, values, mores and ways of life are not beyond criticism, and they need to be evaluated in terms of the outcomes that they produce.

The failure in the market of ideas

Liberalism is a non-authoritarian creed: It draws its strength from the non-coercive power of reasoned argument, in contrast with systems that depend on brute force or intimidation by intellectual or moral authorities. The survival and progress of liberalism depend on free trade in ideas, unconstrained by the cramps on criticism that are imposed by cartels, monopolies and various forms of protectionism in the mind industry. Bartley's (1991) *Unfathomed Knowledge, Unmeasured Wealth* provides a wealth of detail on that topic. On top of this, people tend to be hostages to the first ideas that they take on board.

Ludwig von Mises (1978: 196) argued that 'Every new theory encounters opposition and rejection at first. The adherents of the old, accepted doctrine object to the new theory, refuse it recognition, and declare it to be mistaken. Years, even decades, must pass before it succeeds in supplanting the old one. A new generation must grow up before its victory is decisive'.

This has hardly changed with the advent of mass primary, secondary and lately higher education. Clearly education and instruction alone do not furnish the habits and disciplines that are required for continuing intellectual growth and for the imaginative criticism of received opinions.

Bartley's work provides an explanation and an antidote to this situation. Inspired by Popper's critique of the authoritarian structure of Western thought in epistemology and politics, noted in the extract at the head of this essay, Bartley explored the logical limits of rationality and the problem of bringing criticism to bear upon fundamental beliefs. He confronted the perennial problem of validation and *the dilemma of the infinite regress versus dogmatism*. This dilemma arises as follows: If a belief claims validation by a supporting argument, what justifies the support? Where and how does the chain of justification stop? If one attempts to provide reasons for the supporting argument then an infinite regress can be forced by anyone who presses for more supporting statements which in turn demand justification. *It appears that this can only be avoided by a dogmatic or arbitrary decision to stop the regress at some stage and settle on a belief at that point.*[2]

This dilemma creates conscientious objections to open-mindedness because a logical chain of argument apparently justifies dogmatism and resistance to counter-arguments as the last resort in a debate. To the despair of people who want to make full use of evidence and arguments to pursue both scientific truth and more effective actions, their opponents can defeat the principle of rationality on impeccably logical grounds. Bartley followed up an insight from Popper, who located a barely recognized and previously uncriticized assumption regarding rationality and the justification of beliefs that permeates Western thought; this can be summed up in the formula:

> Beliefs must be justified by an appeal to an authority of some kind, generally the source of the belief in question, and this justification makes the belief either rational, or if not rational at least valid for the person who holds it.

Bartley labelled this theory 'justificationism', and he showed how it created a demand for positive justification which can never be met due to the problem of the infinite regress, which trumps all claims regarding foundational propositions. The solution is to abandon the quest for positive justification and instead to settle for a critical preference for one option rather than others in the light of critical arguments and evidence offered to that point. A preference may (or may not) be revised in the light of new evidence and arguments. This appears to be a simple, commonsense position, but it defies the dominant traditions of Western thought which have almost all taught that some authority provides (or ought to provide) grounds for positively justified beliefs. An important contribution to the literature on this topic is Notturno's (2003) explanation of the way that traditional foundationalism morphed into what he called 'floating foundationalism' in an attempt to take on board the idea that our knowledge is fallible while maintaining the framework of 'justified true belief'.

What are the roots of justificationism? Perhaps there is some biological basis, or it may arise from the fact that we all grow up surrounded by larger people who know more than we do and constantly remind us of this. It may arise from the nature of conventional education, which promotes dogmatic modes of thought. But in addition to all these factors there is the tradition of justificationism itself, which states that we should strive to obtain justified beliefs, a theory endorsed by almost all Western philosophers from Plato to the present day. As Ayer (1982: 134) argues: 'For what would be the point of our testing our hypotheses at all if they earned no greater credibility by passing the tests? We seek justification for our beliefs, and the whole process of testing would be futile if it were not thought capable of providing it'.

So justificationism persists as a subjective attitude or disposition, supported by a pervasive and powerful intellectual tradition. In addition to the influence of academic philosophers in perpetuating this tradition (by example and practice, if not by overt articulation) it is likely that all the 'true belief' religions propagate the same mindset by appealing to the appropriate authority to support the doctrines of the faith.

Responses to the dilemma of the infinite regress v. dogmatism

In the light of the dilemma of the infinite regress versus dogmatism, we can discern three attitudes towards positions: relativism, 'true belief' and critical rationalism.[3]

Relativists tend to be disappointed justificationists who realize that positive justification cannot be achieved. From this premise they proceed to the conclusion that all positions are pretty much the same and none can really claim to be better than any other. For them, there is no such thing as the truth, no way to get nearer to the truth and no such thing as a rational position.

True believers embrace justificationism. They insist that some positions are better than others, though they may accept that there is no logical way to establish a positive proof (justification) for their position. They are prepared to accept that we make our choice regardless of reason: 'Here I stand!' Most forms of rationalism to date have, at rock bottom, shared this attitude with the irrationalists and other dogmatists because they share the theory of justificationism.

According to the *critical rationalists*, the exponents of critical preference, no position can be positively justified, but it is quite likely that one (or more) will turn out to be better than others in the light of critical discussion and tests. This type of rationality holds all its positions and propositions open to criticism, at least in principle (time permitting), and a standard objection to this stance is that it is empty; just holding our positions open to criticism provides no guidance as to what position we should adopt in any particular situation. This criticism misses its mark for two reasons. First, critical rationalism is not a position. It is not directed at solving the kind of problems that are solved by fixing on a position. *It is concerned with the way that such positions are adopted, criticised, defended and relinquished.* Second, Bartley did provide guidance on adopting positions; we may adopt the position that to this moment has stood up to criticism most effectively. Of course this is no help for people who seek stronger reasons for belief, but that problem belongs to them, and it does not undermine the logic of critical preference.

Liberalism has been forced to constantly work against the grain of the received opinions, locked in place by the justificationist or true belief mindset, so the gains of one generation have often been lost to the forces of irrationalism and authoritarianism in the next. But the really penetrating insight provided by Bartley's work is that traditional theories of rationality (based on the assumption of justificationism) perpetuate the justificationist tradition/framework/mindset, which generates the dilemma of the infinite regress versus dogmatism. Hence it seems that rationalists of the justificationist variety like Bertrand Russell (who was described as a 'passionate skeptic') unwittingly nurture the framework that creates so many problems for rationalists.

This helps to explain why the survival of liberalism is precarious, why it needs auxiliaries to support its causes and why civilization lapses into occasional bouts of irrationalism. Episodes such as the Nazi holocaust and the wilder excesses of the generation of '68 are generally regarded as strange aberrations in the normally rational Western tradition, perhaps calling for psychological analysis of the individuals involved, for studies of 'the authoritarian personality' or ruminations on the 'contradictions of developed capitalism' or the decline of religious faith. But seen from the perspective of Bartley's work, such failures of reason are only to be expected in the justificationist framework, which sponsors dogmatism and fanaticism. And as long as that framework remains dominant, our traditions of rationality, tolerance and freedom will remain fragile and liable to collapse at any period of social or political crisis (as in Greece, circa 2012). One of the thought-provoking results of his analysis is to identify academic philosophy and the 'true belief' religions as major vehicles which perpetuate the justificationist framework.

Popper and Hayek retrieved

Some problems regarding apparent tensions in Popper's and Hayek's liberalism can be addressed and resolved in the non-justificationist framework. These are the conflict between Hayek's 'moral iconoclasm' and 'moral conservatism', a similar problem with Popper's theory of tradition and an apparent difference of emphasis between Popper and Hayek on rationality and the scope for critical appraisal of traditions.

The heart of liberalism is the critical attitude towards tradition, but this stance is rendered problematic by the demand for positive justification which critics can use to force the dilemma of infinite regress versus dogmatism. This results in a problem for Hayek, as described by J. N. Grey (1982: 59–61), one of his greatest admirers: 'One of the commonest critiques of Hayek's work (is) that it straddles incompatible conservative and liberal standpoints ... [and] Hayek continues to advocate a strong form of moral conventionalism, resisting the claims of those who see modern morality as in need of radical reform. There is thus tension, perhaps irresolvable in terms of Hayek's system, between his Mandevillian moral iconoclasm and his moral conservatism'.

Similar comments have been made on Popper's theory of tradition and criticism, with the argument running as follows: Popper accepted that we need traditions to provide a framework of expectations and regularities in social life, otherwise we would be anxious and confused. But Popper also urged a rational (critical) attitude towards traditions and beliefs of all kinds. This raises the same questions as that posed above on Hayek's iconoclasm and conservatism.

Kukathas (1989) raised the same issues in his study of Hayek. As a conservative and sceptic, Hayek asserts that ethics is not a matter of choice because 'Our morals are not (and cannot be) the product of design but are the result of a natural selection of traditions' (Kukathas, 1989: 190). However the rationalist Hayek is driven to seek reasons for adhering to traditional morality, and he has a rationalist's concern to defend those principles, such as the market order and the rule of law that are required for his vision of human progress. But to pursue these principles he is obliged to adopt an agenda of radical reform to 'free the process of spontaneous growth from the obstacles and encumberances that human folly has erected'. But if these obstacles belong to our traditional heritage, then where do we stand in order to put the lever of reform under them? Tensions of this kind prompt Kukathas's conclusion that the foundations of Hayek's liberalism will not hold.

This conclusion begs the questions that Kukathas raised about classical liberalism in his final chapter: 'First, is it a defensible ideal and, secondly, how might it be defended?' Kukathas (1989: ix) suggested that 'Liberal theorists should turn away from their preoccupation with uncovering Kantian foundations for liberalism, and look again to Hume'. In Hume we find critical scepticism combined with respect for the truth and for valuable traditions. At the same time he recognized the need for continual improvement in our knowledge, our institutions and our practices. The challenge is to sustain a critical attitude without lapsing into the corrosive and nihilistic forms of moral relativism which deny that there is any rational way to choose between rival theories or moral principles. The usual rejoinder to this latter view is to insist (like Kant) that there is indeed some authoritative source of justified beliefs. Unfortunately, opinions differ on the appropriate authority, and all such theories fall foul of the dilemma of 'the infinite regress versus dogmatism' as described above. However if the stance of 'critical preference' is adopted, the tension between the Humean and Kantian tendencies in Hayek's thought may be resolved. This is very much the position stated previously by Hayek (1978: 19):

> The proper conclusion from the considerations that I have advanced is by no means that we may confidently accept all the old and traditional values. Nor even that there are any values or moral principles which science may not occasionally question. The social scientist who endeavours to understand how society functions, and to discover where it can be improved, must claim the right to examine critically, and even to judge, every single value of our society. The consequence of what I have said is merely that we can never at one and the same time question all its values. Such absolute doubt could lead only to the destruction of our civilization.

This stance is not problematic in the framework of critical preference. With his foundational problems in order, some of the difficulties in the body of his work may dissolve in turn. For example,
the cluster of liberal policies (free trade, limited government, the
rule of law, etc.) may be held on the grounds of critical preference
over their rivals, given the larger objectives of peace, freedom and
prosperity. Such a preference does not rest on faith or foundations,
merely on the evidence of some millenia of conscious or unconscious
experimentation.

Both Popper and Hayek (at least in their better moments) can be
described as advocates of the non-justificationist framework of 'critical
rationalism' which takes account of the limitations of human knowledge and accepts that we need institutions and traditions without
conceding that any of these are exempt from criticism in the light of all
other values. In that mood (or mode), they adopt the stance of 'critical
preference' rather than 'justified belief', and the suggestion of tension
between iconoclasm and conservatism in their work arises from the
implicit assumption that a moral belief can only be held and acted on *if
it is positively justified, beyond doubt*. This assumption is part and parcel
of the justificationist mindset, and people who hold this assumption
cannot comprehend the notion of a tentative belief or a critical preference made on the basis of evidence and arguments but to open to
change in the future.

Jan Lester on liberty, welfare and anarchy

Lester's (2000) *Beyond Leviathan* possibly represents a landmark in the
literature of liberalism on two counts. One is these is the robust statement of his major thesis on the compatibility of free markets, liberty and
welfare. The other is the way he explicitly used the non-authoritarian
theory of rationality with attribution to Popper and Bartley. Lester's
(2000: 2) statement of the 'compatibility thesis' runs as follows:

In practice (rather than in imaginary cases) and in the long term,
there are no systematic clashes among interpersonal liberty,
general welfare, and market anarchy, where these terms are to be
understood roughly as follows: 'interpersonal liberty' is 'not being
imposed on by others'; 'general welfare' is 'people having their
unimposed wants satisfied'; 'market anarchy' is 'unrestricted libertarian trade'; and the underpinning conception of 'rationality' is

'agents always attempt to achieve what they most want under the perceived circumstances'.

The main characteristic of Lester's approach is that he only attempted to achieve what is possible, namely the formation of a critical preference for one option rather than another. He did not attempt to provide a logically conclusive proof of his case. What is possible is to propose a theory or a doctrine and subject it to criticism; then if it stands up we may proceed with that theory or doctrine until such time as an alternative is proposed that has better credentials and stands up to criticism at least as well as the previous candidate. As a result of that approach, Lester pointed out that his book contains a lot of other people's criticisms of liberty, anarchy and free trade, with his rejoinders. One reader described this as a 'set them up and knock them down' method, to which Lester he replied that he did not regard this as a valid criticism because it is precisely what critical rationalists should be doing. This may be contrasted with those who use the justificationist method to 'build it up (yet again) and ignore the counter-arguments'.

A rejoinder to Felperin on deconstructionism in literary studies

Howard Felperin (1987) wrote *Beyond Deconstructionism* to explain and defend the contribution of the deconstructionists in the contemporary dialogue on literary studies. It appears that the deconstructionists have adroitly located the weak point of Western philosophy, that is, the problem of establishing firm foundations for rational or supposedly justified beliefs, and the closely related problem of working out where to stop when a critic persists in asking for a statement to justify the previous statement that was offered in support of a position. Following Bartley, it can be argued that the deconstructionists proceed from a correct premise – *there are no authorities to justify the foundations of belief* – to a false conclusion – *there is no way to form a tentative critical preference for one theory or interpretation of a work of literature rather than another.*

Felperin was prepared to look on the bright side and hope that good will come from the loss of foundations of belief. The challenge of deconstruction in his view is to find some way to move forward without foundations of belief, to achieve progress in knowledge and understanding of literature without expecting to produce a body of positive knowledge that is immune to change and revision. But what is the 'mode of being' that makes this possible? This is where the work of Popper and

Bartley is helpful, because they replied to the deconstructionist challenge at a deeper philosophical level than is usually offered by literary scholars and critics; certainly a deeper level than that to which Felperin ventured. Bartley explored the implications of the breakdown of traditional theories of knowledge and rationality which depend on various authorities for belief. This gives him some common ground with the deconstructionists, because they both reject foundations.

Bartley's work contributes to the current literary debate in two ways. First, it clarifies the logical core of the position that the deconstructionists have occupied to conduct their reign of terror against opponents. But the logical problem caused by justificationism is not generally articulated; it just operates as a powerful but unstated subtext of debate. Second, Bartley has suggested a way to move forward in the comparative analysis of works of literature, forming critical preferences in a kind of philosophical space where the absence of certainty or consensus is not a source of anxiety nor an excuse for obscurantism, seemingly either for its own sake or for the sake of intimidating opponents by 'obscurantist terrorism' (Foucault's term to describe the tactic of writing in an incomprehensible manner and then accusing critics of failing to understand your position).

Conclusion

It appears that Bartley has provided a crowbar to apply to the wall of irrationalism. Where best to apply the point of this instrument? One approach is to challenge irrationalists at every opportunity, but this may not work due to the capacity of people to ignore rational arguments when it suits them. A complementary approach is to focus on rationalists with the aim of ensuring that they (we) cease to be under the influence of justificationism. While rationalists help to perpetuate the justificationist framework and mindset, irrationalism can be seen to be parasitic on rationalism; but if we cease to accept and propagate the framework of justificationism, then irrationalism will have to sustain itself without the unwitting assistance of rationalism. Irrationalism can be regarded as a kind of disease, a form of intellectual AIDS carried by rationalism, waiting only for the right conditions to become manifest (social or political crises of some kind, or even simply personal stress). The rationalist tradition has done remarkably well considering the logical problems in its foundations, and one can only be optimistic about its future prospects as Bartley's work becomes better known.

Given the historical preponderance of authoritarian theories of knowledge, the traditions of democracy and tolerance wherever they exist at present must be seen as truly remarkable developments. They are also highly fragile, which accounts for their tendency to break down during times of serious social dislocation. Similarly, under stress, reasonable and tolerant people can break down and lapse into dogmatic and uncritical thinking. This observation is not a concession to the pessimists who believe in the fundamental irrationality of people. Quite the reverse; in view of the almost universal acceptance of authoritarian theories of knowledge, it is difficult to see why people are ever tolerant, and how a tradition of tolerance ever took root. This situation can be expected to improve if students of philosophy are all exposed to the ideas of Popper and Bartley to ensure wider understanding of Popper's non-authoritarian theory of knowledge and Bartley's contribution to the ancient problem of rationality and belief. It will also be helpful if the 'true belief' religions can explore ways to promote the valuable elements of their doctrines without at the same time propagating the 'true belief' framework.

Notes

1. Popper referred to the moral framework in a paper delivered to the Sixth Meeting of the Mont Pelerin Society in Venice in 1954. It is reprinted in Popper (1963).
2. Bartley developed his ideas in a series of publications, starting with *The Retreat to Commitment* in 1962, reprinted with important additions in 1984, and two major papers (Bartley, 1964; 1982). The two papers and other related material can be found on line at this address http://www.the-rathouse.com/writingsonbartley.html
3. Bartley actually called his theory of rationality *pancritical rationalism*, or *comprehensively critical rationalism*, and contrasted it with *critical rationalism*; however that refinement is not necessary for the purpose of the argument in this chapter.

Bibliography

Ayer, A. J. 1982. *Philosophy in the Twentieth Century*. Counterpoint, London.
Bartley, W. W. 1962/1984. *The Retreat to Commitment*. Knopf, New York, 2nd revised and enlarged edition, Open Court, La Salle.
Bartley, W. W. 1964. Rationality Versus the Theory of Rationality. In Mario Bunge (ed.) *The Critical Approach to Science and Philosophy*. The Free Press, New York.
Bartley, W. W. 1982. Rationality, Criticism and Logic. *Philosophia*, 121 –221.
Bartley, W. W. 1991. *Unfathomed Knowledge, Unmeasured Wealth: On Universities and the Wealth of Nations*. Open Court, La Salle.

Felperin, H. 1987. *Beyond Deconstruction: The Uses and Abuses of Literary Theory.* Oxford, Oxford University Press.

Grey, J. N. 1982. F. A. Hayek and the Rebirth of Classical Liberalism. In *Literature of Liberty*, Vol. V, No. 4 (Winter).

Hayek, F. A. 1978. The Errors of Constructivism. In *New Studies in Philosophy, Politics, Economics and the History of Ideas.* Routledge, London.

Hayek, F. A. 1988. *The Fatal Conceit: The Errors of Socialism.* The University of Chicago Press, Chicago.

Kukathas, C. 1989. *Hayek and Modern Liberalism.* Clarendon Press, Oxford.

Lester, J. C. 2000. *Escape from Leviathan: Liberty, Welfare and Anarchy Reconciled.* Macmillan, London.

McCloskey, D. N. 2010. *Bourgeois Dignity: Why Economics Can't Explain the Modern World.* University of Chicago Press, Chicago.

Notturno M. A. 2003. *On Popper.* Wadsworth, Canada.

Popper, K. R. 1963. *Conjectures and Refutations: The Growth of Scientific Knowledge.* Routledge, London.

Roberts P. C. 1992. A Land Mine in Western Thought. *Commentary* May.

Von Mises, L. 1933/1978. *Epistemological Problems of Economics.* New York University Press, New York.

11
An Interview with Stephen Kresge

Steven Dimmick, Stephen Kresge and Robert Leeson

RL: Hayek's father was a botanist who would have loved to have been a professor; his childhood is full of discussions about university things. Hayek grew up with the view that there is nothing higher in life than to be a university professor. He doesn't really care what subject; it's the lifestyle, the aura, the status, of being a professor?[1] Did he add anything else about his childhood when you were talking to him, or talking to Bill [Bartley]?

SK: No, I think he had a very good childhood. There was no traumas, no conflict. He was the first born. And, although Bill did, I think, talk to his brother, I don't think there was any evidence of intense sibling rivalry, or jealousies, or that sort of thing. And, of course, they had money.

RL: And a title.

SK: The title – on both sides. The money was actually on the mother's side.

RL: So the father was 'marrying up' in a way?

SK: Yes. And it was through the mother that Hayek was related to Wittgenstein.

RL: It was the grandmother's sister who married a Jew?

SK: Yes.

RL: He was very precise about the proportion of someone's 'Jewishness'. Wittgenstein was very precisely 'three-quarters Jewish'.[2] Was it a common attitude at that time in Central Europe, to see people as a proportion Jewish?

SK: That I can't really speak to because, again, it varies to what purpose and what location you were in. And Hayek himself was never totally forthcoming on how all of that worked. Again, because

I think there was a dramatic change after the War. Because he says at some point, for example, that he would have never known Popper when they were young, because at that time, the class that he belonged to, and the group that he spent his time with, would not have fraternized with the group that Popper was a part of.

RL: The Jewish distinction?

SK: Yes.

SD: Was it a Jewish distinction or Jewish occupation, or class status?

SK: Jewish. Popper had a professional father, they had money, they had a good flat. It wasn't class: it was that Popper was Jewish.

RL: There was a Habsburg Jewish nobility – they had their own special title?

SK: Yes. I've come across this in other places, because I'm investigating this period in other detail, because I'm quite intrigued as to how Ernst Mach got the influence that he did, over a whole generation at that time. And it was a very peculiar society that you had in Vienna at that time.

RL: Almost impenetrable from the outside?

SK: Yes.

RL: From an American point of view, this must seem somewhat strange? 'Jewish circles' and 'non-Jewish circles' in California?[3]

SK: Right. It has never been an issue in California. There was a transition at work in the Austro-Hungarian Empire: they knew that it was coming to an end long before the First World War – there was a sense of letting go. The old feudal certainties were weakening. And one of the most curious aspects – something that Hayek never mentioned, and Popper never mentioned – when you start digging, you find that there was almost a cult of suicide prevalent in Vienna. And to get at the roots of that is something that is beyond me: somebody should really dig into it.

RL: Is that related to the 'death wish'?[4]

SK: Well, I think it's why Freud assumed there was something like a death wish, because a lot of it was born out of a sense of betrayal. Even one of Mach's own sons committed suicide. Two of Wittgenstein's brothers committed suicide, Paul Feyerabend's mother committed suicide, somebody else's mother, I think it was Wolfgang Pauli's mother, committed suicide. I mean, it was just widespread.

RL: After the First World War, there was a culture, a sort of Hippie culture, wandering bands of music playing minstrels, strumming around.[5] Did Hayek talk to you about that?

SK: No. By the end of the war, Hayek had matured considerably, and was looking for his placement. And Psychology was not going to be a possibility for him because, as he said, there was nobody in the university at the time with whom he could study – who could pass him through the degree. The other option that he had was the Diplomatic Corps, which he talked about. That, too, was closed, because the training school for that – the Konsular-Akademie – had been disbanded by the government in Vienna. So, what he decided to do, was to take this combined degree, which was an economics and law degree, for the PhD. Then he actually got a second PhD. I would have to look up to see what the difference between these two really was. And by 1923, he decides that he's going to go to America.

SD: What made him want to come to America?

SK: That is a mystery.

RL: He didn't really like America.

SD: He says that when he was in New York, he was in extreme poverty, struggling.

SK: Well, see his first choice – he wanted to go to Munich to study with Max Weber. But the family had no money, because of the inflation.

SD: So they lost whatever they had, through the inflation?

SK: Hayek had saved up enough money for his passage to New York, and he had gotten an agreement through this man Jeremiah Jenks, an American who had been in Europe to advise Germany, I think, on this whole matter of reparations, loans, that sort of thing. The Dawes Commission was set up. Oddly enough, Keynes was also on this commission. Hayek met Jenks, and Jenks said, 'Well, you can get to New York. I can take you on as a research assistant'. So Hayek goes to New York and Jenks is not there – so he has no money, and I think he has to wash dishes or something like that.

RL: Well, within a day of beginning washing dishes, Jenks came back from a holiday.

SK: Yes, just in time!

RL: Presumably he was paid a reasonable middle-class salary, reasonable for a young person at that time, when he actually got the Jenks job?

SK: Yes, well when he got the job, it was all right, but he couldn't afford to stay with only that. You know, he had to really get his career going.

RL: He considered staying in the States but it didn't appeal to him?

SK: Well, there was the romantic issue!

RL: His second wife?

SK: Right.

RL: I've never seen a full discussion of what happened. He was in love with his cousin; she married someone else; on a rebound he married his secretary?

SK: Let's just describe it as a miscommunication.

RL: You devoted several years of your life to the Hayek *Collected Works* project. As editor of Phillips' *Collected Writings* (2000) and co-editor of Friedman's *Collected Writings* (Leeson and Palm, 2012) I can imagine that you had some intense experiences.

SK: Yes – and Walter Morris deserves the lion's share of the credit. Not only did he provide financial support for the *Collected Works* project, he paid Charlotte Cubitt's salary and he became a good friend to Hayek and to Mrs. Hayek as well, telephoning at least once a week. He thought very highly of Bill, and secured an invitation for Popper to give a lecture at the medical school at the University of Arkansas. He got us through some very difficult times. Laurence and Christine Hayek were wonderful. And of course Penny Kaiserlian at Chicago and Peter Sowden (followed by Alan Jarvis) at Routledge.

What Walter and Bill were absolutely clear about was that the *Collected Works* would be the authentic text for transmitting Hayek's legacy to future generations. This meant that the work would have to meet the highest standards of scholarship; verifying all facts and references, separating (and rejecting) rumour from historical reality and making sure that misquotation and quotation out of context did not slip into the transition from manuscript (including Hayek's letters) to published text. Until this task was completed, restrictions had to be placed on other uses of Hayek's papers. This did not sit well in some quarters, but there is never any right to rummage. The desires of personal ambition or political bias would have to defer to Hayek's own wishes, which Walter Morris and Bill Bartley had volunteered to carry out.

One of the things that I had to contend with when I was doing the editing was the weakness that Hayek owned up to: when he read the arguments, the ideas, of other people he had great difficulty reproducing them. As he said, he would take from other writers those ideas that he found congenial, and would promptly forget everything else. What this means is that when he writes something it is not always clear what he is addressing – that sometimes gets lost. I charged my editors: 'We are going to have to spend a lot more time filling in some of these blanks. We need to re-establish the context for the contemporary reader who may not know what Hayek was responding to. That has to be restated. We also have to be clear about his references'. Hayek was very, very careless about his references; sometimes he would remember something but not remember it exactly, and sometimes would not go back and check. Every one of his quotations had to be double-checked.

RL: Hayek suggested that there were two types of minds: 'intuitive thinkers' (like himself and Keynes) and 'masters of the subject'.[6]

SK: Hayek had certain key ideas that acted as a core. He used those core ideas like a magnet when he read other people. When ideas registered he would add that to his cluster. But when he was responding to other arguments he was not very good at stating the original problem. If he was opposing someone's argument he wouldn't state clearly what the problem was that the other person was responding – and that he was rejecting. That he didn't always trouble himself to do.

I have always wondered why he wrote the *Pure Theory of Capital* (1941) the way he did. That was one of his saddest efforts in terms of the response it elicited. He put three or four years of his life into this densely argued book. It fell...I don't know if anybody read it – John Hicks perhaps.

What went wrong? Unless one was thoroughly familiar with the controversies with Frank Knight in the 1930s over capital, with the development of Austrian capital theory etc. you wouldn't have a clue as to why any of that was worth thinking about – because he never restated any of the problems.

English economists could never understand why the Austrian went on about time and the problems of time. For Neoclassical economists you just abstract time away: time collapses. Hayek insisted that capital has a time structure. This notion that you could categorize capital because of the time structure was so bizarre to anyone trained in Neoclassical economics.

SD: Why did Hayek make so few citations to French writers?

SK: He didn't like French thinkers. He thinks Rousseau is the source of a great many evils; he doesn't like Cartesian rationalism; he blames most of the planning dogma and socialism on Comte.

SD: Was he aware of Bergson?

SK: I don't know. I don't think he was. There are similarities between Proust and some of Hayek's thinking. He didn't find French thinkers congenial. Of course, Menger and Walras never got along. Hayek said he had two regrets about work he didn't do. One was not responding to Keynes' *General Theory* (1936) the other was not responding to Friedman's methodology (1953).

RL: In 1953 Hayek and Friedman were colleagues at Chicago and fellow Mont Pelerin Society members. Was that a constraint for Hayek?

SK: Well I think that was part of it. They agreed about so many other things.

RL: There is a – possibly fictitious – oral tradition about a dinner at your Oakland Hills home in which supposedly a confrontation took place between Friedman and Popper. Others were there as well: Sidney Hook, Joseph Berger...

SK: Popper was rather deaf and didn't want to engage in concentrated conversation – he and Hook spoke a lot about their ailments.

SD: Not like Wittgenstein's poker, then?

SK: No! I think it was a rather good evening!

Notes

1. 'My determination to become a scholar was certainly affected by the unsatisfied ambition of my father to become a university professor. It wasn't completely unsatisfied; he was by profession a doctor. He became a botanist, and his main interest became botany. He became ultimately what's called an "extraordinary professor" at the university. At the end of his life it was his only occupation, but through the greater part of my childhood, the hope for a professorship was the dominating feature. Behind the scenes it wasn't much talked about, but I was very much aware that in my father the great ambition of his life was to be a university professor. So I grew up with the idea that there was nothing higher in life than becoming a university professor, without any clear conception of which subject I wanted to do. It just seemed to me that this was the worthwhile occupation for your life, and I went through a very long change of interests. I grew up with biology in my background, I think it was purely an accident that I didn't stick to it. I was not satisfied with the

sort of taxonomic work in botany or zoology. I was looking for something theoretical at a relatively early stage'. 1978 UCLA Hayek interview with Robert Chitester. See also Hayek (1994, 40).

2. Wittgenstein was 'Three-quarters [Jewish]. The common great-grandmother, his and mine, was of a stern country family, who married into these Jewish Vienna connections. So three of his grandparents were Jewish'. 1978 UCLA Hayek interview with Leo Rosten.

3. 'There were also scientific societies and discussion clubs, but even they were in a cruel way split up, and that again was connected with what you might call the race problem, the anti-Semitism. There was a purely non-Jewish group; there was an almost purely Jewish group; and there was a small intermediate group where the two groups mixed. And that split up the society'. 1978 UCLA Hayek interview with Earlene Craver. Hayek never met Freud 'because it was a Jewish circle as distinct from the non-Jewish one. Although I moved a good deal later on the margin of the two groups – there was a sort of intermediate group – the purely Jewish circle in which Freud moved was a different world from ours'. Mises was 'not of the Jewish group. He was Jewish, but he was rather regarded as a monstrosity – a Jew who was neither a capitalist nor a socialist. But an antisocialist Jew who was not a capitalist was absolutely a monstrosity in Vienna'. 1978 UCLA Hayek interview with Armen Alchian.

4. Hayek spent his 'university days' arguing with Marxists and Freudians: 'We had endless discussions, and it was really what I thought was the poverty of the arguments of the Marxists which turned me against socialism. Incidentally, I'll let you in on another thing: both the Marxists and the Freudians had the dreadful habit of insisting that their theories were irrefutable – logically, absolutely cogent. That led me to see that a theory which cannot be refuted is not scientific, and that made me later praise [Karl] Popper when he spelled the same idea out, which he had gained in the same experience'. 1978 UCLA Hayek interview with Leo Rosten. Hayek remembered 'one occasion when I suddenly began to see how ridiculous it all was when I was arguing with Freudians, and they explained, "Oh, well, this is due to the death instinct." And I said, "But this can't be due to the [death instinct]." "Oh, then this is due to the life instinct."'

5. 'I saw [the *Wandervogel*] happen; it was still quite active immediately after the war. I think it reached the highest point in the early twenties, immediately after the war. In fact, I saw it happen when my youngest brother was full time drawn into that circle; but they were still not barbarians yet. It was rather a return to nature. Their main enjoyment was going out for walks into nature and living a primitive life. But it was not yet an outright revolt against civilization, as it later became'. 1978 UCLA Hayek interview with Leo Rosten.

6. 'Böhm-Bawerk was the master of his subject; Wieser was much more what one commonly would call an intuitive thinker. Then, later in life, I have known two types who are typical masters of the subject, and who, because they have the answer for everything ready, have not done as much original work as they would have been capable of. The one is Lionel Robbins; the other is Fritz Machlup. They both, to an extent, have command of the present state of economics which I could never claim to. But it's just because I don't remember what is the standard answer to a problem and have to

think it out anew that occasionally I get an original idea'. 1978 UCLA Hayek interview with James Buchanan.

Bibliography

Friedman, M. 1953. *Essays in Positive Economics*. Chicago: University of Chicago Press.

Hayek, F. A. 1941. *The Pure Theory of Capital*. Norwich: Jarrold and Son.

Hayek, F. A. 1994. *Hayek on Hayek: An Autobiographical Dialogue*. Stephen Kresge and Leif Wenar (eds). London: Routledge.

Keynes, J. M. 1936. *The General Theory of Employment, Interest and Money*. London: Macmillan.

Leeson, R. 2000. *A. W. H Phillips: Collected Writings in Contemporary Perspective*. Cambridge: Cambridge University Press.

Leeson, R. and Palm, C. 2012. *The Collected Writings of Milton Friedman*. Hoover Institution on War, Revolution and Peace.

12
Bill Bartley: Biographer Extraordinary

Werner Erhard

I came to know Professor Bill Bartley in 1972, when he contacted me some months after he had participated in The est Training, a personal development programme I had created. He told me that as a result of what he had accomplished for himself in the programme, he had gotten over his persistent insomnia (as he said, a real problem for a thinker and a teacher). He explained that he was interested in exploring with me the ideas expressed in that programme. Given Bill's stature as a professional philosopher, I was thrilled by the opportunity. He was a rigorous thinker, and the depths to which he interviewed me about my ideas challenged me to express my own ideas more rigorously. In our discussions, Bill introduced me to and helped me to understand the philosophical thought related to the ideas that were presented in the programme, and I used what I learned from him in the programme's ongoing development.

One of the things I enjoyed in the relationship that was developing between us was discussing (battling over) ideas. Bill had not come to his own conclusions lightly, and he could defend them powerfully. At the same time, he was generous in considering new ideas, but insisted on testing them thoroughly. I learned a lot from Bill, and he and I became friends. He was a highly effective teacher, though he never wore his powerful intellect on his sleeve. He once invited me to speak to one of his classes at California State University, Hayward. Before the class we met in his office, and I waited there alone while he and a colleague left to bring back coffee. When Bill returned I told him that sitting alone in his office I had realized that he what got paid for was reading, thinking, and discussing ideas – and I was completely jealous!

In addition to his erudition and scholarship, Bill was a charming and colourful character. He drove a vintage white Jaguar, and he and his partner Stephen Kresge collected stunningly beautiful antique silk imperial Chinese rugs and wall hangings that hung in their striking home. Bill even wrote a highly readable article about Lewis Carroll's logic for *Scientific American* (of all places for a philosopher to be published). Moreover, Bill was a great conversationalist and a wonderful dinner guest.

Once after a dinner gathering, Bill asked to speak to me privately. When we sat down together he said that he would like to write my biography – as he said, the development of the ideas and the person who created the ideas. He warned me that if I agreed what I would be agreeing to would be a full disclosure, warts and all – and with private interviews with my family (including my former wife), my staff, and other people who knew me. He said that I would have no say about what he wrote, and that I would have to be aware that when published, the book might cost me any friendship I might feel for him. Of course, a guy with no formal education – whose only claim to fame was the value people created for themselves out of being exposed to some radical ways of looking at life and self – when asked by a scholar who had done a biography of Wittgenstein if that scholar could write his biography said yes. I was not really worried about the caveats I was agreeing to in agreeing, as I had already been publicly upfront about the many skeletons in my closet.

In addition to the breakthrough of getting over his insomnia, out of his participation in The est Training Bill created another breakthrough for himself from which I came to benefit. He and Sir Karl Popper had been close friends and colleagues – in fact, early in Bill's career, Popper had been Bill's mentor. However, a number of years before Bill and I met, he and Popper had ceased all connection with each other over a clash of ideas. But with a new perspective, Bill found in himself whatever was required to repair and re-establish the relationship with Popper. This was for me another expression of Bill as a 'big person'. He generously introduced me to Sir Karl. I was a bit awed in the presence of the great man, but he immediately put me at ease by discussing some of my ideas that Bill had apparently shared with him. Sir Karl and I actually hit it off, and he was kind enough to have a few more discussions with me when he came to California. He made some powerful contributions to my thinking.

Bill, as you will no doubt already know, died in 1990. My closest colleague and co-author for the last decade has been the Harvard economist, Michael C. Jensen. Then Milton Friedman and I became friends after he made a presentation on Economics for Dummies on the closed circuit satellite network that allowed hundreds of thousands of graduates of The est Training programme to participate. The title of the satellite event (held on 4 April 1987) was 'This business of money'. One of the people we work with has the videos of the various events, but I don't know what kind of shape they are in; when I left the USA, all records went into storage. One of these days the tapes will get sorted out and digitalized where appropriate.

The night before the closed circuit TV presentation that Milton did for us, he came to dinner with a group of people with whom I got together from time to time to discuss ideas, enjoy each other's company, and have an pleasant meal. Milton was a great conversationalist, and great at healthy banter with people for whom he had some respect. As I said in introducing him the next day, the dinner conversation and personalities were so great that I wished we could have shared it with everyone, but for sure it was clear that with Milton Friedman presenting they were in for a memorable two hours.

Some time later I invited Milton to come to another of these dinners, and again he contributed greatly and made the evening wonderful for everyone. I certainly liked Milton, and maybe he enjoyed my company to some extent – or maybe he just liked the food a lot!

Mike Jensen and I worked together on various projects including the Barbados Group (named after a meeting we had in Barbados) on 'A new Paradigm of Performance'. We then created a Leadership Course based on an Ontological Phenomenological model, which has been delivered in a number of academic institutions over the past six or so years and has created quite a stir. We are now writing a book together on integrity, with the working title: *A Positive Theory of the Normative Virtues* (Cambridge University Press). Much of the writing we do by phone, but also in person, either at my home or one of Mike's homes. We get along like a house on fire: I am completely self-educated (high school diploma level) and Mike is a consummate academician and a brilliant teacher.

Some years after Bill Bartley completed his biography of me, he submitted a request to the Werner Erhard Foundation (a public foundation I had established) for a grant to support work he was doing on *The Collected Works of F. A. Hayek*. Bill had spoken about his commitment to this project for some years, and given the importance of Hayek's thinking and Bill's scholarship as editor, the foundation was pleased to lend its financial support.

By the way, tough as the biography was, our friendship did last.

Bibligraphy

Bartley, William Warren, III. 1972. Lewis Carroll's Lost Book on Logic. *Scientific American*, 227 (July): 39–46.

Index

Printed and bound in Great Britain by
CPI Antony Rowe, Chippenham and Eastbourne